From Partition to Solidarity

The first 100 years of Polish football

From Partition to Solidarity

The first 100 years of Polish football

Ryan Hubbard

RAH

First published in 2019 by RAH (Leicester, UK)/Amazon KDP

All text copyright of the author, Ryan Hubbard.

The moral right of all the authors to be identified as the authors of this work has been asserted. All chapters written by Ryan Hubbard.

Copyright © Ryan Hubbard, 2019

All rights reserved. No part of this book may be reproduced in any form without prior permission in writing from the author.

ISBN: 978-1-097492-44-2

E-Book ASIN: B07VLSY393

Front cover designed by Ryan Hubbard

All illustrations drawn by Ryan Hubbard

Body text font: Alegreya/ALEGREYA SC (www.fontsquirrel.com/fonts/alegreya)

Header font: Veteran Typewriter (www.dafont.com/veteran-typewriter.font)

www.ryan-hubbard.co.uk

www.pilka.uk

Twitter: @Ryan_Hubbard

Facebook: @ryanhubbardpol

*Dla mojej żony Melissy i mójego syna Riversa.
Kocham was bardziej niż świat.*

PRONUNCIATION

"W Szczebrzeszynie, chrząszcz brzmi w trzcinie".
[fʂtʂɛbʐɛʂinɛ xʂɔũʂtʂ bʐmi ftʂtɕinɛ]
(fuh-sh-cheb-sheh-shin-ye hr-shon-sh b-shmi fuh-tsh-chin-ye)

IT IS ACTUALLY easier than it looks. Granted, it does look extremely difficult, but don't skip ahead and you'll soon know your 'L's from your 'Ł's.

Firstly, Polish has one advantage over the English language: every word is pronounced exactly as it is spelled. The sounds of the letter don't change either (unless your group certain ones together, but we'll get to that later); so, to repeat the wise words of Mr Roy Walker, "just say what you see"...

On the flip-side, the Polish alphabet has 32 letters: 23 in common with its English counterpart and nine which, although they look familiar, have the potential to cause a few linguistical faux pas.

For the large part, many letters sound exactly the same as they do in English: ***b***, ***d***, ***f***, ***g*** *(always hard, as in the word "go")*, ***h***, ***k***, ***l***, ***m***, ***n***, ***p***, ***r***, ***s*** *(always soft, as in the word "save")*, ***t*** and ***z***. Others, particularly the vowel sounds, are a little more specific: ***a*** is like in "at", ***e*** is like in "bed", ***i*** is a shorter version of the "ee" in "bee", ***o*** is as in "hot", ***u*** is similar to the "oo" in "foot" and ***y*** is comparable to the "i" in "this".

Some, however, take a little more getting used to...

The Polish letter ***c*** is soft—similar to the sound "ts" in the word "lots".

The Polish letter ***j*** is pronounced like the letter "y" in the English word "yet".

Usually the one that catches English speakers out, the Polish *w* is, similarly to German, pronounced like the English "v".

Then we have the mysterious nine—most of which don't have comparable letters in English:

Ą: similar to the word "on", without the hardness of the "n".

Ć: a softer version of the "ch" in the word "chin".

Ę: like the "en" in "ten", without the hardness of the "n".

Ł: a replacement for the English "w".

Ń: similar to the "ni" in "onion", or the Spanish "ñ".

Ó: like the Polish "*u*", the "oo" in "foot".

Ś: a softer version of the "sh" in the word "shin".

Ż: comparable with the "s" in "leisure".

Ź: very similar to the "ż" above, but slightly softer.

Sorted? Well, not quite yet... Just a few letter combinations, or digraphs (and a trigraph), to get through. These are slightly trickier.

ci: like the "*ć*" above—not a soft "c".

ni: the same as "ń".

ch: a throaty "h", like at the end of "Czech"—never like the English "ch" sound in "church".

ck: the soft "tsk"—never hard like at the end of "truck".

sz: like the "sh" in "shoe". Harder than the Polish "*ś*".

cz: as per the "ch" in "check". Think "Czech" again.

PRONUNCIATION

dz: pretty much as it looks—like the "ds" in "pads".

dż: similar to the "dg" in "edge".

dź: slightly softer than "dż", like the "j" in "jelly".

rz: exactly the same as "ż"—like the "s" in "leisure".

dzi: exactly the same as "dź".

And there we have it—a crash guide in Polish pronunciation, which should be more than enough to get you through the rest of these pages. Here are a few of the words you'll see throughout this book, with a quick phonetic translation, to set you on your way:

Śląsk—Sh-lon-sk

Zagłębie—Zag-wem-bee-eh

Piłka Nożna—pee-uw-ka nozh-na

Wisła—Vees-wah

Łódź—Wooj

Legia—Leg-ee-a

Kraków—Krak-oof

Lwów—Luh-voof

Warszawa—Var-shar-vah

Wrocław—Vrots-waf

Zabrze—Zab-shuh

Dziesięciolecia—Jeh-shen-chee-oh-leh-chee-a

PROLOGUE
FOR POLAND

"The thing about football—the important thing about football—is that it is not just about football."
- Terry Pratchett, "Unseen Academicals"

CRUMBLING, WEED-STREWN TERRACES; brittle plastic seating, faded from years of exposure to both the most-blistering heat and the heaviest, coldest snowfall; rusting metal fences with gaps seemingly big enough to render themselves completely pointless. It is almost as if nature has been forever attempting to reclaim this concrete bowl, only to have been halted by the fortnightly footsteps of men, women and children, treading the same seed-shell scattered walkways as their fathers and grandfathers decades before.

From behind, the scent of freshly grilled kiełbasa and cheap, strong lager soon gives way to the overpowering, yet somewhat tantalising whiff of firecrackers and flares; the warmth from which provides merely a brief respite from the biting, prevailing winds which have travelled for miles over the vast Silesian coalfields. In the distance, above the silhouettes of factories, smoke stacks and mining towers, the setting sun shines through the smog to create a beautifully haunting, orange haze. At this point I'm not entirely sure why, but everything just feels... right.

In the prologue of his book *Behind the Curtain*, Jonathan Wilson writes of his developed fondness for Eastern Europe based upon childhood trips to the former Yugoslavia and night trains to Belgrade. He reminisces of a world seemingly stuck in time, where communist iconography still doesn't feel out-of-place, despite the last vestiges of such a system being wiped out in the region decades ago. My own fondness for Poland feels very similar: not in such detail that I yearn to spend time in a Warsaw *bar mleczko* adorned with portraits of Władysław Gomułka or sit atop the roof of the Jubilat in Kraków watching ice floes on the Wisła, but rather in that there feels something special about being in a place so steeped in history that it doesn't take much to imagine what it would have felt like to be there thirty-, fifty-, one-hundred-years ago.

As opposed to Wilson's nostalgia-tinged love for football—and indeed life—in the Eastern Bloc, I suppose my own endearment to Poland is borne purely out of curiosity and intrigue. I was barely old enough to spell my own name as the communist dominoes were toppled across Europe, and so the whole concept of the Soviet Union and its satellite states still seems both alien and other-timely. Being able to pass through remnants of that bygone era—the vast, tree-lined avenues of Katowice's Park Śląski; the elegant, yet imposing halls of Warsaw's Palace of Culture and Science; even the largely empty shelves of that brutalist Jubilat department store on Ulica Zwierzyniecka—gives a slight glimpse of a world that I've otherwise only read about in books.

However, it is the terraces of those decaying stadia that provide, in my eyes, the most-enthralling window into Poland's not too distant past; a past littered with stories of success, defeat, joy, tragedy. The people that occupy them provide an accurate cross section of, not only the history of their particular club, but also that of their city, region and country; where they have come from, what they stand for, how they've become what they are.

With Poland's slightly delayed ascent into the 21st century, those decrepit bowls are necessarily being replaced by grandiose, modern arenas. Some of the best in the world, I hasten to add. But while there are no worries at all that this will signal a loss of atmosphere or identity, there is still the inescapable loss of charm, of history, that for many years has brought those stories to life.

The struggles of Poland's recent past are extremely well documented: Partition, Reunification, Occupation, Oppression, Rebellion and, finally, Freedom; yet outside of its borders, the history of Polish football is not. This book is my attempt to show, however separate the two subjects may seem, that an inextricable link has always existed between them—for better or for worse. It is also an attempt to promote both Poland and its football to an audience which may not normally have looked in its direction.

But most of all it is my 'thank you' to a country which over the last decade I have fallen in love with. If reading the following pages leads one person to take a cheap flight to Modlin, strike up a conversation with their Polish neighbour, watch an Ekstraklasa match or even just order a bottle of Perła at the Polish bar down the street, it will have been more than worth it.

Ryan Hubbard,

May 2018

Act I
A Partitioned Poland

CHAPTER ONE
THE BEGINNINGS

"I like maps, because they lie.
Because they give no access to the vicious truth.
Because generously, good-naturedly
they spread before me on the table a world
not of this world."
- Wisława Szymborska, "Mapa"

WŁODZIMIERZ CHOMICKI IS HARDLY a name synonymous with Polish football. In fact, the mere mention of him to the average Pole would still likely be met with either a blank look or a shrug of the shoulders. Yet, on 14 July 1894, he wrote his name into the very beginnings of Polish football history.

Under the rule of the Austrian Empire since the First Partition of Poland in 1772, the Galician city of Lemberg had remained a hotbed of both Polish and Jewish culture well into the late 19th century. Over 85 per cent of the population named Polish as their preferred language, and it was still regarded as an important Polish city, despite the country having not officially existed for over a century. Polish culture was so ingrained into its society that the city continued to be widely referred to by its Polish name, Lwów.

Unlike the partitioned Polish lands which lay under both Russian and Prussian control, the Austrian region of Galicia was granted a certain amount of autonomy by the authorities: Polish was considered an official language and taught in schools, while nationalist parties were allowed to participate in the politics of the empire. Yet many Poles and Jews, as well as Galicia's Ukrainian population, remained concerned about the potential destruction of their cultures. As a result a number of pro-nationalist organisations were established.

One of the larger groups created to help promote Polish nationalism was the Gymnastics society, Sokół. Founded in 1867, its main aim was to help spread the importance of physical education amongst Poles, and renowned for attracting large crowds, thousands would flock to witness their displays of athletic ability. Sokół's jamboree in Lwów had originally been due to take place two weeks earlier, but had been delayed due to poor weather. With much improved conditions for the rescheduled event on 14 July, around three thousand spectators were estimated to have descended upon the city's Park Stryjski for the usual display of various sporting disciplines. Amongst them, a team of athletes from Sokół's Kraków branch had been invited to make the 200-mile journey eastwards, to exhibit a game which had already risen to popularity across much of Western Europe.

That game was football, however in its most primitive form. There were no strategies, tactics or formations, just a spectacle of twenty two men chasing a ball around a specially prepared, almost-square field. Both sides wore plain white jerseys, with the colour of their shorts the only differentiating factor—the team from Lwów wearing grey, and their Cracovian opponents sporting a dark shade of blue. The rules weren't entirely clear either, with the majority of the audience's knowledge of the game limited to the basic idea that it was required to kick the ball between the opposition's goal posts. After just six minutes of play, an uncontrolled scramble close to the Kraków goal resulted in the ball breaking loose. It fell to Chomicki, a sixteen-year-old Leopolitan high school student, who fired off a right-footed effort towards the Kraków goalkeeper. Unable to react quickly enough, the shot sailed past his outstretched arms and between the two sticks.

"Suddenly, the ball rolled in front of my right foot. Without thinking for too long, with a bang, I sent the ball sailing over the heads of the players of both

teams, which all of a sudden turned out to be straight in front of the Kraków goalkeeper. He tried to put his hands on it, but it was too late—the ball had already passed."
- Włodzimierz Chomicki

Having originally been planned as a three-day event, the postponement had forced the jamboree to be whittled down to two, and as a result a number of events were either condensed or forced to be scrapped altogether. With the prestigious gymnastics event—the showpiece of the meet—scheduled on the same field straight after, the commotion surrounding Chomicki's strike was seen as the perfect excuse for the organisers to conclude proceedings. The signal was made by the event organisers for referee Zygmunt Wyrobek to bring the game to a premature halt, which he did, with his fellow Cracovians protesting in vain.

***

Though the six minute exhibition is regarded as the first officially recorded game in Poland, football had been played before, but informally in playgrounds and schools rather than as a competitive sport. One of the most important figures in bringing the game to the attention of the Polish public was a doctor and philanthropist by the name of Henryk Jordan. Dr Jordan was both well educated and well travelled: a staunch pro-Polish campaigner even in his teenage years, when threatened expulsion for joining protests in favour of a reunited Poland forced him to move to Italy to continue his high school education. From there, university in both Vienna and Kraków followed, before relocation to Berlin, and then New York, broadened his horizons further.

In the USA, Jordan both began his medical practice as an obstetrician, and also opened a school for midwives. After returning to Kraków via England and Germany, Jordan continued his work, presiding over both the Kraków Gynaecological Society and the Society of Medical Doctors, and then later the Association of Polish Teachers of High School Education. Due to his status as one of the empire's most renowned obstetricians, he was called upon by a princess of Austria's ruling Habsburg dynasty, who happened to be passing through Kraków as she went into labour. Jordan made such an impression on the family that he was called to Vienna for all subsequent births—earning the nickname 'The Stork of the Habsburgs'.

Jordan's practice and honours earned him a small fortune—much of which he ploughed into his true passion: encouraging children to take up a more active lifestyle. Jordan strongly believed that a child's physical development was as equally important as their intellectual development; and after successfully helping to campaign for Physical Education to be made mandatory in schools, he set about ensuring that exercise was seen as a fun pastime rather than a chore.

By 1889, on a patch of land to the north of Kraków's Park Błonia, Jordan had begun to fund the construction of a sports facility—the first of its kind in the Polish lands, and possibly even Europe. With twelve sports fields of various sizes, running tracks and a swimming pool, children up to the age of fifteen were given the opportunity to try their hand at sports including the javelin, archery, stilt walking and gymnastics.

Park Miejski Gier i Zabaw w Krakowie, known informally as 'Park Jordana', would be open to youths from all backgrounds, privileged or poor. All would be treated equally, too: handed a uniform on enrolment, given a glass of milk and a bread roll after games sessions, and allowed use of the facility's showers during the warm summer months. Sessions were run by students of Kraków's universities, and an emphasis placed on pleasant exercise rather than competitiveness. No one was forced to take part in activities, while participants were encouraged to practice their favourite disciplines away from the park. Jordan himself was credited with bringing the first football to Kraków after a trip to the Prussian city of Brunswick in 1889, and introduced the game to the park soon after.

According to local newspaper reports, Park Jordana's first game of football in front of an audience eventually took place on 30 August 1891.

Though Jordan pioneered football in Kraków, it is Edmund Cenar, a lecturer at Lwów's College for Teachers and an active member of Sokół, who is widely attributed as being the catalyst for bringing the game to wider Polish attention. In 1891 Cenar published the book *Gry gimnastyczne młodzieży Szkolnej*— 'Exercises and games for School Children'—a list of physical activities in which young people could participate. Within its pages, the Cambridge rules of football were translated into Polish for the very first time, and were later re-printed in booklet form by newspaper *Gazeta Sportowa*. Like Jordan, Cenar had also returned from a short spell abroad with football equipment, providing Lwów with its first leather ball after a trip to England in 1892. It was with his influence that Sokół's exhibition game took place two years later, while he also helped to coach Chomicki and the victorious Leopolitan team.

> "The youth of the IV High School are already playing intelligently, and if they continue, it is expected that they will become excellent football players."
> - Edmund Cenar, Gazeta Sportowa, 1900

With Sokół's exhibition deemed a success, more-and-more Leopolitans began to take up the sport in the local schoolyards, and football began to quickly spread across Galicia. Games were arranged between students of different schools around the city, spearheaded by a teacher at IV High School, Eugeniusz Piasecki; yet, after Cenar's words were published in *Gazeta Sportowa*, it took a further three years for the first clubs to be created.

Lechja Lwów (later adjusted to 'Lechia') were first, with Sokół members of Lwów's III and VI middle schools coming together days after the conclusion of the summer break. Just days later, Sława—soon to become Czarni Lwów, titled after their black uniforms—were formed by pupils of the city's I and II real schools, with Piasecki's highly rated IV High School students establishing Klub Gymnastyczno-Sportowy IV-ego Gimnazjum the following year. In their early days, the clubs regularly played against each other, as well as taking on other school teams around Lwów, and the three became members of Towarzystwa Zabaw Ruchowych—a Lwów-based society with similar aims to Park Jordana—soon after its establishment in 1905. However, it wasn't until the Spring of 1906 that any of them ventured further than the outskirts of the city, and by then the game had also begun to spread westwards.

Thanks to the influence of Park Jordana, Kraków's young players had too begun to develop well and, like in Lwów, schools would often form games against each other. In May both Czarni and KG-S journeyed over 300 kilometres across Galicia to Kraków, to play against the best of the city's students. As was the case in the inaugural game twelve years earlier, both of the Leopolitan teams were too strong for their Cracovian opponents; Czarni defeating 'Studencki' 2-0 and KG-S 4-0 victors over 'Academicki'. But despite their defeat, the visit had a profound effect in encouraging Kraków's students to establish their own clubs. By mid-June Akademicki Klub Footballistów had been formed by the students who had been defeated by KG-S just a week earlier. Wearing a pale blue uniform complimented by a white sash—the colours of the city—AKF were widely considered as the first club in Kraków, and just three months after their establishment they adopted the Latin name of their home city: Cracovia.

Having participated in Polish football's unofficial first 'international game' in August—a 1-0 victory over members of the passing Buffalo Bill Travelling Circus who had set up camp on Park Błonia—the Studencki players adopted the red-and-white colours of the Polish flag, becoming known as Biało-Czerwoni. It was under this guise that they travelled to Lwów in late September, gaining revenge on Czarni with a surprise 1-0 victory.

With the sport's popularity increasing, other teams were swiftly created, and in October a tournament was organised for them by Taduesz

Konczyński, an author and Doctor of Philosophy at Kraków's Jagiellonian University. Alongside the two better-known clubs, newer teams such as Czerwoni, Czarni, Gimnazjum Święty Jacek and Gimnazjum Święta Anna took their place amongst the sixteen participants. Having been established months earlier, the tournament was also one of the first recorded appearances of the students from Kraków's II Szkoła Realna who, led by their professor Tadeusz Łopuszański, had taken the name Wisła—both their title and blue uniforms a reference to the river which runs through the city.

While Biało-Czerwoni emerged victorious from Konczyński's tournament, by 1907 they had already begun to struggle with the financial and organisational side of running a club. With Cracovia too finding themselves in a similar situation the pair joined forces, taking the former's red-and-white colours (*Pasy*, the Polish for 'stripes', becoming the nickname), and the name of the latter—traditions that the current incarnation of the club maintain to this day.

Wisła may too have quickly changed away from their original colours following a couple of mergers, however both they and Cracovia have maintained links with their origins by basing themselves within close proximity to their spiritual home in Park Jordana. Cracovia set up their stadium on the south border of Park Błonia in 1912 while, ten years later, Wisła moved in less than a kilometre away on the north side of Błonia, adjacent to Jordan's Park. The Leopolitan clubs too harked back to Polish football's roots, and the Sokół Jamboree of 1894, when establishing their homes; Czarni and Klub Gymnastyczno-Sportowy—the latter by then rebranded—both basing themselves around Park Stryjski, in 1909 and 1913 respectively.

However, despite his role as the catalyst for which was to follow, Polish football has never paid a fitting tribute to its beginnings, and Włodzmierz Chomicki never truly honoured as he perhaps should have been. Not seeking fame or recognition, after graduating he took up a modest job as a sports teacher in Lwów, before retiring in 1938. Like many

Poles from Eastern Galicia he was forced to move at the end of World War Two, settling in the Lower Silesian town of Chocianów, close to Legnica. There he passed away in 1953—two days before the 59th anniversary of his maiden goal.

With the Sokół rally having taken place on what is now Ukrainian territory, in 1999 the country's Football Association saw fit to honour 'Volodymyr Khomytsky', and the rest of both the Leopolitan and Cracovian teams, by declaring 14 July 1894 as the beginning of Ukrainian football. Poland now too regards the day as the start of its country's footballing journey, though it has still never been publicly honoured.

On 19 April 1988—what would have been his 110th birthday—Chomicki did finally receive some minor form of posthumous recognition in his motherland when, at a candlelit vigil, players from local amateur club Stal Chocianów adorned his grave with a crystal football and a plaque honouring his feat—albeit, somewhat fittingly, with the incorrect date carved into the stone:

> *"14 March 1894, in Lwów's "Sokół" stadium, was the first official football match between teams from Kraków and Lwów. The first goal in the match, and at the same time in the history of Polish football, was scored by Włodzimierz Chomicki."*

CHAPTER TWO
GALICIA

"Compared to the Polish regions ceded to Prussia and Russia, Galicia became for many Poles a mythical land of relative independence, where 'old' Polish social structures were maintained along with Polish habits, and where progressive and revolutionary thoughts were born and ripened... Historically and traditionally, this was a Polish centre of conspiracy, revolution, stubbornness, political debacles, and memories of the glorious past of Poland."
- Literary Images of Galicia in 1846: Marie Von Ebner-Eschenbach and the Polish Nation, Agnieszka Nance

BY EARLY 1907, Towarzystwa Zabaw Ruchowych was close to collapse. Both Lechia and Klub Gymnastyczno-Sportowy had begun to grow weary of its board's perceived favouritism towards Czarni—the largest and most marketable club in Lwów—and as such had set the wheels in motion to leave. Further to their potential exit, a handful of members from each club had also discussed informally about joining together to create a bigger and stronger entity that could truly rival, or even better Czarni. While those discussions had previously been nothing more than idle chatter, the disassociation with TZR provided a spark for talks of a merger to become more official.

A hastily arranged meeting at the Ulica Zamoyski apartment of Lechia president Maksymilian Dudryk proved positive, as a group of eight —four representatives from each club—thrashed out the details of the new one. It was decided that the new club would be presided over by KG-S coach Eugeniusz Piasecki, while Dudryk's suggestion of the name Pogoń —a reference to the Lithuanian coat of arms, showing a knight on horseback in pursuit—was favoured by the majority. Club colours were also decided upon: the delegation settling on white-and-red striped shirts and blue shorts—a combination of KG-S's red-and-blue and Lechia's white-and-red. Before long the white elements were discarded, and Pogoń became known as the *Niebiesko-Czerwoni*.

Though many members of the two clubs were in favour of the merger, some were strongly against it. As the oldest club in Lwów, several Lechia players refrained from joining Pogoń and instead continued their club's traditions under its former name. Klub Gymnastyczno-Sportowy too had members opposed to the merger, with central midfielder Marian Bilor instead moving to Czarni to join his brother Henryk. While the loss of Bilor—regarded as one of the best midfielders in Galicia—was disappointing, the retainment of Lechia's Tadeusz Kuchar proved to be much more important. Though a talented midfielder himself, Kuchar's involvement with Pogoń became more notable for attracting the interest of the club's first sponsors: his parents.

Following the birth of Tadeusz in 1891, Ludwik and Ludwika Kuchar relocated from Kraków to the small town of Łańcut, where they had a further four offspring: sons Karol, Władysław and Wacław, and daughter Kazimiera. Soon after the latter's arrival in 1898, the family moved on once more to Lwów, where another two boys, Mieczysław and Zbigniew, completed the family. In 1907 the family opened the 'Dreamland' theatre on the corner of Lwów's Plac Mariacki and Ulica Kopernika—the first cinema in the city. It was instantly popular among Leopolitans, and over the next several years it created a demand for a further two cinemas in Lwów. 'Lew' and 'Pasaż' were soon added to the family's theatre portfolio, while they also went on to open the 'Wanda' cinema under the shadow of Kraków's Wawel Castle.

With their eldest son involved both on- and off-the-pitch, the generous Kuchar parents were only too happy to offer their sponsorship of the club. Seeing that Pogoń's operation was based entirely around the enthusiasm of its young members, and with their five other sons keen to become involved, it was a project which they heavily supported.

FROM PARTITION TO SOLIDARITY

***

The joining of Lechia and KG-S wasn't the only Galician merger to take place during 1907; although now unfathomable, a surprise amalgamation between Cracovia and Wisła also occurred—albeit only a temporary one. Originally under the premise that they were to become Cracovia's second team, Wisła's players withdrew from the merger after just a few months with relationships soured, having mostly played fixtures that had been organised for Cracovia's third and fourth teams.

Though regarded as the city's two most prominent clubs, Cracovia and Wisła didn't actually face off—or at least no meeting was recorded—until 20 September 1908, when a sodden Błonia field hosted what would become regarded as the first *Derby Krakowa*. A goal apiece left the sides inseparable at the break, and neither were able to force a second-half winner to claim the unofficial title of 'Kraków champions'.

Cracovia's rapid development had been aided by the arrival into the city of an Englishman, William Calder, earlier in the year. Having formerly been on the books of London club Fulham, Calder joined the Pasy almost immediately upon his arrival in Kraków and quickly made a mark: his experience rubbing off on his new teammates as he, in broken Polish, would explain the importance of teamwork and tactics picked up from his time in the British game. A left-back known for both his long throw and marauding runs into the opposing half, the 'Polish Englishman' maintained both a coaching and organisational role in the club. Along with Wacław Wojakowski and Józef Lustgarten, he was also involved in the designing of Cracovia's red-and-white striped flag—the club's emblem for almost their entire history.

Like another Kraków-based Englishman, Dawson (whose forename is unfortunately not preserved in history), Calder also occasionally took to the field in a refereeing capacity. Just days after taking part in Cracovia's first trip away from Polish soil—a 4-2 defeat against Czech-Silesian club Troppauer FV—he umpired a match on Park Błonia between Wisła and

Pogoń Lwów's reserve eleven. Despite his links to Cracovia, Calder also took charge of both the second and third Kraków derbies towards the end of 1908; Cracovia emerged 3-1 victors from the first, while they shared a 2-2 draw just under a month later. In the months that followed, Wisła, Pogoń and Czarni would all go on to follow Cracovia's lead by venturing outside of their cultural borders to play against non-Polish opponents. Wisła too travelled to Moravia, losing 3-0 to Troppauer at the back-end of 1908, while Pogoń later travelled to Košice where they conceded five without reply against Hungarian champions Kassai AC. Czarni's trip to the Bohemian capital of Prague proved the most disappointing of them all, finding themselves on the wrong end of a 10-1 hammering by Slavia.

Although initial results against 'foreign' opposition may have not been encouraging, the Polish clubs knew that if they wished to improve, they would need to regularly compete against the best that the empire had to offer. In order to establish better relationships with the more-experienced clubs, Cracovia, Wisła, Pogoń and Czarni all made connections with the Österreichischer Fußball-Verband (Austrian Football Association) and by February 1910 had joined their ranks. The quartet were joined by Hasmonea Lwów, a Jewish club which had been established two years previously by members of the Sokół movement's Jewish equivalent, ŻTGS Dror.

Under the auspices of the ÖFV, jaunts outside of Galicia became commonplace, while the door was opened for clubs from Ostrava, Brno, Budapest, Vienna and Prague to visit Kraków and Lwów on a regular basis. Membership of the ÖFV also brought with it the added benefit of membership of FIFA, and subsequently games with clubs from outside of the empire's borders. During 1910 Kraków hosted a number of German teams, with Cracovia defeating Diana Kattowitz, and Wisła trouncing both Preußen Kattowitz and Preußen Breslau.

While all of the clubs benefited from their newly broadened horizons, Wisła's membership of the ÖFV quickly became uncertain. With their presence in the organisation conditioned by the future establishment of an autonomous Polish association under the Austrian umbrella, a lack of movement on the matter was deemed as a broken promise by the Wisła authorities. Frustrations grew and cracks appeared, and only eight months after joining, the club withdrew its membership.

Though it wasn't forced, Wisła's arm had certainly been twisted, by an organisation known as the Česky Svaz Fotbalovy (Czech Football Association). Established in 1901, the ČSF was a patriotic association focused solely on the Czech clubs located within the Austro-Hungarian Empire; however, formed away from the ÖFV, Vienna was less than pleased with the competition. With the ČSF having been provisionally accepted into FIFA in 1907, the ÖFV quickly filed a protest, citing the rule that only one association from each country could be allowed into the framework of FIFA. With the Czech lands lying under Austrian jurisdiction, FIFA sided with the ÖFV and the Czechs were expulsed just a year later.

Undeterred, the ČSF—along with amateur groups from both France and England—created the Union Internationale Amateur de Football Association (UIAFA), an organisation established with the intention of rivalling FIFA. The Czechs were sympathetic to the wishes of the Polish clubs to create a nationalist football association, and in 1910 sent a number of clubs to Kraków in order to convince the Galicians to break away from the FIFA-backed ÖFV. Smichov Prague played five games in the city (three against Wisła, two against Cracovia), while Union Žizkov, Slavia and Sparta Prague also played games on Błonia. Being given orders by the ÖFV not to play their November game against Slavia was the final straw for Wisła. After ignoring the request—and losing 10-3—they seceded from the organisation, becoming members of UIAFA just a few days before Christmas.

In order to aid their new allies' establishment within the organisation, the Czechs continued to dispatch teams to face Wisła; however, with the gulf in class, the journeys quickly became an inconvenience. Despite this, the ČSF were integral in getting professional side Aberdeen, who had just finished second in the Scottish First Division behind Glasgow

Rangers, to stop off at Park Błonia on their trip through Central Europe. ÖFV protests that the Scots should not play against non-FIFA members fell on deaf ears, and their tour through Prague and Kraków went ahead in May. However, Wisła's amateurs were outclassed on two occasions, losing 9-1 on the Saturday and 8-1 a day later.

On the day of Aberdeen's arrival in the city, Kraków's newspapers had reported about Wisła's intentions to form a Polish nationalist football association within UIAFA. Just one month later, Wisła joined ten other clubs not already affiliated with the ÖFV—Sandecja Nowy Sącz, Diana Podgórze, Polonia Kraków, Krakus Podgórze, Resovia Rzeszów, Skawa Wadowice, Kresy Biała, Wisłoka Dębica, Klub Footbalistów Mielec and Klub Footbalistów Tarnów—and established Związek Footbalistów Polskich, the 'Polish Footballer's Association'. In addition to their footballing independence, the creation of the ZFP also offered a chance to establish a Polish representative team, just as UIAFA's Czech, French and English members had done.

Having seen Wisła break away, the ÖFV were eager for the remaining Galician clubs to stay onside, and strong persuasion was required to prevent them from joining the *Biała Gwiazda* in secession. In 1911, they appointed editor of the Polish magazine *Czas*, and recently appointed Cracovia president Stanisław Kopernicki as a vice-president; in turn this helped to pave the way for an Austrian Select XI to visit Kraków in May. During their short stay in the city, the Austrians emerged comfortably victorious in a three-team series against Cracovia and Czarni Lwów; defeating the Cracovians 6-3, and putting twelve past a hapless Czarni without reply. The visit, though, had no effect on Czarni, as the Leopolitans had already been swayed by Wisła's early independent successes. Having left Kraków before the traditional post-competition banquet, it wasn't long before they too left the ÖFV.

Czarni's exile was short, as within a month of leaving, the ÖFV had finally been forced to give in to the demands for Polish clubs' autonomy. On 25 June 1911, the Związek Polski Piłki Nożnej was established, again with Kopernicki's influence; and with four clubs—Cracovia, Pogoń, Czarni and Robotniczy KS Kraków—under its jurisdiction.

The Austrians' U-turn effectively spelled the end for UIAFA, as by allowing autonomy for the Polish clubs, they would also be required to do so for those of other nationalities. Secret talks between the ÖFV and the ČSF began during FIFA's June 1911 Congress in Dresden, eventually resulting in the Czech clubs' accession to Austrian rule. Now left without the contact of Czech, Austrian, Hungarian or Polish clubs, Wisła—and indirectly the ZFP—were forced to make a decision on their future. After the club's general meeting at the end of July, Wisła issued a statement declaring their intention to rejoin their fellow Galicians within the ZPPN.

The Austrians rewarded Kopernicki's Cracovia for their loyalty to the association by handing them a position amongst their 'First Class' teams. This new-found status effectively put them on the same level as the strongest teams in the empire, including Viennese sides Cricketers, Sportklub and WAF; Prague's Slavia and Sparta; and Budapest's Törekves, BAC, NAC and Nemzeti. With more prestigious teams now heading to Kraków, the Pasy required a new permanent home to host them, and in March 1912 their new grandstand on the south side of Błonia was inaugurated with an exhibition game against Pogoń Lwów.

While at the forefront of the establishment of the ZPPN, Cracovia were not required to play in the first official competition organised by the association: a qualification round robin for 1913's inaugural 1st Class of Galicia Championship. Five teams took part, aiming to fill the three positions alongside Cracovia: Wisła, Pogoń, Czarni, Robotniczy KS and AZS Kraków, with a sixth, Lechia Lwów, missing out with their application to join the ÖFV still incomplete. By September though, the competition had been cancelled and the strongest clubs—Wisła and Pogoń—hand-picked to join Cracovia in the 1913 Galician Championships.

A week before starting their Galician Championship campaign at home to Wisła, Cracovia returned a favour to Pogoń Lwów by helping to open their new stadium on Park Stryjski, not far from the stadium which Czarni had built four years earlier. Pogoń claimed a 3-1 victory in a match notable for the debut of Wacław Kuchar—Ludwik and Ludwika's fourth son—who lined up alongside his older brothers Władysław and Karol. While Pogoń's victory had been impressive, the Niebiesko-Czerwoni couldn't repeat their victory when the two sides met in a competitive environment, drawing 2-2 in Kraków and 1-1 in Lwów. Defeats to Wisła ensured Pogoń finished bottom of the table, while Cracovia's 2-1 victory over Wisła left the Kraków pair level on four points at the top of the championship, with the title to be decided in the return fixture at the Stadion Cracovii.

Despite the bulk of the attacking play being in Cracovia's favour, a second half goal from striker Tadeusz Przystawski was enough for Wisła to claim a 1-0 victory over their rivals. Their elation, however, was short-lived, as it was discovered that they had played three unregistered Czech players, who had arrived on the morning of the game and left immediately after. Upon a protest being lodged, Wisła were stripped of their victory. Subsequently handed a 5-0 walkover, it was Cracovia who became the first official champions of Galicia.

CHAPTER THREE
PRIVISLINSKY KRAI

―

"If you see to it that no Pole can ever become a Russian, I guarantee that Russia will not subjugate Poland."
- Jean Jacques Rousseau, French philosopher

AT A TIME OF DIVISION across Europe, the city of Łódź was a shining beacon; a multicultural melting pot in which people of multiple religions and nationalities co-existed. Polish, German, Russian, Yiddish; all were widely spoken on the streets. Catholicism, Protestantism, Orthodoxy, Judaism; all were practised in the city's many different houses of worship. If a visitor was unaware, they would have been hard pushed to tell to which of Europe's ruling empires the city belonged.

It did, however, belong to the Russian Empire; handed over during the Congress of Vienna in 1815, in the ashes of the former state known as the Duchy of Warsaw. Having been established by Napoleon Bonaparte in an attempt to drum up support for an invasion of Russia, the Duchy was swallowed by Europe's great powers after the attacks failed, and as Napoleon's empire crumbled behind his retreat.

Formally known as the Kingdom of Poland, the Russian-governed area of the former Duchy took the unofficial title of 'Congress Poland' in a nod to the meeting which had divided the region. During the congress, the Kingdom had been granted a large amount of political autonomy, thanks to a constitution regarded as one of the most liberal in Europe. However, in reality the Russian Emperors treated it with disdain, effectively controlling the Kingdom as a puppet state. Following a series of uprisings in the 1800s, the constitution was disregarded altogether and Russification of the Kingdom was attempted.

In the years that had followed the Russian annexation of Łódź, the town grew at a remarkable rate. Home to fewer than 800 people on its incorporation into the Duchy of Warsaw in 1807, by the turn of the 20th century it had grown almost four-hundred-fold and accounted for approximately 10 per cent of the region's entire population. Much of the growth came through industrialisation, with Łódź's transition from a small, dilapidated town to a modern industrial hub beginning in the early 1820s. Partly in thanks to the early efforts of Stanisław Staszic—a multi-talented statesman and supporter of industrial development in Poland—Łódź eventually became one of the most important manufacturing centres, not only in Congress Poland, but with the abolition of customs barriers in 1850, the whole of the Russian empire.

With its thriving textile industry, Łódź soon earned the nickname *ziemia obiecana*—the 'Promised Land'. Many immigrants arrived from Germany, Silesia and Bohemia, all in search of work in the booming metropolis; while smaller, yet still significant numbers also arrived from as far away as France, Portugal, Ireland and England. With the influx of workers from Western Europe came the first introductions of football to Russian-partitioned Poland. English and German workers arriving in the late nineteenth century brought with them word of the new sport gaining popularity across their homelands, which quickly spread throughout the workforce of Łódź's manufacturing industry.

It is therefore of little surprise that the first proper football clubs in Łódź were of foreign origin; namely from the German community. Towarzystwo Cyklistów-Turystów, also known as 'Touring-Club', are considered one of the first sports clubs in Łódź, with a footballing section established in 1906 as an extension of the cycling club of the same name, founded eleven years previously. Stowarzyszenie Sportowe 'Union', another German club promoting cycling and tennis, was established in 1897, with football again following in 1906. It was these two clubs which played the first official football match in Łódź: a 1-1 draw in August of that year, played on a grassy square inside Union's cycling track in Park Helenów. Touring-Club then followed up a year later with a trip to Częstochowa; in what is believed to have been the first game in the shadow of the Jasna Góra monastery, they defeated workers from a French machinery company by five-goals-to-one.

The following years saw a wave of clubs emerge in Łódź, again led by the city's migrant workers. As the city's biggest minority group, the German population were once more the most proactive: Turnverein Kraft, FC Victoria, LTG Jahn and LTG Achilles being among the many factory-based teams appearing between 1907 and 1910. Even expatriates from Great Britain were able to make their mark on the city's game, most notably with the founding of Newcastle Łódź by an engineer from north east England in 1911. Despite the increase in popularity of the sport, the absence of Polish teams was telling of the authorities' restrictions on Polish-based organisations in Privislinsky Krai (the name given to the region after it was stripped of its autonomy and Russified). After the major uprisings of the nineteenth century, the Russian leaders clamped down on displays of Polish nationalism. The Łódź insurrection in 1905, riding the wave created by the Russian revolution of the same year, only strengthened the government's stance.

Some, however, were determined to find a way around the restrictions imposed upon them. Henryk Lubawski, a young Łodzianin who had finished his studies in Prussian-partitioned Poland, returned to his home town in 1908 as a convert to the game. After reacquainting with many of his former friends, the group would regularly meet behind the city's factories to play football, and confiding with two of those most trusted, Arnold Heiman and Jerzy Hirszberg, he detailed his plans to establish the first Polish football club in Łódź. The group of players, which quickly numbered as high as 25, would become known as 'Łódzianka': a collection of men from different backgrounds, nationalities and religions. However, headed by an ethnic Pole, approval of the club's statute by the General

Governor would be difficult; an assumption which proved correct, with Lubawski waiting weeks for any word on his application before its inevitable rejection—both his age (at 21, he was still classed as a minor to the tsarist authorities), and the club's links to Polish nationalism (the white-and-red colours seen as a reference to the Polish flag) thought to be behind the decision.

The failed statute was not entirely a waste of time, as Lubawski's incessant attempts to speed up the application brought him in contact with a fellow Pole, working at the Governor's office in Piotrków Trybunalski. Mr Adamczewski (his first name unfortunately not recorded) is said to have been sympathetic to the plight of the group, and offered to advise Lubawski on how to draft a statute so that it would not draw any objections from the authorities. Anything that may have been perceived as a display of nationalism was removed, firstly with the white-and-red colours becoming white-and-black instead. The name was also amended to Łódzki Klub Sportowy—ŁKS for short. More importantly, Adamczewski advised on the names which should be signed on the document to make its chances of approval more likely: those of Jewish or German origin. With new names attached—Feliks Markus Wasserzug, a middle-aged German bookkeeper at the city's I.K. Poznański factory and Arnold Heiman, himself a Pole of Jewish origin—in mid-1909 the statute was accepted by the Governor's office, and ŁKS was officially born. As recorded in the statute, the club was welcoming to all nationalities and religions—just as the original Łódzianka group had been. While not entirely the Polish club which Lubawski may have originally imagined, ŁKS truly was a club which represented multi-ethnic Łódź.

ŁKS maintained a close relationship with the I.K. Poznański factory throughout its early years, with many of its early members employed by the company. The first honorary members of the club were a pair of Englishmen: James Galaway and Thomas Horrocks—the latter being I.K. Poznański's executive director. It was with the backing of Horrocks and I.K.P. that ŁKS were eventually able to move away from Kraft's Ulica

Dzielna pitch, at which they had been temporarily residing. In 1912, they moved to their own ground, located on the city's Ulica Srebrzyńska, just a few miles west of the I.K.P. factory.

Together with their former landlords, ŁKS became founding members of the Łódzka Liga Sportowa—a competition organised by the Lodzer Fußball Verband (Łódź Football Federation) for the biggest clubs in the city. They were joined in the inaugural 1910 competition by Union and Victoria, with Kraft emerging victorious. As a prize, they claimed a trophy donated by Robert Smith and Alexander Gillchrist—another pair of Englishmen living and working in the city.

With Łódź's textile industry booming well into the twentieth century, I.K. Poznański was just one of many factories in the city; and with the first city-wide championships helping to increase football's popularity, employees at other factories began to establish football sections too. The manufacturing plants of Geyer, Scheibler and Grohman all became footballing hotbeds, and some even attempted to sign other factories' players with offers of employment. The Heinzel & Kunitzer factory in the eastern district of Widzew was yet another in which football became extremely popular, and in 1910 Polish workers there too decided to forge a new club. On 25 November the club's statute was approved, and Towarzystwo Miłośników Rozwóju Fizycznego na Widzewie—the 'Society for Lovers of Physical Development in Widzew'—joined Łódź's footballing landscape.

TMRF Widzew participated in the now-seven-team championship in 1911, along with Newcastle and Lodzer Sport-und Turnverein (LSTV)—the latter also formed in late 1910 from a merger between Jahn and Achilles. However, the new additions had contrasting fortunes in their first campaign: while Newcastle lifted their countrymen's trophy, LSTV and Widzew occupied the bottom two positions. In 1912, Touring-Club became the competition's eighth team, finishing in third; meanwhile, ŁKS lifted their first title, before going on to repeat their success the following year.

Although, like Łódź it was located within Privislinsky Krai, the development of football in Warsaw was more akin to the development in Galicia a few years earlier, as opposed to the industry-backed beginnings just 100 miles away. Despite being governed by the same laws stating that anyone aged under 21 could not become a member of a sports club, it was the Warszawiak youth who led the way in developing the game in the capital.

Based on Henryk Jordan's model in Kraków, Warsaw too had areas for youth to participate in physical activity: Ogródy Gier i Zabaw Dziecięcych (Gardens for Children's games and activities)—known informally as Rau's Gardens. The idea for the gardens came in 1899, on the initiative of a group known as Warszawskie Towarzystwo Higieniczne (Warsaw Hygienic Society); and the inaugural garden was founded the same year by the heirs of industrialist Wilhelm Ellis Rau. As well as being a co-owner of the Lilpop-Rau-Löwenstein metallurgy factory in Warsaw, Rau was also a keen advocate of encouraging young people to take up physical activities; and upon his death in early 1899, 250,000 roubles of his estate were allocated for the garden's construction. Before 1914, a further fourteen of these parks were built around the city, offering young people from all over the city the chance to take part in various sports and games in a non-competitive environment.

Warszawie Towarzystwo Higieniczne itself obtained permission for registration from the authorities in 1899; however, without rights to conduct classes for young children, that permission was almost immediately withdrawn. Two years later, upon appeal in the Russian capital St Petersburg, WTH did obtain its permit; but stating, in line with the law, that minors could not be registered as members. The authorities were even stricter when it came to registering associations solely for young people, and while some lucky applicants were able to get their applications processed in months, in most cases it would stretch into years. Even the

Sokół movement was not exempt from the scrutiny of the Russian officials: after the legalisation of the group in Privislinsky Krai during 1906, it was banned just a year later, under the belief that the society's true purpose was to prepare for a Polish nationalist uprising.

With the WTH's influence, a number of Warsaw students created school teams, and faced off on the city's open squares. From 1905 these games quickly gained momentum, and within a few years the number and frequency of games had increased dramatically. The growing sporting rivalries between schools were supported, and indeed encouraged, by the Warszawskie Koło Sportowe (Warsaw Sports Circle)—an association registered in December 1907, originally geared towards the participation of adults and those from the higher classes.

Warszawskie Koło Sportowe had been founded by 50 of Warsaw's wealthiest elite, including economist and future Chancellor of the Exchequer Jerzy Zdziechowski, Liga Narodowy member Seweryn Świętopełk-Czetwertyński, and member of the Stock Exchange Committee Michał Bergson. Similarly to other Warszawiak sports associations, the group's primary activities included traditional sports such as pigeon shooting, horse riding and tennis; however, due to the approaching Olympic Games in London, the practise of modern disciplines had also begun. Soon after its registration, WKS leased a patch of land on Ulica Myśliwiecka—in the south of the city, close to Park Łazienki—from the Horse Racing Society. Upon its opening in April 1908, 'Agrykola' would become the focal point for the development of football within the whole of the city.

Sekcja Gier Ruchowych (Section of Games Movement) presided over football within WKS, and became responsible for organising tournaments between students from the city's top schools. In its first year, eight of these school teams entered, rising to around 20 just two years later. Held in April, the yearly tournament became the unofficial Cup of Warsaw; with prizes ranging from scholarships for individual players, to a trophy for the winning team donated by Leon Goldstand, the Polish Consul in

London. Representation teams were later formed under the banner of WKS, with the best players selected to face visiting teams from the Austrian partition; Pogoń Lwów being the first to visit in June 1912, and winning 6-2.

At its peak, it is estimated that around 100 school teams played in competitions under the auspices of WKS. The organisation was described as an incubator, in which teams grew and learned to operate independently; and though many of those school teams fell apart, some did eventually go on to become separate entities. Korona were the first: an extension of the team from the Masovian Land Society School (Szkoła Towarzystwa Ziemi Mazowieckej), and founded in 1909. Quickly identified as the strongest team within WKS, Korona recorded multiple victories in the *Puchar Goldstanda* (Goldstand's Cup); during one tournament they even posted a massive 32-0 victory over Syrena. By 1911 they had established second and third teams, made up from a number of school teams which lacked proper organisation, and also gained many supporters.

But not all was entirely well within Korona; by the end of 1911, a number of players had grown unhappy with the direction of the club, and decided to leave. Led by team captain Wacław Czarnocki, a small group amalgamated with players from two of the disorganised school teams, Stella and Merkury, to create a new entity: Polonia. The new club quickly began operations, playing its first game on 19 November 1911 at Agrykola, against Czarnocki's former club. Although an informal meeting, with Polonia yet to be registered within WKS, the new team put up a spirited fight, losing 4-3. One weekend later they even travelled to Łódź where they were heavily beaten, 7-2, by Newcastle.

The registration of the club was eventually completed in the spring of 1912, and as a part of the process Polonia were required to submit colours in which they would play. At a meeting consisting of the team's founders including Czarnocki; Jan, Wacław and Tadeusz Gebethner; and Janusz Mück, the latter was tasked to find suitable uniforms. As there were not yet any Varsovian stores stocking sports equipment, Mück enlisted the help of an acquaintance, Józef Górnicki—son of the owner of a nearby shipping company who regularly travelled abroad for work. Fitting with Polonia's nationalistic themes, Górnicki was asked to search for shirts, shorts and socks that were red-and-white in colour; however, after consultation with Bronisław Kowalewski, head of Sekcja Gier Ruchowych, it was advised that such an act would likely see the club incur the wrath of the tsarist police, and Górnicki was instead given free reign to choose a different colour.

Górnicki eventually returned from Königsberg with shirts of black-and-white longitudinal stripes, which along with home-sewn black or white shorts, Polonia wore for approximately a year. By early 1913 though, due to a combination of poor quality and the muddy Agrykola pitches, the club once again sent Mück to source new jerseys. While folklore states that Polonia's now-traditional shirts were chosen as a symbol of mourning for their partitioned homeland, they were primarily chosen for aesthetic reasons: Mück had been briefed to find a shirt which was dark in colour, and therefore would not show mud stains as easily. The black uniforms with which he returned from Łódź are to this day synonymous with the club, and are the basis for their nickname, *Czarne Koszule*. Though Kowalewski had vetoed the idea of red-and-white shirts, there was another display of Polish nationalism which Polonia were allowed to show: it was agreed that a red-and-white shield would be attached to the shirt—not sewn, but pinned; allowing for its hasty removal should the police arrive.

Polonia's new black attire received its first outing on 23 February 1913, once again with Korona the opposition. The two teams played in unusually warm conditions, for a trophy donated by Count August Potocki, president of WKS. With Polonia running out 4-0 victors, one newspaper later reported that, had it not been for the Polonia strikers' hesitancy in front of goal, the result could have even been much higher.

CHAPTER FOUR
THE PROVINCE OF POSEN

"Hit the Poles so hard that they despair of their life; I have full sympathy for their condition, but if we want to survive we can only exterminate them."
- Otto von Bismarck, 1861

WHILE THE CONGRESS OF POLAND in 1815 had handed the eastern two thirds of the Duchy of Warsaw to Russian Tsar Alexander I, the western third found itself under Prussian rule once again, only eight years after its secession. Although supposed to be administered as the semi-autonomous Grand Duchy of Posen, any freedoms that Poles had were swiftly removed, and before the decade was over the Prussians had recommenced with a strict policy of Germanisation following on from the work begun by King Freidrich II more than thirty years earlier.

The Prussians were well aware that the Poles longed for independence, and under the leadership of Chancellor Karl August von Hardenberg, the Prussian elite attempted propaganda gestures aimed at earning the trust and support of Polish land owners and aristocracy. These gestures included guarantees in regards to maintaining Polish cultural institutions, continued use of the Polish language and the right to practise Catholicism within their largely Protestant state. In reality though, their rights were defined very strictly; as soon as 1819 the Polish language had begun to be eliminated from schools, while both Polish teachers and educational programmes were replaced with German equivalents.

Over the next ten years anti-Polish policies increased in both quantity and intensity, and following the 1830 November Uprising in Congress Poland, Prussian leaders began to fear a similar nationalist movement in their own partition. As a prevention measure, as well as sending aid to Russian troops battling against the Poles, they moved 80,000 of their own soldiers into the Duchy to quell any troubles. Germanisation then increased even further through the 1830s, under the Grand Duchy's new governor Eduard Heinrich von Flottwell—a self-described "enemy of the Poles". During his tenure Poles were removed from courts, offices and administration, while Polish peasants were forced into military service within the Prussian forces. At around the same time, the Prussian government changed their stance on the province's Jewish population by removing limitations on their freedom and integrating them into Prussian society. In turn, Jews began to look upon Prussia as a liberal state and joined the Prussian opposition to the Polish calls for independence.

After two further failed uprisings in 1846 and 1848, the Duchy was finally stripped of its semi-autonomous status, renamed as the Province of Posen and incorporated, firstly into the newly formed Northern German Confederation, and after the Franco-Prussian war of 1870, the unified German Empire. Under new chancellor Otto von Bismarck oppression of the Poles continued, and Catholicism, the religion of the majority, was targeted by his *Kulturkampf* policies. Though the majority of these laws were abolished by the time that Bismarck lost power in 1890, the seed of hatred against Prussia's Poles had already been well laid in German society: the establishment of the far right German Eastern Marches Society in 1894, and further legislation passed allowing the confiscation of property, ensuring the Poles' status as second-class citizens continued into the twentieth century.

***

As in much of the world, football had arrived in the German lands thanks to British immigrants during the second half of the 1800s. In the quarter-of-a-century following the 1874 creation of the Dresden English Football Club, the game spread rapidly across the country; this led to the establishment of many German clubs, and subsequently the German Football Association—the Deutscher Fußball Bund—in the first month of the new century. Although a number of Prussian clubs were amongst the 86 founder members of the DFB, not a single one was from the ethnic Polish areas of Pomerania or Greater Poland. While no laws forbade Poles from playing, the years of Germanisation policies and programmes and the Poles' hostility towards German rule left the authorities unwilling to allow the creation of Polish clubs.

As a result, the first clubs in the Greater Poland region were of German origin, and while Poles were permitted to join, those who did were treated with disdain by some compatriots who doubted their patriotism. Britannia Posen, SC Union and Victoria Posen were three of the biggest clubs to bring Poles and Germans together, while Deutscher Sportverein (DSV) Posen were strictly anti-Polish, accepting only Germans within their ranks. DSV were also by far the strongest team in the region, winning five of the six Posen qualifying tournaments for the Sud-Östdeutscher Fußball Verband's regional competition between 1909 and 1914—only once succumbing to Britannia, in 1913. Neither, though, managed to make it past the semi-final stage of the Prussian national competition, both losing out to stronger clubs from the Silesian city of Breslau.

Due to the oppression of the German government, the first Polish teams were forced to form in secrecy, attached to the clandestine organisations founded to continue the teachings of the Polish language and cultures. Soon the game sprung to life in Posen's Gorczyno, Wilga and Stare Miasto quarters; but with the teams' unregistered status, games were forced to be arranged away from both the city and the vigilance of the Prussian police.

With the rapidly growing popularity of the game amongst Poles, it was only a matter of time before the first Polish-majority clubs were accepted; however, these would still be heavily monitored and restricted by the authorities. The German language was made mandatory for both club correspondence and on-the-pitch communication, while any perceived links to Polish nationalism were heavily punished. Polish names were also forbidden, with the early pioneers of the Polish game in the region tending to opt for Latin monikers rather than German.

Normania were the first club of Polish origin in Prussia, established in May 1907 by young men from the city's merchant and craftsmen communities. Although both established and dominated by Poles, the prerequisite for membership was actually Catholicism; as such there were several Germans present within the club. Normania also opted for red-white-and-blue, as opposed to the usual red-and-white, for their colours, in order to allay any suspicions of Polish patriotism.

Outside of Posen, Ostrów Wielkopolski also became a hub for Polish football, with a pair of clubs established during 1908 and 1909. Twelve months after Normania, Gymnazjalny Klub Sportowy Venetia appeared thanks to students of the Royal Catholic Gymnasium, including Wacław Konarski—a native of Kempen (Kępno) who had experience of the game both in Germanic clubs and as a referee. The club were largely patriotic, and linked to the Tomasz Zan Association, while the name was taken from the Latinised version of 'Wenecja', a settlement on the outskirts of Ostrów in which the team meetings were held in secrecy. Venetia's Catholic links were hinted at by their choice of colours: blue-and-yellow, the Papal hues. Like Normania they too were not a club solely for Poles, with a handful of both Germans and Jews also accepted as members. Ostrovia appeared soon after; founded by workers and craftsmen attached to Towarzystwo Terminatorów. The players invested their own money in order to purchase the club's first uniforms—the popular choice of red shorts and white shirts; although these quickly needed to be changed, with the club instead opting for red-and-white striped jerseys obtained from Berlin. Unlike the clubs which came before, Ostrovia was solely Polish; for that reason it was unable to register with the German FA. Elsewhere in the province a number of clubs welcoming both Poles and Germans were also able to flourish. Fußballklub Victoria Kempen (1910) and SV Preußen Krotoschin (1909) both opted for Germanic names despite a largely Polish core: the former established by Poles, before their statute was padded out with German-sounding names; the latter formed by a mixed group, before Poles began to dominate.

The establishment of Warta Poznań in June 1912 was a turning point for Polish football in the region. For the first time players actively left German clubs in order to create a Polish alternative, with a number of 16- and 17-year-olds exiting both Britannia and Union to join the *Warciarze*. Within just a few months of its formation, the club—named after the Polish name for Posen and the river on which the city lies—had already claimed the scalp of Germans Hertha Posen with a comprehensive 9-2 mauling. With Warta's early successes, Poles began to leave German clubs in their droves, either joining their compatriots or establishing clubs of their own. Pogoń Poznań and Sparta Poznań were two of those formed in the city, whilst Polonia Leszno, Fervor Kościan and Victoria Jarocin were amongst the many more that emerged elsewhere in the province. As a result of the mass exodus, many German clubs were forced into liquidation.

With more-and-more Poles taking up the game, persecution by the Prussian authorities increased dramatically. Clampdowns on displays of nationalism—and even just 'Polishness' in general—eventually became an everyday occurrence. During a game against Turnverein, supporters of Polonia Leszno were found in possession of small red-and-white flags; when Prussian police interrupted the game, each player was fined 3 marks—a sum eventually paid in its entirety by one of the club's patrons. Continued persecution later forced the club to change its name to Pogoń. Venetia also found trouble during a game against Preußen Krotoschin when, after a Preußen player broke his leg, the club were accused of both aggressive behaviour and speaking Polish during play. The club were initially banned, but after a series of appeals the prohibition was eventually lifted.

The most severe punishment, however, fell to Normania, who saw one of their players, Marian Sroka, expelled during a game against Britannia for communicating in Polish. After the rest of the team followed in protest, fines and disqualifications were handed out, and by late 1912 the club was forced to disband altogether. Normania were not absent from the footballing landscape for long, as by November the club was reformed solely by its Polish members. In January 1913 the name again disappeared, but only to be replaced by a new one: Pierwszy Polski Klub Sportowy 'Posnania'. The new entity also diversified more than its predecessor, with sections created for tennis, swimming, fencing and boxing.

In early 1913 Warta, Posnania and Ostrovia were integral to the establishment of the Związek Polskich Towarzystwo Sportowych (Union of Polish Sports Association), an organisation created with the aim of forging relationships between Polish clubs while at the same time opposing the German nationalistic sports movement. The ZPTS were an instant attraction to Polish club across Wielkopolska, later in the year founding the inaugural Wielkopolska Championships in which Warta emerged victorious ahead of Posnania in second and Ostrovia in third. The organisation was also responsible for establishing relationships with Polish clubs outside of Prussia, and towards the end of 1913 a representative team was chosen—largely players from Warta, supplemented by a handful from both Posnania and Ostrovia—to travel for an exhibition match in Galicia. Although soundly beaten by both Wisła Kraków (4-0 and 9-2) and Czarni Lwów (5-2 and 4-0), merely building these relationships was seen as a success in itself.

Meanwhile, Warta's mauling of Hertha in 1912 had seemingly left German clubs unwilling to play against them—a decision that the Poles took as a sign of weakness. For almost two years, Warta unsuccessfully attempted to arrange games with the two former clubs of their founders, Britannia and Union; eventually though, in March 1914 Union did put together a team of soldiers stationed in the city to take on the Warciarze. With political tensions rising across the continent, German might and dominance was of prime importance, and a Union victory was supposed to be yet another display of superiority over the inferior Poles. But Warta did not roll over. Many years later, Warta president Edmund Szyc commented in his memoirs of his players "getting ready for the battle" and "fighting like lions"; and describing their surprise 4-2 victory, he continued that "perhaps it was the decisive blow against German football in Poznań".

CHAPTER FIVE
THE GREAT WAR

—

"Only the sword now carries any weight in the balance for the destiny of a nation."
- Józef Piłsudski, 1914

By 1914, Polish football was blooming across all three partitions. The championship of Wielkopolska was beginning its third term, although this time with only Warta and Posnania taking part. In Łódź they were into a fifth campaign, again with eight teams and with Polish-orientated ŁTS-G Łódź taking the place of Germanic club LSTV. Galicia's largest clubs too continued to grow, with Wisła opening their new stadium at Oleandrach and Pogoń travelling to test themselves against the established Hungarian clubs Toerekves (losing 1-4 and 0-2) and Budapesti AC (0-2 and 0-5).

The third Galician championship saw Cracovia and Czarni emerge as the dominant teams, with two victories each and a draw against each other; however, Czarni's fourth game of the campaign, away at Wisła, never took place. A misunderstanding as to the kick-off time was the reason: having arrived at the correct time—and crucially the same time as the referee—Czarni were handed a 3-0 walkover victory. Although this was disputed by the home side, before any appeal could be heard, events in Austro-Hungarian Bosnia and Herzegovina drew the attention of all in Europe away from sports. They also eventually led to both the cancellation of all football competitions in partitioned Poland, and the closure of many clubs.

Political tensions were understandably high following the assassination of Austrian Archduke Franz Ferdinand; and with the Serbian government unwilling to bow to Austro-Hungarian demands for a thorough investigation into the murder, conflict quickly became inevitable. As the Austro-Hungarians deployed a section of their army to take on the already-mobilised Serbs, both the Russians and the French were obliged to mobilise their own forces. In turn, the Germans dispatched their troops in support of their Austrian allies, and just a month after the assassination, Europe was plunged into a bloody war which Poles of all three partitions found themselves at the heart of.

Still, Polish nationalism remained of a prime concern, and circumstances now dictated that the Poles had much more bargaining power amongst their three partitioners. In return for their support and loyalty in the war effort, Germany, Austro-Hungary and Russia were all willing to make concessions and future pledges of Polish autonomy.

As the German armies fought their way into Privislinsky Krai during the early stages of the conflict, many Poles in the region became hostile towards their new occupiers. Having watched their compatriots in the German partition being subjected to the harsh Germanisation policies of Bismarck, while themselves being partially liberalised following the 1905 revolutions, there were sympathetic feelings as the Russian soldiers were forced out of the territory. Many too had seen the change in Russian attitudes towards them and believed that their proposals were the best hope of a Polish state in the near future.

This was an attitude which frustrated Józef Piłsudski, the Austrian-orientated founder and commander of the Polish Legions. Piłsudski's aim was for a reunited, independent Poland, free from all of its partitioners, and believed that to achieve such a target it would require the annihilation of all three of the ruling powers. By aligning his Legions with the Austrians they focused on fighting the retreating Russians in the east, while also quietly hoping that Russia's allies from Great Britain and France would defeat both the Austro-Hungarians and the Germans on the Western Front. Such a result would effectively create a vacuum in Central Europe from which a Polish state could be recreated. Piłsudski even went as far as informing the governments of both Britain and France that they would never engage in battle against them—only the Russians. As Piłsudski's men liberated firstly Kielce, and then both Radom and Lublin from Russian control, the welcome was not as warm as they had imagined; it was only by late 1915 that support for the Russians began to wane, as they carried out a plunder and decimation policy of the Polish lands from which they retreated.

***

German rule may have been far from welcome in Warsaw, however, the city's still unregistered football teams were able to use their occupiers' desperation to their own advantage. Soon after taking the city, the German and Austrian forces began to see a period of inactivity on the eastern front lines. This allowed a small amount of normality to return to daily life. Football once again returned to the fields of Agrykola, and with the Germans keen to give locals the impression that they were more compassionate than the Russians, while also wishing to attract support for the war effort in the process, both Korona and Polonia attempted to take advantage of an opportunity to make their statuses official.

While the registration of Korona was reasonably straightforward, there were still questions over whether the registration of Polonia was even possible. The club had attempted to register with the Russians in 1914, and with the draft being reviewed in St Petersburg by early 1915, it was thought there may be a possibility that the now-much-more-liberal tsarist authorities could be open to the idea of a club with such a name. Yet as the city came under German occupation before the process could be completed, there were renewed doubts over whether the stricter German authorities would entertain the idea. Polonia didn't give up and continued to try to register under the city's new occupiers; and on 8 October 1915 it proved worthwhile, as the club's application was processed and its statute adopted. However, German acceptance of Polish nationalism didn't extend far: in Wielkopolska, Venetia were disbanded in November 1915 due to disapproval of their links to Polish nationalist movements, while Ostrovia were forced to continue their activities in secrecy after 1917 citing similar pressures.

To the south, the outbreak of war could have seen Galician football almost devastated, with fighting aged players from Wisła, Cracovia, Pogoń and Czarni spread across Europe in either Piłsudski's Legions or among the Austrian divisions. Once hostilities in the region calmed, the sport was once again resumed and General Piłsudski himself was eager to see his men participate. In Kraków, the Legions' regiments established a couple of teams to take part in a tournament against two teams of civilians, beginning in August 1915. Before those teams from the artillery and the infantry met, two squads both under the 'Cracovia' umbrella—made up from not only pre-war players of Cracovia, but also Wisła and other smaller teams from Kraków—faced off in what would effectively be the club's first game since the outbreak of war.

Wisła had not been able to maintain the same infrastructure as their Cracovian neighbours and were largely inactive until the summer of 1918, with Pogoń Lwów president Rudolf Wacek writing in his journals that "while Cracovia remained loud, the sound of Wisła was lost". Some later reports—mainly from ex-Wisła players—do claim that there were attempts to rekindle the club as early as 1915, when a then-little-known striker named Henryk Reyman returned wounded from Italy, and made contact with some of his former teammates. With their Oleandrach ground firstly used as barracks by the Polish Legions and then destroyed by fire, the Wisła players were said to have been allowed to train on Cracovia's field; but with a new Austrian offensive in Italy beginning before the end of the year, any activities once again ceased.

In 1916 Pogoń Lwów sprung back into life and, perhaps learning from Wisła's experiences, under the initiative of Wacek they were split into two squads: *'Wojskowa'* (Military) for those players called into service, and *'Cywilna'* (Civilians) for those too young or unable to fight. The Military team would contain the bulk of the pre-war Pogończycy, while the Civilian team would be able to play scheduled games should the soldiers be unavailable due to their duties, and would also play a role in developing young players for the future. The Civilian team welcomed Cracovia to Lwów in early October 1916, suffering a 2-0 defeat. A week later, the youngsters made the return trip to Kraków, and were soundly beaten by eight-goals-to-nil, with both Józef Kałuża and Tadeusz Dąbrowski scoring hat-tricks.

Cracovia continued their form into 1917, starting out with a hard fought draw against Pogoń's stronger Military team in early June, while throughout June and July, and then into mid-August, they participated in a number of matches against regiments of the Legions, starting with Piłsudski's prided 1st Brigade on 10 June. The Commander himself was there to witness his men fall to a 5-1 defeat, along with his wife and the 1st Brigade's Colonel Edward Rydz (later Rydz-Śmigły); while the Third, Fifth and Sixth Brigades were also beaten heavily over the next two months.

* * *

With a view to increasing the number of Poles fighting against Russia, which would subsequently allow German troops to be sent to the western front to fight the Allied Armies, the Germans and Austro-Hungarians jointly proclaimed the "independence" of Poland with the creation of the Kingdom of Poland in November 1916. Piłsudski even took the position of Minister of War in the newly formed Regency Government; however, in reality the Kingdom was merely little more than a German puppet state. But with the Russian Revolutions of 1917 leading to Vladimir Lenin's Bolshevik Party taking control of the empire, fighting on the eastern front came to an abrupt end as the new leader ultimately withdrew from a war of which he had from the outset wanted no part of. Piłsudski now sensed the time to begin the switch of his legions' allegiance from the Central Powers to the British and French '*Entente*', and in July 1917 he forbade his soldiers to swear an oath of loyalty to either the Germans or the Austro-Hungarians. As a result of his actions he was arrested by the former and detained in the prison at Magdeburg for the remainder of the conflict. This only served to enhance his reputation amongst the Polish people, who had originally been wary of his ideas as—unlike his great rival Roman Dmowski, who had previously declared that the best way to establish a Polish state would be by siding with the Russians—he was willing to take on all of Central Europe's powerhouses in order to achieve Polish independence on their own terms. This did, however, spell the end of the Polish Legions, as within days they were disbanded and the troops absorbed into the Austro-Hungarian Army. Dismayed, a number of soldiers went on to join another organisation created by Piłsudski—the Polish Military Organisation—continuing espionage and sabotage operations against German positions.

In addition to the PMO there was a second organisation which also survived the disbanding of the legions: a football club referred to as *Drużyna Legjonowa*—'the Legions' Team'. Under the initiative of Galician footballers amongst the Legions, training sessions had begun around Piotrków Trybunalski in 1915. The team itself was established during a respite from fighting in April 1916, in the forests surrounding Maniewicze (now Manevychi, Ukraine). Within its ranks sat players from Cracovia, Wisła, Pogoń, Czarni and Lechia—the very best players that the Legions had to offer. Their early games were played in the forest's clearings, but with hardly any active teams in the area they were organised against teams of players cobbled together from elsewhere within the Legions. Their symbol —a white 'L' on a black shield—was taken from the Legions' own, while a black diagonal sash on their white shirts was said by the club's co-founder Stanisław Mielech to be inspired by that of Czarni Lwów.

What had been a makeshift 1916 season was interrupted in June and July, as Russian troops launched a desperate offensive action led by General Alexei Brusilov. So successful was the surprise advance that, as well as gaining the occupation of Lwów, Łuck and Kowel, it forced both the Austro-Hungarians and the Polish Legions to retreat as far westwards as the Carpathians and Warsaw. Many of the Legions' soldiers eventually found themselves in the historical Polish capital, including the key members of Drużyna Legjonowa. After the Russian push had subsided in 1917 they settled in the city and once again resumed their activities—now going by the shortened name, Legia.

The team had by now assembled some of the best pre-war players from across Galicia, notably the Cracovian trio of midfielder Mielech, left-sided winger Tadeusz Prochowski, and striker Antoni Poznański, who had all been a part of the Pasy's 1913 Galician championship-winning team. In addition, Tadeusz Kowalski and Henryk Bilor had been important players for Czarni Lwów, Tadeusz Tyrowicz and Jan Tarnawski had too played in Lwów for Lechia, and Edmund Hardt and Kazimierz Wójcicki were alumni of Pogoń; while other players from Kraków, Bochnia and Przemyśl made up the squad. Legia took up residence at Agrykola and made their debut on its fields in April 1917, with Mielech grabbing a last-minute equaliser to draw 1-1 against Polonia.

Despite the arrest of Piłsudski and the disbanding of the Legions in the summer, Legia continued their activities and were able to arrange a first friendly game outside of Warsaw in September: travelling to Kraków to face Cracovia. In addition to the aforementioned trio, two of their Cracovian teammates—goalkeeper Stanisław Mikosz and midfielder Stanisław Wykręt—joined them in the Legia line-up, with leading news journal *Nowa Reforma* commenting on its peculiar nature in their post-match report:

> "Legia consists of the best players from Cracovia three years ago. Yesterday's game had the character of a family, fraternisation, and sometimes regression and errors; perhaps explained by the fact that the players often forgot against whom they were playing."

The game ended in victory for Legia, with second-half goals from Prochowski and Poznański against their 'parent' club. Cracovia could only manage a late consolation through attacker Tadeusz Dąbrowski.

***

Pogoń Lwów and Cracovia continued through 1917 with mixed successes. The Leopolitans challenged a number of Austrian Army units, before both the Military and Civilian teams were defeated by Vasas Budapest and a combined team were narrowly beaten by a Vienna representative eleven. Cracovia, meanwhile, were able to earn victories against Česky Lev Plzen, SC Donaustadt, and Viennese sides Hertha and Wacker; although they too saw defeat against a representative team, from Budapest. In late October, Cracovia then hosted Pogoń's Civilian team, beating them 5-1 in a tempestuous encounter which saw the expulsion of four players.

In early 1918, Czarni Lwów returned to action, and in June they were challenged with a game away at Cracovia; but despite the resurgence of Galician football, the lack of a Wisła team had been noticeable. Pogoń president Rudolf Wacek sent a letter to Wisła's activists in November 1917, encouraging them to re-establish the club; however, the reply from Marian Kopeć was far from optimistic, stating: "We don't have our own pitch, we have nowhere to train, we don't have half of our old players. We can't even move". Some of these players had found themselves training across the city at Cracovia, and according to Józef Lustgarten could have even signed for the club; but even for Cracovia it was important that a strong Wisła re-emerged from the wilderness.

> "A strong Wisła is required for Cracovia. Strong competition is an essential factor for progress in the sport... Some players from Wisła had been training [with Cracovia], and played well; and who without any resistance would remain permanently in our club. I thought, however, that you should

not break a competitor, because depriving them of their greatest athletes could mean the burial of Wisła".
- József Lustgarten, 1918

Eventually, Henryk Reyman returned to Kraków from his army duties, and in the Spring of 1918 contacted Kopeć, along with two former *Wiślacki*, Stanisław Adamski and Michał Szubert, with the intention of re-establishing the club. They gathered together as many of the club's pre-war players as they could, from those who were either on leave, wounded or had been released from the forces, and in mid-July convened for the club's first meeting in four years, just prior to a 4-0 victory against Czarni Jasło. However, it was decided that the team would not go by the name of Wisła, but rather Sparta Kraków—unwilling to ruin the pre-war opinion of their beloved club, Kopeć and Reyman had opted to use a different name while they built themselves back up from the ashes. It was also under this name that they travelled to Lwów at the request of Wacek, to face Pogoń's Civilian team. After a 3-0 victory, they were asked to return to Lwów for a rematch by the Pogoń president, but under the proviso that they "next time come along as 'Wisła'". Following August games against Cracovia II and DSV Opava they fulfilled Wacek's request—repeating the scoreline from their first visit.

By now aged 21, Reyman netted his first goals for Wisła in a late-September Kraków derby—the first meeting between the rivals since the outbreak of war. His brace, however, was not enough to prevent them losing to a strong Cracovia team containing the likes of Kałuża, Poznański and Prochowski, in what both the *Ilustrowany Kuryer Codzienny* and the *Nowości Ilustrowane* newspapers described as a "very honourable" 3-2 defeat. The pair later met on 10 November, with Wisła claiming a 1-0 victory; however, given the socio-political situation at that very time, reporting of the game paled into insignificance…

***

As the year had progressed, the political landscape in Central Europe shifted dramatically. With the Russian Empire collapsed and both the German and Austro-Hungarian Empires on the verge of joining them, many Poles sensed the re-emergence of their nation. Relationships between cities, which for so many years were separated by borders, had already begun to develop in anticipation of the re-establishment of a Polish state. Journeys between them may have been arduous, but formerly partitioned Polish football clubs were amongst the many organisations which started to extend hands towards their re-found compatriots. The most notable, and seen as a symbolic meeting of Poland's consolidation, was that of Polonia Warsaw and Pogoń Lwów, with the Warszawiak club traversing the former Russian/Austro-Hungarian border to spend eight days in Lwów. After victories against the Military and Civilian teams, the Black Shirts came unstuck against Pogoń's combined team, losing 5-2, with the Leopolitan press commenting on the meeting as "very important to Polish sport's development".

Meanwhile, with the allied armies of Great Britain, France and USA steam-rolling towards German territory, the German- and Austrian-created 'Polish Regency Council' announced its intention to restore Polish independence. As the Central Powers crumbled, the new Polish Second Republic began to fill the vacuum, just as Piłsudski had predicted. Battered and bruised, and with faith lost in Kaiser Wilhelm II, the incoming German government soon began negotiations with American President Woodrow Wilson in the search for peace. Hoping to find an ally in the new Polish state, Piłsudski was released from Magdeburg on 8 November to great fanfare, and placed on a direct train to Warsaw. He arrived two days later, while within 24 hours—on the 11th, the day of the German armistice—with the backing of the majority of the Polish political parties, the Regency Council ceded all responsibilities to him. Piłsudski took the role of Provisional Chief of State, and before long all of the local governments created in the previous few months had declared their loyalty. For the first time in 123 years, the independent Polish state had become a presence on the map of Europe. Still though, peace was not quite within reach just yet...

Act II
A Reunified Poland

CHAPTER SIX
POLSKI ZWIĄZEK PIŁKI NOŻNEJ

"It has been said that Poland is dead, exhausted, enslaved, but here is the proof of her life and triumph."
- Henryk Sienkiewicz

EVEN BEFORE THE GREAT WAR had reached its conclusion, strides towards the establishment of a united Polish Football Association had already been made. From the ashes of the Galician ZPPN, Wisła activist Jan Weyssenhoff, Cracovia's Józef Lustgarten and Pogoń Lwów's Stanisław Polakiewicz had laid the groundwork for the creation of a nationwide organisation, and just before Christmas of 1919 the PZPN—*Polski Związek Piłki Nożnej*—was born. Due to pressure from the state authorities wishing to stress the importance of the revived national capital, Warsaw was chosen to host the inaugural PZPN Congress. On 20 December, representatives from across the newly reformed nation convened for a two-day meeting to shape the future of football in Poland.

On the first day of the congress, the board, led by Edward Cetnarowski, ratified the creation of five district organisations: in Warsaw, Lwów, Kraków, Łódź and Poznań—the pre-war hubs of Polish football. Later, steps were outlined for the PZPN's acceptance into FIFA (which was eventually achieved in 1923), while it was also agreed that Kraków would become the home of the organisation for at least three years, as the city and its footballing authorities held much more experience than those in the capital. Finally, the rules and regulations for the first Polish championship were outlined, to take place the following year. The five districts were to hold regional championships in the spring, with the winners advancing to a five-team national competition in autumn.

Due to the loss of documents in the years that have since passed, it is not known exactly which clubs were represented at the inaugural meeting. As there had been no comprehensive list of clubs which had played prior to the war, let alone those which had been established since, the organisers were instead forced to rely on the better-known clubs to invite teams of which they knew. By the signing of the first statute—drafted by Polakiewicz, and amended by both Weyssenhoff and Lustgarten—a total of 31 clubs had been gathered. Before the first competitions got underway in the spring of 1920, several more had joined the organisation's ranks.

Kraków's district championship was the first to begin in late April 1920, with six Józef Kałuża goals and an Adam Kogut brace giving Cracovia an 8-0 victory at home to Jewish club Jutrzenka Kraków. Wisła began their campaign a week later, and were held to a goalless draw by another of Kraków's Jewish teams, Makkabi Kraków. After less than two months Cracovia emerged victorious, three points ahead of Wisła, and became the first team to qualify for the national competition.

The Poznaniak teams began their competition in early May, with Warta and Unia Poznań dominating ahead of Posnania, Ostrovia Ostrów Wielkopolska and Pogoń Poznań. Pogoń Lwów, Czarni Lwów, Polonia Przemyśl and Rewera Stanisławów had to wait a further month, until 9 June, to begin the championship of the Lwów district, while Warsaw and Łódź both scheduled their regional competitions to begin a month-or-so later. Yet before any other clubs could earn the right to join Cracovia in the finals, an attack from the army of Soviet Russia stopped the competition in its tracks.

***

For a number of years, Galicia's Ukrainian population had quarrelled with their Polish neighbours; with a majority to the east, they too were hoping to emerge from the embers of the Austro-Hungarian Empire with a state of their own. Many Poles had been surprised at this, having thought that the Ukrainians would form a part of the new Polish nation. However, upon seeking the establishment of their own cultural institutions in the early 20th Century, conflict between the two developed rapidly.

With the collapse of the Austro-Hungarian government in October 1918, Eastern Galicia's Ukrainians seized an opportunity: on the evening of 31 October a group of officers took control of Lwów, and declared it the capital of the West Ukrainian People's Republic. The thought of one of Poland's cultural capitals not being under Polish rule had been unimaginable, and as such the majority of its population awoke shocked to find themselves in the middle of a proclaimed Ukrainian state. Soon, the city's Polish residents had formed self defence units consisting of war veterans, students and even children, and battled the poorly organised Ukrainian soldiers until reinforcements could arrive. Though the city eventually did return to Polish hands, it took over six months to completely exile the WUPR; cut off from Czechoslovakia, their only source of supplies and ammunition, they were forced to retreat eastwards. On 21 November 1919 Eastern Galicia was officially handed to Poland for a period of 25 years, after which a plebiscite would be held to determine its future. Exactly five months later Piłsudski signed an alliance with Symon Petlyura, the leader of the Ukrainian People's Republic based in Kiev, giving support in their fight against Soviet Russia in exchange for an agreed border on the River Zbruch.

Lenin had by now begun to view the recreated Polish state as a bridge that must be crossed in order to implement his communist movements in Western Europe. Following a joint Polish-Ukrainian offensive in July 1920, the Soviets launched a counter-attack which proved so powerful and successful that the Poles were forced all the way back to Warsaw. The impending battle on the streets of the capital was widely predicted to end in a Soviet victory, and the fall of Warsaw would have almost certainly seen the capitulation of the Polish state. But, against all odds, it was the Poles who emerged victorious. A surprise attack by Piłsudski's men disrupted the Soviet advance, forcing them into a disorganised withdrawal; 10,000 Soviet soldiers were killed, 30,000 injured and a further 66,000 captured in what Lenin called an "enormous defeat", and Poles have since referred to as the "Miracle on the Wisła". Several subsequent Polish victories followed, pushing the Soviets back further and further. With the signing of the Treaty of Riga on 18 March 1921, the country's eastern border was once again secured—although to Piłsudski's dismay, much further west than had been hoped, and at the sacrifice of Poland's Ukrainian allies.

With the Russian border no longer under threat, Poland had been able to return to some semblance of normality by the end of 1920 and many clubs arranged friendly games both nationally and internationally. Tensions did, however, still remain between Poland and their northern neighbours Lithuania, over the disputed region surrounding the city of Vilnius; though attempts to solve the situation at discussion tables rather than on battlefields were enough for the PZPN to give the go ahead for the 1921 Polish championships to take place in the spring.

A total of 22 teams took part in their regional competitions: seven in Łódź, four in Kraków, six in Poznań, three in Warsaw and just two in Lwów. By the summer these had been whittled down to just five, with few surprises as Cracovia, Łodzki KS, Pogoń Lwów, Polonia Warsaw and Warta Poznań all progressed to the autumnal finals.

Cracovia's advance had come without dropping a single point from their six games and with a goal difference of +30; as a result they were rightly seen as favourites to become the first Champions of Poland. Like it had been a year earlier, Cracovia's attack was spearheaded by Józef Kałuża and Adam Kogut, who netted a combined 22 times in the Kraków championship—once more than they had during the 1920 campaign. The pair were joined in attack by 23-year-old Bolesław Kotapka, who weighed in with eight goals of his own, despite having made only one competitive appearance the previous year. Many of Cracovia's 1920 squad also reprised their roles in the 1921 team: defenders Ludwik Gintel and Stefan Fryc; midfield trio Stanisław Cikowski, Zdisław Styczeń and Tadeusz Synowiec; and forwards Stanisław Mielech and Leon Sperling.

However, under the tutelage of Hungarian coach Imre Pozsonyi, they were arguably even more of an intimidating proposition than they had been previously. As a former striker for both MVE and MTK Budapest, and a Hungarian international four years before Cracovia had even been established, Pozsonyi brought a wealth of experience to the club. His knowledge of tactics were beyond anything that the Cracovia players had seen before, while a new emphasis was also placed on physical fitness. Mielech later commented kindly on Pozsonyi's teaching methods in his memoirs:

> *"Dipping his fingers in beer, he portrayed on the tabletops the position of players; and explained how in a given position you need to play, how to adjust, how to free yourself from an opponent. It was a great tactics school."*

The Pasy's dominance of Polish football was confirmed by November, as their unbeaten record was extended until the end of the season. In total they won seven and drew one of their eight championship games, becoming the first official *Mistrz Polski* with a couple of games to spare. The only team able to take a point from Cracovia during the calendar year was Warta, who managed a 2-2 draw in Poznań—although Gintel had missed a late penalty which ultimately prevented them from recording a perfect season. Polonia finished the campaign five points behind in second place, while Warta, Pogoń Lwów and ŁKS ended on eight points, six points and one point respectively. Kałuża topped the scoring charts with nine goals; one ahead of Wacław Kuchar, and two from both Kotapka and Warta's Marian Einbacher.

While Cracovia's season on-the-field was as successful as it could have been, it had been preceded by off-the-field tragedy. Their championship-winning squad was missing one big name from the previous season. Previously a soldier in Piłsudski's Legions, and then a pilot in the Polish Army, Antoni Poznański's eleven-year affiliation with Cracovia had been repeatedly interrupted by the ongoing conflicts to the east. Despite his regular displacement, Poznański continued to practice the sport; in addition to his prior involvement with Legia, he would also often turn out for Sparta Lwów while stationed near to the city. Still though, on his forays back to Kraków, he would pull on the red-and-white stripes of the club which he considered his own. The last time he did so, in a May 1921 friendly win against Jutrzenka, he received hardly a fitting send off; having barely recovered from a broken leg—which newspaper *Tygodnik Sportowy* claimed "was still failing", and as a result his performance "showed no positive attributes"—he was overshadowed by Kałuża and Kogut, who scored five of the six Cracovia goals. Following the game Poznański returned to Lwów where, less than a month later, he was killed as a result of injuries sustained during a plane crash, aged just 29.

***

From its very inception, the PZPN's main aim had been to establish a Polish national football team, and encouragements in their attempts to do so came from the Polski Komitet Olimpijski (Polish Olympic Committee). Established two months prior to the PZPN, the PKOl had been tasked in its inaugural meeting with preparing athletes for the 1920 Olympic Games in Antwerp—the first following Poland's independence. Included among the many track and field disciplines, a spot was allowed for a Polish team to take part in the football competition. Prior to leading Polonia Warsaw to the vice-championship of 1921, American fitness specialist George Henry Burford was selected to lead the Poles to the Olympics; meanwhile, two squads were chosen by the PKOl for a game in Kraków, to decide the players who would make the trip to Belgium. Once named, the

Olympic team then hammered a representative team from Lwów 12-1, and much sterner tests against the national teams of Austria, Hungary and Czechoslovakia were discussed. However, before these could be agreed, the war against the Bolsheviks led to the withdrawal of all the country's athletes from the games.

Once the hostilities had calmed, Cracovia embarked on a trip to Vienna in October 1920, facing friendly games against Admira and WAF. During the tour Cetnarowski and Lustgarten renewed contact with their former colleagues in the Austrian FA, who subsequently agreed to send their national team to face a Polish representation in Kraków the following July; however, a swift withdrawal of their offer left the PZPN eager to find a replacement. As political tensions with neighbours on all sides remained frayed from the various conflicts, the difficulty of the task increased dramatically. Negotiations with both the French and Swedish FAs were touted, while in a column for the recently established sports journal *Przegląd Sportowy*, Tadeusz Synowiec stated his belief that the Czechoslovakians should be contacted as they were "boldly regarded as the best on the continent". But it was an offer from the Hungarian association which was deemed the best. While the Magyars had suggested a meeting in Budapest at Christmas, a counter suggestion of Spring 1922 was made by the Poles. Eventually though, realising that the Hungarian offer was too good to decline, the PZPN agreed to a 1921 date, and 18 December was set in ink for the inaugural meeting of the Polish National Football Team.

The choice of Hungary as the Poles' first opponents may too have been due to influence from Cracovia coach Pozsonyi, who in the summer of 1921 was selected by the PZPN to lead the *Białe-Orły* into the game against his countrymen. Pozsonyi was joined by the president of the Łódź association, Józef Szkolnikowski, who took a role as selector of the squad; and between them they selected two squads' worth of players to run the rule over during a pair of November trial games. After 4-1 and 5-1 victories for the 'A' team, the squad was whittled down to just thirteen, with the likes of Cracovia's Kotapka, Fryc and Popiel; Warta's Wawrzyniec Staliński; Pogoń's Ludwik Schneider; and Witlold Gieras of Wisła all missing out despite their impressive form.

Poland (v Hungary)
Friendly Match; Stadion Hungaria, Budapest;
18 December 1921:

Goalkeeper: Jan Loth (Polonia Warsaw).

Defenders: Ludwik Gintel (Cracovia), Artur Marczewski (Polonia Warsaw).

Midfielders: Zdisław Styczeń (Cracovia), Stanisław Cikowski (Cracovia), Tadeusz Synowiec (Cracovia), Stefan Loth (Polonia Warsaw).

Attackers: Stanisław Mielech (Cracovia), Wacław Kuchar (Pogoń Lwów), Józef Kałuża (Cracovia), Marian Einbacher (Warta Poznań), Leon Sperling (Cracovia), Mieczysław Batsch (Pogoń Lwów).

Two weeks prior to their maiden outing, Pozsonyi's side began a three-game tour of the south of Poland, facing representative teams from major cities. Firstly they travelled to Bielsko, defeating the best of the city's players 3-1; then they headed to Lwów, routing theirs 9-1. Finally it was to Kraków where, one week before facing the Hungarians, a team made up largely of players from Wisła, Jutrzenka and Makkabi were beaten 7-1. After a few days rest, the squad then gathered at Kraków Główny railway station to begin the 36-hour journey to Budapest. The group of 21 (in addition to Pozsonyi and his squad; four PZPN officials, two journalists and one supporter) travelled in third class in order to save money, and only arrived in the Hungarian capital at midnight, the night before the game.

While the importance of the meeting for the Poles was insurmountable, for the Hungarians it was merely another game—their 80th, in fact.

With the appalling weather, and the Poles hardly considered as prestigious opponents, the terraces of MTK's Stadion Hungaria were significantly empty compared to the thirty-or-so-thousand which had witnessed some of Hungary's more recent games. The 8,000 locals who did brave the freezing wind and rain witnessed their team unable to play the free-flowing football with which they were associated.

> *"...it was nasty weather. A layer of snow covered the city, and while the pitch was cleared, it remained very difficult, muddy and heavy. It was our trump card, because the hosts had better technique, and it was harder for them to show their class on the ground".*
> *- Edmund Szyc, founder Warta Poznań and journalist for "Sport Ilustrowany".*

Whilst the Hungarians may not have been able to play to their strengths, the Poles suffered from stage fright; just eighteen minutes into the game, slack defending allowed Jenó Szabó to turn in a Jenó Wiener cross to give the hosts a lead which proved unassailable. That isn't to say that Pozsonyi's team completely floundered—they did have chances of their own to score. The biggest fell to Wacław Kuchar, whose powerful shot smashed against the head of goalkeeper Károly Zsák; yet receiving the rebound, the Pogoń striker nobly opted to tend to the injured player rather than tap into the empty net. Even so, the result was justified, with many more chances falling to the hosts. Before half-time, Artur Marczewski brought down György Molnár in the Polish box, leaving Czech official Emil Grätz with no option but to point to the spot. Defender Károly Fogl couldn't make use of the penalty, while a combination of the goal frame and an inspired second-half performance from Polonia custodian Jan Loth kept the scoreline static until the final whistle.

Commemorative pennants were exchanged at the post-game banquet, while representatives from both Football Associations discussed the possibility of an upcoming rematch, eventually scheduled for five months later in Kraków. Although defeated, the Poles were able to hold their heads high, having given one of European football's top representations a challenge in a game they were expected to lose heavily. While the records show that Poland's first game ended with defeat, after the partitions and wars which had engulfed the country, the fact that such a game even took place at all should be regarded as a victory in itself.

CHAPTER SEVEN
NEW BORDERS AND HORIZONS

—

"Germany can generally only pay [its war reparations] if the corridor and Upper Silesia are handed back to Germany from Polish possession, and if besides, somewhere on the earth colonial territory will be made available to Germany."
- Hjalmar Schacht, German economist, April 1929

POST-WAR UPPER SILESIA could hardly have been considered an area of great beauty or elegance. It is for similar reason that British novelist P. G. Wodehouse stated in the 1940s that "[i]f this is 'Upper' Silesia, then one must wonder what 'Lower' Silesia is like". Yet in the years following the Great War, both Germany and Poland were desperate to gain control of the region.

Formerly a part of medieval Poland, Silesia had transferred between Bohemian and Austrian rule, before finally being allocated to Germany in the late 18th century. Under German rule the region established itself as one of the nation's centres of industrialisation, fuelled by the wealth of natural resources—coal, copper, iron and zinc—which lay beneath its surface. It was for this reason that the Germans had been unwilling to surrender Upper Silesia as easily as they had done Poznań, Bydgoszcz and Eastern Pomerania.

Home to the majority of Silesia's mines, foundries and factories, the so-called 'industrial triangle' of Kattowitz, Beuthen and Gleiwitz was planned to be key to Germany's economic recovery; however, it was also home to a large Polish population, who believed that their nation too had some claim to the region. Though the Treaty of Versailles decreed that a plebiscite should be held to determine the region's borders, Polish Silesians remained far from happy, and soon a series of uprisings were organised, bringing even more instability.

German claims to Upper Silesia were backed by both the British and Italian governments, who feared that should it fall to Poland, their former enemies would default on their reparation payments. France, meanwhile, supported the claims of their long-standing Polish allies, wishing to do anything in their power to weaken the Germans. Though the vote for self determination in March 1921 ended with a decisive German victory, a further Polish uprising forced intervention from the League of Nations, who put together a multi-national committee to decide Upper Silesia's fate. After a six-week investigation, the border was finally drawn just east of Beuthen and Hindenburg: the larger western portion, containing Gleiwitz and Oppeln, remained with Germany; the more-industrialised eastern slither, containing Kattowitz, Königshutte and Tarnowitz (now Katowice, Chorzów and Tarnówskie Góry), fell to Poland.

There were also troubles in the north-east of the country, where Lithuania continued its disagreements with Poland over the regions surrounding the cities of Vilnius and Suwałki. Piłsudski had hoped that he could create a commonwealth of countries stretching from the Black Sea to the Baltic—*Międzymorze*—which could unite against the Russians; however, the Lithuanians saw the plans as a threat to their independence, and relations rapidly worsened. The Soviet advance of 1920 had allowed the Lithuanians to creep behind, gaining the territory encompassing Vilnius, and soon afterwards the Republic of Central Lithuania was established. With a Polish majority remaining in the city itself, Poland were keen to recover the region quickly, and with the League of Nations' suggestion of a plebiscite dismissed by both sides, the conflict between the two continued into 1922. Eventually, in January, elections in the self-declared Republic were scheduled. With non-Poles boycotting the vote, a landslide victory was declared for the Polish-orientated candidates. By the end of February, the new parliament had convened and voted for reincorporation into Poland as the Wilno Voivodeship.

With the expansion of the Polish territory, the creation of new Polish football clubs was inevitable. In Upper Silesia, this came even before the region's future had been decided. Throughout 1919 and 1920, pro-Polish activists attempted to boost claims for ownership of the region by encouraging Poles to establish their own cultural organisations; and almost immediately, football was identified as one of the most effective ways for Polish Silesians to display their nationalism. A number of new clubs were created, with many opting for Polish-patriotic names: Szombierki's KS Poniatowski (named after Józef Poniatowski, the nobleman who fought to defend Poland during the partitions), and Polonia Bytom (co-founded by Tadeusz Gebethener, one of the original founders of Polonia Warsaw) among them. The Silesian Uprisings also became a common theme, notably with Ruch Wielkie Hajduki ('*Ruch*' being the Polish word for 'movement') appearing in April 1920. The title was also adopted in 1921 by Ruch Radzionków, who had been formed as Towarzystwo Gier i Zabaw two years earlier.

The game in Upper Silesia developed rapidly, and was aided in 1920 by visits from both Pogoń Lwów and Cracovia: Pogoń played games against a Silesian representation team, and Germanic sides Diana Kattowitz and SC 09 Beuthen, while Cracovia defeated a Katowice XI, as well as Polish sides Słupna Mysłowice and Naprzód Lipiny. The number of clubs continued to increase dramatically through the year, and by 1921 there were more than enough to form two unofficial Upper Silesian championships. In the 'Katowice' tournament, Słupna, Poniatowski and Naprzód all finished behind Pogoń Katowice. Ruch Wielkie Hajduki emerged victorious in the eight-team 'Chorzów' competition, against clubs including Śląsk Świętochłowice, Unia 20 Mysłowice and Iskra Siemianowice.

Yet still, even after the calls from Polish activists, a number of traditionally German clubs remained populated heavily by Poles. Some of these continued operation following the definition of the borders, became Polonised, and were eventually accepted into the PZPN. Two Katowice-based clubs changed their identity, with Zalenze 06 becoming KS Załęże 06, and Sport Club 1911 Eiche changing to Dąb Katowice; VfR Königshutte transformed into Amatorski KS Chorzów; while the Mysłowice pair of Sport Club 09 Myslowitz and Borussia 06 Myslowitz became Górnik 09 and Lechia 06 respectively. The revised national boundaries also had massive repercussions for those Polish clubs which now lay outside of their country's territory; the biggest of which were Polonia Bytom, who were forced to disband completely as they were absorbed into Weimar Germany.

Like Upper Silesia, Wilno too saw the establishment of clubs before the borders were entirely confirmed; but, due to the city's location some distance away from areas of heavy footballing activity, they developed at a slower rate. Growth was helped by the arrival of Jan Weyssenhoff, who moved from Kraków in 1921 to become a Professor of Theoretical Physics at one of the city's universities. He took the presidency of the Wilno Football Association not long after his arrival, and also gathered players from the city's most-active club, KS 'Sokół', to form a new one: Strzelec Wilno. In addition, heavy military presence in the region led to the creation of army clubs around the city: WKS 1p.p. and WKS 6p.p. being the most active, while AKS Wilno also sprung into existence.

At the PZPN's Congress in February 1922, the associations of both Upper Silesia and Wilno—alongside that of the centrally located region of Lubelski—were incorporated into the national organisation, with all three establishing league competitions to qualify for that year's Polish championship. Ruch Wielkie Hajduki, Strzelec Wilno and WKS Lublin qualified to make their debuts in the reworked 1922 national competition, against the same five clubs who had taken part the previous year; however, the gulf in class was easily apparent. The debutants could only muster a solitary victory each: Strzelec against Polonia Warsaw in the northern group, and Ruch and WKS against each other in the south. A similar pattern would ultimately continue for several seasons, with Lauda Wilno (a successor to Strzelec), Pogoń Wilno, Lublinianka Lublin and Iskra Siemianowice all progressing from the regional groups, only to struggle on the national stage.

***

Despite being struck by tragedy for a second time with the death of young striker Bolesław Kotapka, Cracovia were still widely expected to retain their national title in 1922. The 23-year-old's grieving teammates were able to gather themselves after a couple of defeats to progress into the national championship's southern group, and started their defence with four successive wins—home and away against both Ruch and WKS Lublin. Even with the absence of Kałuża through injury, Adam Kogut, Leon Sperling and Zygmunt Chruściński were scoring goals aplenty, and looked as though they were still confident of bringing the championship back to Kraków in honour of their fallen comrade.

Pogoń Lwów, though, were even more impressive. Under the leadership of Austrian coach Karl Fischer, the *Pogończycy* were almost unstoppable in front of goal, with the ever-present front trio of Wacław Kuchar, Mieczysław Batsch and Józef Garbień netting 35 of their 37 group stage goals. After putting twelve past a hapless Ruch, they became the first team in the tournament to take points off of Cracovia with a 3-2 victory. Having started their campaign late, they were then required to play both fixtures against WKS in Lublin on successive days—still managing to rack up all four points and fifteen goals without concession. Cracovia did later defeat them 4-1 in Kraków to go two points ahead in the table; however, the Niebiesko-Czerwoni still had one game left to play, and travelled to Wielkie Hajduki two days later needing to win by four goals to progress to the national final. They scored six without reply—one each for Batsch, Garbień and Józef Słonecki, and an eight-minute Kuchar hat-trick—to set up a tie against Warta for the championship. Following a 1-1 draw in Poznań, Pogoń's first title was claimed with a 4-3 victory in Lwów; Kuchar again scoring a second-half hat-trick, including two in the final five minutes which ultimately turned the game on its head. It also confirmed his status as the tournament's best striker with 21 goals.

The 1922 championship began a period of dominance for the Leopolitans. Fischer once again led them to the title in 1923, after collecting maximum points from an eastern group containing Warta, ŁKS and Iskra Siemianowice; they did. however, require both a third game at Warsaw's Agrykola, and then extra time, to defeat Wisła for the trophy. Despite the competition's absence in 1924, Pogoń remained just as dominant on its return in 1925, overcoming Pogoń Wilno and Lublinianka Lublin in the first round, before again defeating Wisła and Warta in the final group for the title. Finally, a fourth successive championship was earned in 1926, after navigating past Cracovia and Lublinianka in the southern group, and then Polonia Warsaw and Warta in the final round.

While Pogoń were busy claiming domestic honours, Cracovia's dwindling successes gave them the time to help promote the Polish game on the continent. Having started 1923 with a New Year's tournament in France against Red Star Paris and Swiss club Servette FC, they also toured Denmark and Sweden in April, meeting clubs such as Aarhus GF, Helsingborgs IF and Malmö FF. However, with the loss of coach Pozsonyi, who left for Spain in February, the start of their Kraków *A-Klasa* campaign was nothing short of disastrous. Losses at both Wisła and Wawel Kraków left them trailing the former from the outset; by the time they installed a new coach—former Southampton striker and Polonia Warsaw boss George Kimpton—they were too far behind to catch up. Even a victory at home to their biggest rivals in May was not enough to bridge the gap, and the Pasy failed to progress to the national tournament for the very first time.

With no part to play in the autumn, Lustgarten and Cetnarowski once again enlisted the help of Pozsonyi, this time as an intermediary to arrange a three-week tour of the Iberian peninsula for September and

October. While the majority of results went, as expected, against them (4-0 and 4-2 against Valencia, 4-0 and 4-2 against Real Madrid, and 3-0 and 3-1 against Celta Vigo), they bookended the trip with their most impressive performances: starting with a 1-1 draw against FC Barcelona in the Campo de Les Corts, and concluding with a 3-2 win over Sevilla. It should also be considered a distinct possibility that the trip had benefits for Pozsonyi: just a few months later, the Hungarian was appointed by *Barça* to lead them into their 1924 season.

***

Following on from the national team's defeat in Budapest, the PZPN opted for a new approach to team selection, and appointed a trio from Kraków to choose the squads for their next games. Cracovia president Józef Lustgarten, Kraków FA secretary Adam Obrubański and former Wisła player Stanisław Ziemiański—the so-named 'committee of three'—were chosen to ensure a fair selection process for the squad; a request that had been made by the PZPN's Leopolitan representatives, who felt that some of their best players had been unfairly overlooked for the trip to Budapest. Still, though, nothing changed, and the selection for the rematch against Hungary was filled with even more Cracovians. The Pasy five of Gintel, Cikowski, Synowiec, Kałuża and Sperling all kept their places, while Henryk Reyman and Stefan Śliwa of Wisła, and Józef Klotz and Zygmunt Krumholz of Jutrzenka made their debuts. Polonia Warsaw keeper Jan Loth and Pogoń attacker Wacław Kuchar too returned, and were the only players in the selection to be based outside of Małopolska; though before his untimely passing, there was speculation that Kotapka could have been in line to replace Kuchar in the second striker's role.

Sixteen thousand Polish supporters crammed into the Stadion Cracovii on 14 May, but bearing witness to a much more effective performance from the visitors, they were given little to celebrate. Unlike in Budapest, the better conditions allowed the Hungarians to play in their traditional way; even so, the Poles' performance was said not to have warranted the 0-3 scoreline. Despite scoring an early own goal, Ludwik Gintel was reported to have been one of the best players on the pitch, while the pre-match agreement to not allow substitutions caused some bother for the White Eagles when Śliwa picked up an injury and was forced to stay on the field. After the game, the visitors commented kindly on their hosts' hospitality, and even visited Kotapka's grave to lay a wreath and pay their respects. With relations blooming, it should be of no surprise that the two countries would go on to meet four more times over the next four years.

But the Poles needed to test themselves against other opposition, and two weeks later a modified squad travelled to Stockholm to face Sweden. Six kept their spots from the game in Kraków: Klotz, Cikowski, Synowiec, Kuchar, Kałuża and Sperling; and when after 25 minutes a Sperling cross was adjudged to have hit the outstretched arm of a Swedish defender, Jutrzenka defender Klotz stood up to score his country's first ever international goal. The Swedes equalised after half-time, but with a quarter-of-an-hour left on the clock, one of the four debutants —Pogoń Lwów's Garbień—earned Poland's maiden victory, slotting home after rounding a couple of defenders.

Neighbouring Romania were the Poles' next opponents, in a game organised at just a few days notice, at the request of the Foreign Ministry. As a compromise, the border town of Cernăuți was chosen to host the match, helping to reduce travel costs for the PZPN. Due to the lack of preparation time, a whole host of new faces were called up, including Spoida, Niziński, Staliński and Prymka of Warta, and Korona Warsaw's Russian-born midfielder Jerzy Bułanow. At the request of Lustgarten, five Cracovia players were released from their planned game against BBSV Bielsko; while the least experienced of the squad, Leopold Dużniak, had only been playing in the Kraków B-Klasa with Olsza Kraków when he was chosen to make up the numbers. It was he, though, who scored the Poles' only goal —the opener in a 1-1 draw.

Four weeks later, many of the regulars had returned as Zagreb played host to the Białe-Orły's 3-1 victory over Yugoslavia. The eleven for this trip were the only squad selected by the trio of Lustgarten, Cetnarowski and Władysław Jentys, after Obrubański and Ziemiański had left their posts citing differences of opinions. Obrubański returned as a selector at the beginning of 1923, elected alongside Pogoń Lwów founder Tadeusz Kuchar and ex-Venetia Ostrów player Kazimierz Glabisz; however, in their five games just one victory was recorded. Their tour to face both Finland and Estonia, where they picked up that lone victory against the latter, was notable for the lack of representation from Cracovia—not due to a change of direction from the selectors, but rather because the players were otherwise engaged on their club's tour of Spain. The Pasy contingent did, however, return for a 2-2 home draw against Sweden in November.

With its lack of success, the idea of a selection committee was abandoned at the 1924 PZPN Congress and, following another election, Obrubański gained sole control of selecting the squad. Makkabi Kraków's Jewish-Hungarian coach Gyula Bíró was also employed, and handed the task of preparing the players for the upcoming Olympics in Paris, while time was afforded to the pair by the cancellation of the 1924 Polish championship.

After trials, 21 players were chosen, and they travelled via Stockholm where a warm-up game was scheduled. This approach didn't prove any better as they succumbed to a heavy defeat against the Swedes—a result which would set the tone for the Olympics. The 5-1 scoreline became Poland's largest defeat, yet it was a record which would last for only eight days. Bíró sent his team out to face Hungary at Paris' Stade Bergeyre where, despite a competent first-half showing, a collapse in the second period left the Polish players heading home on the back of a 5-0 mauling.

> "What was the reason for the breakdown? I believe that the reason was nothing other than it was their first appearance in the Olympics... I am convinced that if they had the opportunity in the next few days to play with

the same team, and with the same opponent, it is certain that the result would be quite different—more honourable."
- Edward Cetnarowski

Despite failure on the pitch, Poland's appearance in the Olympics helped to forge new relationships. Within a month, games were scheduled against the USA in Warsaw and Turkey in Łódź. Having failed to return from Paris in time to lead the team, Obrubański was replaced, firstly by Tadeusz Orzelski, and then Ignacy Rosenstock. While Orzelski could only succumb to a hard-fought 3-2 defeat against the American team, Rosenstock's line-up went on to claim a 2-0 victory against the Turks—the *Biało-Czerwoni*'s first ever victory on home soil.

CHAPTER EIGHT
THE PROFESSIONALS

IDEAS FOR A NEW COMPETITION to compliment the Polish championship had been bandied about for a number of years before plans finally came to fruition. It was Adam Obrubański, a devout Anglophile, who suggested the creation of a knock-out competition based on the English FA Cup; however, a few changes were needed before the inaugural 1926 competition was given the rubber stamp by PZPN President Cetnarowski.

The new tournament would be contested by the winners of nine regional cup competitions scheduled for the autumn of 1925 and, rather than a standard knock-out competition, it was given a much more unconventional format. Firstly, the nine teams would be split into groups of three—one of which was given a bye to the second round, where they would meet the winner of the game involving the other two. The winner of that match would then advance to a final group, where the same process would be repeated. In the end, just eight regional winners took part: Toruński KS, Warszawianka Warsaw and Warta Poznań in the northern group; Sparta Lwów and Sokół Równe in the eastern group; and ŁKS Łódź, Wisła Kraków and Ruch Wielkie Hajduki in the south western group. WKS 1p.p. Wilno had been due to join Sparta and Sokół in Group 2, but their withdrawal was forced before the competition had begun.

Wisła ultimately claimed the *Puchar Polski* trophy following a 2-1 victory against Sparta Lwów, with Henryk Reyman's deciding strike coming in the final minute and giving the visitors little time to respond. It was, however, a competition shrouded in controversy, starting with Wisła's opening game against ŁKS which was abandoned in the 83rd minute when Łodzianin supporters attacked the referee after disagreeing with a penalty decision given against them. Penalty decisions and crowd trouble were again at the centre of proceedings a week later in Toruń, where Warta Poznań activist Edmund Szyc took the whistle for his club's game against TKS after the scheduled referee had failed to arrive. After handing Warta a chance to score from twelve yards, the threat of trouble from the home support encouraged him to renege on his decision. Upon Warta's protests, the PZPN forced the game to be replayed, with the Poznań club advancing to the final group by virtue of a 7-0 victory.

Partly in thanks to the PZPN's lack of organisation, Warta's adventure in the competition didn't last much longer. While they were taking on Sparta in Lwów, two of their key players—Wawrzyniec Staliński and Michał Flieger—were back in Poznań, representing the Polish national team in a friendly against Romania. Staliński had scored four of the Warciarze's seven in Toruń, and they severely lacked his influence as Kazimierz Murski's late goal condemned them to a 1-0 defeat.

Even with a helping hand from the PZPN's poor scheduling, Sparta's accession to the final had been a big surprise among Poland's footballing circles. The club had only advanced to the Lwów A-Klasa at the end of the 1924 season, and with the 1925 regional tournaments not played due to the break for the Olympics, by the time that they lifted the Lwów ZPN Cup they were still yet to play a game amongst the region's elite teams. Sparta's advance to the final was owed largely to those clubs' failure to take the competition seriously, in the midst of a scandal which had rocked Leopolitan football to the core.

**

In an attempt to break Pogoń and Czarni's dominance in the region, Lwów's largest Jewish club, Hasmonea, appointed Austrian Friedrich 'Fritz' Kerr as their new coach in February 1924. As well as earning seven international caps, Kerr had spent his playing career in two of Vienna's top clubs: WAC and Hakoah. In the latter he had performed alongside future coaching legend Béla Guttmann, and was a part of the travelling Hakoah squad that became the first foreign club to win on British soil with victory over West Ham United in 1923. But while the Hasmonea board had hoped his playing experience would transfer into his first coaching role, the club could only manage third place in the 1924 Lwów A-Klasa. After a number of high-profile friendly games against prestigious foreign opposition over the next 12 months, Kerr left his position.

Though unable to make a significant impression during his eighteen-month stint in Lwów, Kerr was almost single-handedly responsible for bringing the Polish game to its knees within weeks of his departure. In an open letter published by Lwów-based afternoon journal *Wiek Nowy*, the Austrian accused his former club—along with both Pogoń and Czarni—of contravening PZPN rules by paying wages to a number of their players. The clubs retaliated, claiming a smear campaign against them. Hasmonea president Ignacy Roman even tried to distract from his club's guilt by claiming that Kerr's dismissal from the club was for reasons traversing the sport:

> *"The letter by Mr Kerr is an act of vengeance from our excluded coach. Because of his actions interfering with the criminal code: dealing with contraband and the trade of illicit goods; immediately after the disclosure of these acts, we expelled him [from the club]."*
> *- Ignacy Roman, President of Hasmonea Lwów*

Having previously been forced to fend off attempts to see the headquarters of the PZPN moved away from their city, the association's Cracovian representatives now sensed the perfect opportunity to discredit their Galician neighbours, and following a series of investigations around a dozen players were implicated across the three clubs. Appeals followed and sentences were eventually reduced, with three—Zygmunt Steuermann, Izydor Redler and Ludwik Schneider—even going on to appear for the Polish national team soon after. Instead, PZPN officials chose to direct the most severe punishments at those in backroom roles, with a number of administrative staff across the clubs handed suspensions ranging between bans of a few months to, in the most severe cases, lifetime disqualifications. With the PZPN's stance against professionalism in the sport unwavering, the first proper Polish professionals were forced to go abroad to earn a living from the game: in late 1925, the Pogoń attacking pair of Emil Görlitz and Józef Słonecki leaving the restrictive rules in Poland behind, to join their former coach Karl Fischer at Italian club Edera Trieste.

The scandal may have destroyed any hopes of Lwów becoming the home of the PZPN, yet it was under the initiative of the three clubs at the heart of the row that a conference took place on 2 December 1926, with the intention of making changes to the structure of Polish football. The format of the Polish championships had regularly been brought for debate during the 1920s, with an increasing number considering it outdated, obsolete, and inadequate for the development of Polish football. With clubs growing at a tremendous pace, yet only one from each region able to progress past the regional competitions, a number of larger clubs were regularly denied the chance to compete for honours. As such, a league system was seen as the only way forward.

Tadeusz Kuchar chaired the inaugural meeting, and the three Leopolitan clubs were joined by representatives of a further nine from across the country: Wisła Kraków, Polonia Warsaw, Legia Warszawa, Warszawianka, ŁKS Łódź, Klub Turystów Łódź, Toruński KS, Warta Poznań and 1.FC Katowice. Of the country's largest clubs, only Cracovia and Ruch Wielkie Hajduki remained absent—Ruch still open to the idea of a national league, but Cracovia vehemently against it. The same twelve clubs then convened two days later in Warsaw to create the '*Polska Liga Piłki Nożnej*', with activists from military-backed Legia taking prominent roles.

Cracovia maintained their opposition going into 1927, and after failure to come to an agreement during crucial talks at the PZPN's general assembly in February 1927, the members of the PLPN decided to go it alone. Within days, Legia president Roman Gorecki had been appointed as the president of the new entity, while by the end of the month a total of 57 clubs—now including Ruch—had confirmed their participation in the new structure. Fourteen teams were to be placed into the league, with the remainder to participate in regional competitions, and then a national play-off, in order to earn promotion to the top tier. In the hope that a deal could be done, a space in the *Liga Polska* was set aside for Cracovia; however, with confirmation of the club's self-omission it was given instead to another Kraków club, Jutrzenka.

Reactions to the breakaway were highly charged, with the PZPN handing indefinite suspensions to every player and official which had affiliated themselves with the league. As a result, the national team's June friendly with Romania—their sole game of 1927—featured several debutants, only from clubs which had remained loyal to the organisation.

The first round of league matches took place on 3 April, with derby games in Łódź, Lwów, Warsaw, Kraków and Upper Silesia; the commonly accepted chain of events having the game in Łódź, between Klub Turystów and ŁKS, as the first to kick off at 3pm. But while Jan Durka's 36th minute strike—the opener of ŁKS's 2-0 victory—was for a long time considered as the first goal to be scored, evidence has since been uncovered that TKS Toruń's 4-3 victory over Polonia Warsaw began at the same time, giving TKS's Paweł Gumowski the honour with his goal after just six minutes of play. Meanwhile, the highest-scoring match of the seven opening day games came in Lwów, with Pogoń's 7-1 victory over Hasmonea; however, with new recruits on either side having not completed their registrations from Lechia Lwów, the game was forced to be replayed two months later, ending with a narrow victory for Hasmonea.

Supporters received the new format well: over twenty thousand witnessed the opening weekend's play, with the number increasing as the warmer summer months arrived. The clubs also enjoyed the new structure, profiting from both increased competition on the field and increased revenues off of it. However, the issues which had preceded the league's maiden season continued to cast a dark cloud, and when Cracovia hosted Pogoń Lwów in an unsanctioned mid-October friendly, the latter were punished by the PLPN with forfeits in their final three games of the season.

Finally though, as the inaugural season reached its climax, both Cracovia and the PZPN succumbed to the competition's undeniable success; and at the signing of an agreement between the two parties, in the final days of 1927, a tumultuous year was brought to a close. The Polish championship would once again fall under the remit of the PZPN, and Cracovia would retake their rightful place among the country's elite. However, as a compromise, it would also signal the end of the old era in Polish football, with a vote to transfer the PZPN's headquarters from Kraków to Warsaw.

* * *

The punishment handed to Pogoń Lwów for their unsanctioned game prevented them from continuing their five-year dominance of Polish football. Instead, cup winners Wisła Kraków fought with 1.FC Katowice for the championship, and due to their respective backgrounds the battle between the two became widely viewed as a nationalist affair.

1.FC had been established in 1903 as Preußen Kattowitz, whilst the city was still under German rule. Along with Diana Kattowitz and Germania Kattowitz, Preußen had formed from the embers of the region's oldest club, Sportverein Frisch Auf Kattowitz; and it was those three clubs that created the Kattowitzer Ballspiel-Verband in 1905. Preußen proved to be the stronger of the trio, winning the KBV's only championship, while also advancing to the finals of the Südostdeutschland Fußballverband Championship on three occasions before the outbreak of World War One. Upon Katowice's incorporation into Poland, passport issues left Preußen no longer able to fulfil their fixtures in German competition. Before long they had joined the PZPN and renamed themselves as 1.FC—'Erster Fußball Club'—representing Upper Silesia's German minority. Due to the redrawn borders, the club's players now became eligible to play for the Polish national team—something that Emil Görlitz had done before his move to Pogoń Lwów, followed by Karol Kossok several years later. However, their Erster teammate Eryk Heidenreich—regarded as one of the best defenders in Europe at the time—declined the same offer, stating that "[he did] not feel even slightly Polish, but only German".

Despite being considered as Wisła's closest challengers, by the middle of August 1.FC had spent less than a week at the top of the table. Wisła had previously led the pack since a 4-0 trouncing of Czarni Lwów on 8 May, and they soon returned to the summit with a number of dominant performances including a 15-0 hammering of Toruński KS, with the help of a league record double hat-trick from Henryk Reyman. By the time they met 1.FC a fortnight later in Katowice, their lead had been extended to five points.

Erster had been almost formidable at home: their record of nine wins from ten was bettered only by Wisła themselves; but with the Biała Gwiazda's away form temperamental, predictions on the outcome of the result were varied. Judgements were also clouded by the socio-political overtones surrounding the game, with Wisła claiming their "duty to defend Polish colours, and prevent the Polish title passing into foreign hands". The thought of such taking place irked with most: if the only majority German team in Poland were good enough to lift the championship, it would prove a huge blow for the Polish game.

> "...it would be an unpleasant humiliation, and would hurt something more than just the sport's ambitions."
> - Henryk Reyman

Although mathematically the result of the game could not determine the direction of the championship, it was to have a significant bearing on its eventual destination. While a Wisła victory would send them seven points clear, a win for Erster would close the gap to just three; and with two games in hand, would earn them a chance to rise to the summit at the expense of the Poles. Reyman, who had fought against the Germans in the Uprisings just a few years earlier, called it "the most important game in the history of TS Wisła".

The importance of the game wasn't lost on the fans either, with various estimates of between fifteen- and twenty-five-thousand supporters descending on Katowice ahead of the kick off. 1.FC had called upon all of Upper Silesia's German population to attend the game, and could even count on the support of a number of fans from across the border in Gleiwitz, Hindenburg and Beuthen. Meanwhile, several trains were laid on for Wisła supporters to make the 50-kilometre journey westwards, while they also received the backing of Polish Silesians, who flooded in to cheer on their countrymen.

The game itself kicked off at 4pm sharp and quickly developed into a cagey affair, with neither team willing to give up an advantage early on. Even with Erster reduced to nine men in the first half due to injuries to both striker-turned-goalkeeper Emil Görlitz and attacker Teodor Jończyk, Wisła struggled against a stubborn Germanic defence. By the time that the pair had been readied to return to the action, Łodzianin referee Zygmunt Hanke had signalled for half-time, with 1.FC's clean sheet remaining unspoiled.

As the game progressed, the Erster fans' hostility towards their guests had steadily increased in intensity. Polish newspaper reports would later go on to comment that they had "behaved poorly", hurling insults and threatening the Wisła players. At one point they even descended on the pitch, only to be forced back by mounted police. Though the 1.FC players also emerged for the second period fired up, "in spite of the vulgar game played by the Germans" it was Wisła who took the lead within ten minutes of the restart. Starting in the centre with Jan Kotlarczyk, the ball found its way, via Reyman, to Mieczysław Balcer on the right-hand side. His cross caused a great deal of confusion amongst the Erster defence and allowed midfielder Stanisław Czulak to shoot into the loosely guarded net. Deflated, Erster were soon left with a mountain to climb: five minutes later Reyman himself advanced through the middle, before sending Görlitz in the wrong direction to put Wisła two goals to the good.

The crowd grew increasingly raucous—even more so with around twenty minutes remaining on the clock, when Erster striker Artur Geisler saw what he believed to be a goal waved away by Hanke. Almost immediately, as Wisła advanced to the other end of the pitch, a shot from Balcer struck the arm of defender Kurt Pohl. This time the referee was quick to reach for his whistle.

The Erster players were incensed. Frustrated, sensing defeat and also feeling the victim of an anti-German conspiracy, rather than face Reyman's penalty, goalkeeper and captain Görlitz left the field of play and was swiftly followed by his teammates. Unsure of how to proceed, the Wisła striker tapped the ball into the now empty net, while Hanke signalled the end of the game despite only 73 minutes having passed. Instantly the Polish fans flooded the pitch to celebrate with the Wisła players, hoisting them onto their shoulders, protecting them from the threat of attacks from the German support.

On arrival back in Kraków, the Wisła team were treated as heroes; but though the 2-0 victory had been confirmed, the title still hadn't. As it turned out, that was wrapped up a week later with a 7-1 victory over Polonia Warsaw, while Erster suffered a 5-0 loss in the capital against Legia. Henryk Reyman's four-goal haul pushed him closer to his season-ending total of 37—a record which still remains intact.

Having helped to usher in the new era of Polish football, Wisła went on to capture a further title in 1928 ahead of Warta Poznań, Legia Warsaw and league newcomers Cracovia, before relinquishing the trophy to Warta the following year. Erster, meanwhile, suffered a sharp decline. After a fifth-placed finish in 1928, relegation to the regional leagues followed a year later—never to return—with a number of fans once again claiming that an anti-German bias amongst referees and officials had been partly to blame for their downfall.

CHAPTER NINE
EZI, THE TERCET AND THE FIFA WORLD CUP

"He is probably the only player in the world who scored more goals than he had chances."
- Fritz Walter; West Germany, 1940-1958

LONG BEFORE BECOMING THE POSTER BOY of Polish football, Ernest Wilimowski could quite easily have found himself on a different path. Born during the Great War to German parents, while his hometown still lay within the German Empire, it was only tragic circumstances and political turmoil which presented him the opportunity to wear the White Eagle on his chest.

Given the Germanic name Ernst after his father—a soldier killed on the battlelines of the First World War before having the chance to meet his son—he was brought up in Kattowitz by his widowed mother Paulina. When the family home was drawn within the newly defined Polish borders and renamed Katowice in 1922, Paulina opted to stay put rather than move westwards, allowing both mother and son to take Polish citizenship.

While the mandatory Polish lessons in Silesian schools helped young Ezi to learn his new language, Paulina ensured that he maintained his German upbringing by continuing to speak their native tongue at home, and it was only when she remarried a native Pole that Ernst began to use the Polish spelling of his name. Still, like many Silesians, his national identity was never particularly strong; so-much-so that Ernest would often speak the Silesian dialect of the Polish language among friends, while referring to himself as *'Górnoślązak'*—'Upper Silesian'—rather than specifically German or Polish.

Ezi's footballing education mostly came in the unorganised street games on Katowice's Ulica Francuska where, being one of the youngest, he was often forced to play in goal. When he did finally venture on to the outfield his talents were immediately noticeable, and before long he had signed for the youth team of the local Germanic club, 1.FC. With his bright red hair and protruding ears, even as a youngster Wilimowski was instantly recognisable amongst his Erster teammates. Impressive performances in the inside-left position also made him stand out on the pitch, attracting the attention of a number of clubs, all wanting to secure the signature of the teenage prodigy.

Ruch Wielkie Hajduki were one of them. After surpassing 1.FC to become the biggest team in Upper Silesia, the *Niebiescy* had gone on to claim their first national championship in the reformulated competition of 1933. Led by the attacking trio of Edmund Giemsa (15 goals), Teodor Peterek (12) and Alfred Gwodsz (11), Ruch finished second behind Cracovia in the league's Western Group, before defeating the Pasy in their final game of the season to pip Pogoń Lwów to the title by a single point. Following the forced retirement of Gwodsz, who had suffered a broken leg in the penultimate game of the season against Legia, Ruch sought the signature of seventeen-year-old Wilimowski as his replacement. To secure his services, Ruch paid Erster a then-eye-watering 1000zł, as well as handing them the gate receipts from two friendly games to be organised between the clubs. The fee was mostly covered by the club's sponsor Huta Batory—Wielkie Hajduki's enormous steelworks factory. Ezi quickly justified the outlay too, scoring seven times in his first four games for the club, including five in a single outing against Podgorze Kraków.

Wilimowski immediately struck up a partnership with two of Ruch's biggest stars: Peterek and Gerard Wodarz. At six feet tall, 23-year-old Peterek was an imposing figure on the Ruch front line and was known for his competitive and success-driven nature. In part due to his height, Teo was extremely talented in the air, with many of his goals coming as headers. In a one-year spell spanning the end of 1937 and most of the 1938 season, Peterek scored in sixteen consecutive league games—a world record until broken by Barcelona's Lionel Messi in 2013. Of his 22 goals during those twelve months, nine were scored with his head, and a further five as a result of his role as the team's penalty taker. The frontman became so notorious with his efficiency from the spot that just drawing a penalty was often considered as good as a goal; however, according to legend, on one rare occasion against Śmigły Wilno in which his spot kick was saved, Peterek became so incensed that he threw mud into the goalkeeper's face.

Three years younger, Wodarz was much more reserved than Peterek, yet the understanding between the two, and later also Wilimowski, was almost telepathic. Although less prolific in front of goal, it was left-winger Wodarz's crosses which assisted many of Teo's headers. For this reason, Stanisław Mielech went on to proclaim him as "the ideal of a player in that position".

Wilimowski, Peterek and Wodarz soon earned the combined nickname *Królewski Tercet*—the 'Three Kings'—and their formidable performances led Ruch Wielkie Hajduki to a second league title in 1934. Ezi dominated the scoring charts with 33 goals, while Teo wasn't much further behind with 28. Adding in Wodarz's ten, the trio accounted for all-but-sixteen of Ruch's 87-goal haul for the season.

National team coach Józef Kałuża needed little convincing of Wilimowski's talents, and the striker joined both Peterek and Wodarz in the Poland squad for a tour of Scandinavia despite having only been watched by the coach twice. Wodarz and Wilimowski played every minute of the successive 4-2 defeats against Denmark and Sweden, with Ezi netting Poland's second against the Swedes. Before the year was over, the trio all participated in the 4-1 loss to Yugoslavia, while Wodarz and Wilimowski were amongst a Polish eleven which succumbed to Germany in Warsaw, with Ezi again scoring consolations in both games.

Ruch successfully defended their title in 1935, however, on this occasion it was much more laboured. Peterek top scored with 13, while Ruch's squirm to the championship was largely unassisted by Wilimowski, who had picked up and injury that limited his participation to just seven games. Ezi also missed all six of Poland's internationals during the year, but when he eventually returned to action for the 1936 season, he quickly rediscovered his shooting boots.

With the impending Olympic Games in Berlin, the national team spent the early part of the year concentrating on preparations for a second outing in the competition. Kałuża's charges started with a February victory over a talented Belgian team in Brussels, yet were defeated in three unofficial friendly games in May: twice against Austrians Admira Vienna and once against London club Chelsea. Less than a month before their opening game of the XI Olympiad, Kałuża and his German coach Kurt Otto gathered 36 players for a training camp at Legia's Stadion Wojska Polskiego, which after a week would be whittled down to 25, and then finally 18 for the tournament. After returning from both injury and a two-month suspension for allegedly striking an opponent during a league game, Wilimowski was included among the 36; but by the time the final group had been selected, the Katowiczanin was once again ruled out of contention.

Wilimowski's omission from Kałuża's final eighteen is most-widely attributed to a 9-0 friendly defeat to Cracovia, just a few weeks before the tournament. Several Ruch players were alleged to have been "hardly even able to stand" on the pitch in Kraków, after celebrating the previous day's league victory over title rivals Wisła by drinking alcohol into the early hours of the morning—reportedly funded by 50zł bonuses, which were adjudged to have contravened both PZPN and Olympic rules surrounding professionalism. For both "inappropriate behaviour as a member of the

Olympic team, and violation of the Olympic oath", Wilimowski incurred a six-week suspension that ended his competition before it had even begun.

In his place, Kałuża selected another Silesian: Hubert Gad of Śląsk Świętochłowice. During 1935, Gad had scored 14 times as newly promoted Śląsk managed a fifth-placed finish. Kałuża saw the 21-year-old as the ideal replacement for Wilimowski, and after scoring on his debut against Belgium, he was bequeathed a starting role for the tournament.

POLAND SQUAD
1936 Olympics; Berlin, Germany:

Goalkeepers: Spirydion Albański (Pogoń Lwów), Edward Madejski (Wisła Kraków).

Defenders: Henryk Martyna (Legia Warsaw), Antoni Gałecki (ŁKS Łódź), Władysław Szczepaniak (Polonia Warsaw).

Midfielders: Józef Kotlarczyk (Wisła Kraków), Jan Wasiewicz (Pogoń Lwów), Edward Dytko (Dąb Katowice), Wilhelm Góra (Cracovia), Franciszek Cebulak (Legia Warsaw).

Strikers: Ryszard Piec (Naprzód Lipiny), Fryderyk Scherfke (Warta Poznań), Teodor Peterek (Ruch Wielkie Hajduki), Hubert Gad (Śląsk Świętochłowice), Gerard Wodarz (Ruch Wielkie Hajduki), Walenty Musielak (HCP Poznań), Walerian Kisieliński (Polonia Warsaw), Michał Matyas (Pogoń Lwów).

Berlin's Poststadion played host to the Poles' opening game of the Olympic tournament, where they were paired with their old foes from Hungary. Against a significantly weakened amateur eleven, Kałuża's squad claimed a comprehensive 3-0 victory—Gad scoring twice and Wodarz adding a third late on. The two goalscorers were again instrumental during the Poles' quarter final victory against Great Britain three days later: Gad's first-half equaliser followed by Wodarz's ten-minute hat-trick—one goal before half-time, and two after. Ryszard Piec made it five just before the hour mark, and though the Brits rallied with three quick goals to set up a tense final ten minutes, Kałuża's rattled Eagles held on to the 5-4 scoreline, to earn a semi-final meeting against Austria.

Kałuża hadn't wanted to make changes to his starting eleven ahead of the Austria game, but his hand was forced after Fryderyk Scherfke suffered cracked ribs following a number of robust British tackles. In his place, the coach opted to hand a debut to Walenty Musielak rather than the more experienced Michał Matyas—a decision which came as a surprise to many. Meanwhile, the Austrians made two changes to their team which had controversially progressed past Peru, in a game which the South Americans had won comfortably in extra time before their withdrawal from the tournament in protest, after the match was forced to be replayed on extremely dubious grounds.

As in the previous two rounds, Gad again found himself on the score sheet, yet this time his strike with seventeen minutes remaining proved merely a consolation. Incoming striker Karl Kainberger had given Austria the lead early on, while his Salzburger AK teammate Adolf Laudon doubled it just after the break with an impressive shot from outside of the area. Following Gad's strike the Poles pressed for a late equaliser, but in doing so left themselves exposed in defence; with just two minutes remaining the Austrians were able to counter and Franz Mandl struck to put the game beyond Poland's reach. Ending 3-1, Kałuża's demoralised squad fell into a consolation game for the Bronze Medal against Norway where, despite first-half goals from Peterek and Wodarz, Poland returned home empty handed after a 3-2 defeat.

For Gad, the Olympics proved to be the highlight of his tragically short career; less than three years later, just weeks short of his 25th birthday, he drowned after suffering a heart attack whilst swimming. For his funeral procession, thousands lined the streets of Świętochłowice, whilst three of his Olympic colleagues—Peterek, Piec and Dytko—helped to carry his coffin into the church. The striker was even laid to rest in his Olympic uniform.

***

FINALLY, A FAIR DECISION—WILIMOWSKI REHABILITATED!

"The League of the Polish Football Association has decided to end the investigation into the Wilimowski incident, and cancel his penalty. As you know, Wilimowski was wrongly implicated in the scandal at Ruch, which looked not for justice, but to bully the club, which for the fourth time is fighting for the Polish championship... It is a pity that the decision of the sports authorities came so late. Polish sport suffered great loss because of Wilimowski's suspension. The lack of this player in the national team made it very difficult during both the Olympics and in recent international matches."
- Gazeta Polonia, Katowice, September 1936

The importance of Upper Silesia to the international squad was ever increasing. Despite only contributing six of the 18-man Olympic squad, all eleven Polish goals in the tournament had been scored by Silesians: five for Wodarz, four for Gad, and one apiece for Peterek and Piec. Many fans and players also believed that if Wilimowski had been available for selection, the Poles would have undoubtedly claimed gold.

Wilimowski's reprieve may have come too late for Poland, but for Ruch it was almost perfectly timed. With the break for the Olympics, Ezi only actually missed two league games—defeats to ŁKS Łódź and Warszawianka. Even after that temporary loss of form, they went into September still atop the league, a point ahead of nearest challengers Garbarnia Kraków. Ezi's return coincided with an Upper Silesian double header—victories against Dąb Katowice and Śląsk Świętochłowice—in which all three of the Królewski Tercet netted. The trio also chipped in with goals a few weeks later in a comprehensive 6-1 win at home to Legia, setting up the chance to win their fourth-straight title in their following game against a stumbling Garbarnia. It was a chance which they grasped with both hands; despite Wilimowski's early opener being cancelled out before half-time, the Niebiescy responded with five unanswered goals—both Ezi and Wodarz completing hat-tricks—to claim the championship with two games to spare.

Possibly for fear of reprimand, Kałuża had kept fairly quiet about Wilimowski's suspension; however, once the ban was lifted, the 20-year-old's immediate call up for the late-1936 friendly game against Denmark reaffirmed the striker's importance to the team. Ezi went on to take a key role in the program of friendlies scheduled through 1937, both starting and scoring in victories over Sweden and Denmark, and then maintaining his position against Bulgaria and Romania.

These games were effectively a warm up for Poland's attempt at qualifying for the World Cup: a two-legged tie against Yugoslavia beginning at the back end of 1937. As a result of a 9-3 victory in their previous meeting, the Yugoslavs arrived in Warsaw filled with confidence—a confidence which soon disappeared, as one goal apiece for both Wilimowski and AKS Chorzów striker Jerzy Wostal, and a double for the latter's clubmate Leonard Piontek practically put the tie beyond doubt by the halfway point. Svetovar Popović's side were able to collect themselves before the return leg in Belgrade in April 1938, but their narrow 1-0 victory was never close to preventing Poland's advance to the finals for the very first time.

Even before qualification was confirmed, Kałuża's squad were provisionally paired against South America's sole representatives, Brazil. *Los Canarinhos* had not even needed to qualify for the competition; having originally been scheduled to play against neighbours Argentina, they were granted free passage after *Los Albiceleste* withdrew in protest over FIFA's decision to host a second successive tournament in Europe. The first round game had been originally scheduled in the southern French city of

Toulouse, but with the incorporation of fellow qualifiers Austria into the expanding German state, several minor alterations to the tournament were required. These included the relocation of the Poles' game to the more north-easterly town of Strasbourg—a change which suited Polish officials, as they had worried that Toulouse's warmer climate would prove more of an advantage to the Brazilians.

As per FIFA's rules, Kałuża and his assistant Marian Spoida named their 22-man squad in early May, with only fifteen of those planned to make the trip to Strasbourg for their opening game due to financial reasons. A week prior to their departure, Ireland were welcomed to Warsaw for a warm up game, for which Kałuża selected his strongest available eleven. The 6-0 victory, with goals from Wilimowski, Jan Wasiewicz, and two each for Wodarz and Piontek, gave confidence that the Poles were suitably prepared for their first appearance in FIFA's showcase tournament.

POLAND SQUAD

1938 FIFA World Cup; France:

Goalkeepers: Edward Madejski (unattached), Walter Brom (Ruch Wielkie Hajduki).

Defenders: Władysław Szczepaniak (Polonia Warsaw), Antoni Gałecki (ŁKS Łódź), Edmund Giemsa (Ruch Wielkie Hajduki).

Midfielders: Wilhelm Góra (Cracovia), Edward Nyc (Polonia Warsaw), Edward Dytko (Dąb Katowice), Wilhelm Piec (Naprzód Lipiny).

Strikers: Ryszard Piec (Naprzód Lipiny), Leonard Piontek (AKS Chorzów), Fryderyk Scherfke (Warta Poznań), Ernest Wilimowski (Ruch Wielkie Hajduki), Gerard Wodarz (Ruch Wielkie Hajduki), Stanisław Baran (Warszawianka).

Kałuża's hope of sticking with the same squad that earned qualification was scuppered due to injuries: Polonia Warsaw midfielder Edward Nyc was called up just a few days before departure after Wasiewicz picked up a knock whilst playing for Pogoń Lwów, while Jerzy Wostal's long term absence allowed Warta Poznań frontman Fryderyk Scherfke to retain his place having already covered against the Irish. Elsewhere, goalkeeper Edward Madejski continued as Kałuża's first choice, despite being banned from club football due to a scandal relating to his transfer across Kraków from Wisła to Garbarnia. The coach also opted to call up two uncapped 17-year-olds: Ruch Wielkie Hajduki custodian Walter Brom and Warszawianka striker Stanisław Baran. After a short training camp. the fifteen players, along with Kałuża, Spoida and the team's Head of Preparations Tadeusz Foryś, departed westwards, arriving in Strasbourg two days prior to the game.

Less than two-thirds of the Stade de la Meinau was occupied for the Sunday afternoon kick off, with several thousand Polish expatriates among the 15,000 in attendance. Meanwhile, many locals were out in support of the South Americans, hoping to see some of the attractive football which had led to them being named among the favourites to win the competition. But while it was expected that the cooler climes would prove to be an advantage for the European teams, soon after kick off it became apparent that the change didn't faze the Brazilians one bit. Their high-paced attack caused problems for Poland from the first whistle, and it took only eighteen minutes for star striker Leônidas da Silva to breach the Polish defence, latching on to a through ball before firing into the top corner with his left foot.

Poland's response came just moments later when, after skipping through two challenges, Wilimowski was hauled to the ground by a rugby tackle from *Canarinhos'* defender Domingos. Up stepped Scherfke to side foot into the bottom left corner, leaving goalkeeper Batatais without a chance. Unfortunately they were level for only two minutes before Romeu Pellicciari rose highest to head past Madejski; and then, just a minute before the break, fellow striker José Perácio found himself with space in the Polish box to comfortably extend the Brazilians' lead.

Rather than head back to the locker room upon the whistle, Kałuża opted to keep his charges out on the pitch for his half-time team talk. Calm and unaffected by nerves, the coach encouraged his team to fight, and perhaps was even able to restore some of the confidence which they had lost after falling behind. Coinciding with the break in play, the heavens also began to open, pouring rain on to the pitch; when the Brazilians emerged from beneath the stands they immediately began to struggle with the change in conditions, regularly slipping on the wet turf.

Within fifteen minutes of the restart, Wilimowski had Poland back on level terms. Escaping Domingos' marking in the 56th minute, the Ruch frontman neatly slotted past Batatais to reduce the deficit. Three minutes later he cancelled it out completely: in a move described later in the press as "circus-like", flicking the ball with the outside of his right foot over the advancing Brazilian keeper and into the bottom corner.

Yet with around twenty five minutes remaining, the rain stopped as suddenly as it had started. Poland's period of dominance had passed without them being able take the lead and, although not controlling the game, the Brazilians began to once again test the Polish goal. It now seemed only a matter of time before they would reclaim the lead. In the 71st minute they did:

> "Well, I remember this goal! Perácio shot. I played without gloves, as always—I did not have this habit. He struck the ball with great force, it hit my fingers and the momentum carried it on to the bar. However, the ball bounced off of it, and then fell on to my neck and into the net! From the stands it may have looked funny, but I was not laughing."
> - Edward Madejski

"They coped well with the ball" remembered Gerard Wodarz, "but we made up for this shortcoming with fighting spirit, militancy and incredible ambition". Indeed, after falling behind once again, the better chances fell Poland's way: Wodarz himself going close, while a Wilimowski effort struck the post. Just as it looked like they might run out of time, their persistence was rewarded—in the final minute of the game—as Wilimowski completed his hat-trick to send the match into extra time.

In a desperate attempt to counter the effects of the saturated turf, Leônidas had removed both of his boots during the second half—as he later confirmed, wishing to play barefooted as he had done as a boy on the beaches of Rio de Janeiro. Once alerted to the fact, referee Ivan Eklind reprimanded the striker and forced him to replace his footwear. Still, it was without his right cleat—disguised by his black sock being caked in mud—that he scored his second goal of the game to put Brazil back into the lead.

Poland continued to press, and were twice almost rewarded with an equalising goal: firstly Wodarz edging a free kick wide, while Nyc's shot from distance rattled the crossbar at its junction with the post. Yet just before the end of the first half of extra time, it was the South Americans who found the net. After a Brazilian shot clattered the upright and fell to safety, a mix up between Antoni Gałecki and captain Władysław Szczepaniak resulted in the latter attempting to clear, only to kick the ground and nudge the ball into the direction of Leônidas. The *Diamanté Negro* gleefully accepted his invitation, and went on to drill a low shot into the empty net, effectively eliminating Poland from the competition with fifteen minutes to spare.

Though Poland's first World Cup experience steadily petered to an end, Wilimowski still had time to grab a share of the headlines before the game could be brought to its conclusion. With just a couple of the 120 minutes remaining, Ezi embarked on a solo run which resulted in him netting his fourth, and Poland's fifth of the tie. It may not have altered the outcome, yet in doing so he was able to set an individual record for the most goals in a World Cup match—one which stood for 56 years, until finally broken in 1994 by Russian striker Oleg Salenko.

CHAPTER TEN
THE FINAL GAME

Following their World Cup exit, the Polish national team fell into a sharp decline. Losses to Germany and Ireland, a second string's defeat in Latvia, and high-scoring draws with Yugoslavia and Norway ensured that they ended the calendar year without a win in six attempts. 1939 didn't begin any better either, as a full-strength eleven were demolished 4-0 by a dominant French team in Paris' Parc des Princes. Subsequent draws against Belgium and Switzerland in Łódź and Warsaw ensured the winless streak was eventually extended to nine games, leading to questions being asked over Kałuża's continuing suitability for the role.

The *Selekcjoner*, however, remained unconcerned, and had actually been encouraged by his side's battling performances. The Poles had played with only ten men for 83 minutes against the Swiss after Warta Poznań defender Edmund Twórz broke his leg, and yet still managed a credible 1-1 draw. The defeat against France had also come on the back of the long Polish winter break, with players unfit and unprepared, but still displaying an eagerness to play against such prestigious opposition.

The exhibition games had also given Kałuża several chances to test new players from the second tier, with one eye looking towards the 1940 Olympics in Tokyo. Brygada Częstochowa goalkeeper Adolf Krzyk was brought in following injuries to both first choice Edward Madejski and his backup Roman Mrugała, while faith was kept in the experienced Ryszard Piec and Ewald Dytko despite stuttering seasons for their clubs. The coach had also acknowledged Śląsk Świętochłowice's promotion-chasing campaign by handing call ups to their 18-year-old striker Zygmunt

Kulawik and utility man Edward Cebula. With late Summer friendly games against strong opposition such as Hungary, Bulgaria and Yugoslavia in the offing, it was a risky tactic by the coach. Yet it was one he continued to employ as Cebula was once again named, whilst Paweł Cyganek and Michał Dusik were plucked from Fablok Chrzanów and KPW Poznań respectively.

Still, Kałuża was counting on his experienced stars to lead Poland into their third Olympics, and while they may have not been in the best of form with the White Eagle on their shirt, in club colours they were flourishing. Wilhelm Góra had been an ever present for Cracovia as they lifted the 1937 championship at their first attempt after promotion, and continued his good form through 1938 and into 1939. Leonard Piontek also hit a purple patch, with 21 goals despite his AKS side slipping to a bottom-half finish. He too carried on into 1939, hitting the net eleven times before joining up with Kałuża's squad.

Yet no one went into the international break with as much confidence as Ezi Wilimowski. On the back of his four goals against Brazil, he went on to average more than one goal a game as Ruch reclaimed the Polish championship in 1938, and in 1939—as the club were rebranded as Ruch Chorzów—he proceeded to dwarf that figure. In thirteen games before the August international break, Wilimowski plundered a stunning 26 goals, including a hat-trick at home to Cracovia and four goals at Warszawianka. Yet neither of these were his highest of the season—that came on 21 May, as Ruch hosted Union-Touring Łódź at Ulica Cicha. Ezi broke the deadlock after a quarter-of-an-hour, and by half-time had gone on to complete his hat-trick. An astounding seven more goals in the second half helped Ruch to a 12-1 victory, and himself to yet another record—one which may never be beaten.

***

As the Poland squad prepared for the visit of the Hungarians, the political situation in the country was looking bleaker and tensions were increasing with each passing day. Throughout the year, relations between the Polish government and both their German and Soviet neighbours had deteriorated dramatically, and war was becoming more-and-more likely.

Steps had previously been taken to try to prevent conflict. In January 1934—a year before the death of Józef Piłsudski—the Polish government had welcomed the accession of the recently elected German National Socialist Party with the co-signing of a non-aggression pact. The ailing Piłsudski had initially believed that the new Chancellor, Adolf Hitler, was less dangerous than his Prussian predecessors had been; but with Germany re-arming itself in violation of the Treaty of Versailles, and the Poles' French allies stating their wish to only maintain a defensive stance should they enter a conflict with Germany, the pact was seen as Poland's only option to defend its western border. An agreement had also been signed with the Soviet Union a few years earlier, and despite Piłsudski's historical disdain for Poland's eastern neighbours, it was later renewed until 1945. Co-operation with the two neighbouring powers may have been far from ideal, but politicians on both sides of the Polish parliament saw the agreements as a necessary evil in order to protect the country on all frontiers.

In practice, the Polish-German pact lasted for just over five years before being swiftly torn up by Hitler in 1939: the Nazi government had demanded that they be allowed to re-annex the Free City of Danzig as well as build both road and rail links through the Polish Corridor, connecting Germany's eastern border with the East Prussian exclave—demands which Poland flat out refused. Following the Nazi occupation of Czechoslovakia in March 1939, Hitler turned his attention to Poland and war became almost a certainty, even if the British and French believed there was another, less-hostile outcome possible. The two held talks with the Soviet Union on how to curb Nazi Germany's expansionism; however, Soviet leader Josef Stalin had hesitations, fearing that his state would become Hitler's next target. If that was to be the case, consensus in Moscow was that Britain and France would maintain neutrality in order to see both capitulate. Yet, in reality, Hitler needed the Soviets onside. Without them, Germany would not have had the resources to engage in a war, and behind the back of the Allied Powers the two entered secret negotiations, in which the Germans advised the Soviets that they could offer much more favourable terms.

***

Poland (v Hungary)
Friendly Match; Stadion Wojska Polskiego, Warsaw;
August 27, 1939.

Goalkeeper: Adolf Krzyk (Brygada Częstochowa).

Defenders: Władysław Szczepaniak (Polonia Warszawa), Edmund Giemsa (Ruch Chorzów).

Midfielders: Wilhelm Góra (Cracovia), Edward Jabłoński (Cracovia), Ewald Dytko (Dąb Katowice).

Forwards: Henryk Jaźnicki (Polonia Warszawa), Leonard Piontek (AKS Chorzów), Edward Cebula (Śląsk Świętochłowice), Ernest Wilimowski (Ruch Chorzów), Paweł Cyganek (Fablok Chrzanów).

Substitutes: Stanisław Baran (Warszawianka), Piotr Danielak (Warta Poznań), Michał Dusik (KPW Poznań), Marian Jankowiak (Warta Poznań), Franciszek Pytel (AKS Chorzów), Jerzy Wostal (AKS Chorzów).

Aside from a couple of victories against weakened amateur selections, Poland's record against Hungary had been dismal. Defeated in all six of their full international meetings, and with their opponents having earned World Cup silver medals just thirteen months earlier, the Poles were hugely unfancied for the tie; *Przegląd Sportowy* even exclaimed before the game that their team were "without a chance, but prepared to fight". Kałuża's position may have been under threat, but no one was demanding a victory against a team regarded as one of the world's best, only a proud performance to boost the morale of a nation caught in the midst of political turmoil.

The team's preparation for the game had been largely positive. League football had stopped for the one-month summer break on 16 July, allowing the national team to get together for a number of training camps before the game. The PZPN had also managed to persuade former Arsenal and Scotland inside forward Alex James to sign a six-week contract, and he worked with Kałuża to coach and improve the fitness of the team, while also attempting to implement a three-man defensive system operated widely in England. James made such an impression on the team that, after the expiration of his contract, the PZPN sent an invitation to attend the game against Hungary; however, with the precarious political situation, he was keen to return home to London as soon as possible. James did, however, leave messages with the team, telling them to "concentrate on defence" and "hope for a draw". Meanwhile, the Hungarian squad also showed their apprehension about being in Warsaw by making the short trip via aeroplane—the first visiting team to arrive in Poland in such manner—in order to be able to exit the country without hesitation should the situation arise.

In the build up to the game, reports of German troops mobilising at the Polish borders were rife, and the meeting had begun to be viewed as merely a temporary distraction from the escalating tensions. A visible number of the 21,000 crowd in Warsaw were even dressed in military uniform, on standby for a call up which was becoming increasingly likely with each passing day.

As expected, from the moment that the Finnish referee blew to signal the start of the game, the Hungarians dominated proceedings. Shot after shot peppered Adolf Krzyk's goal and after fifteen minutes he was beaten, with Gyula Zsengellér allowed space in the Polish box for a simple tap in. The visitors gradually continued to tighten their grip on the game, and on the half-an-hour mark their lead was doubled when Géza Toldi played in Sándor Ádám, who fired a low shot from the right-hand side of the box past Krzyk. Dénes Ginzery's team had begun with speed and guile, and had only grown stronger as the game progressed, while Kałuża's Poles were showing nerves and playing chaotically. The bulk of the Warsaw crowd was almost sure their team was about to suffer a mauling.

It would take that second Hungarian goal to finally spur the Poles into action. Almost immediately following it Kałuża was forced into a change, with Warszawianka forward Stanisław Baran replacing the injured Henryk Jaźnicki. Within minutes the home side began to show their true capabilities; receiving a header from Piontek, Wilimowski took a few strides forward before smashing the ball over the head of goalkeeper Ferenc Sziklai, pulling the Poles immediately back into the game. Optimism returned to both the players and the fans, and all of a sudden they transformed into a team which played without fear or pressure; by the time that the half-time whistle blew, Poland had begun to dictate play, while a confidence slowly spread around the stadium that the Hungarians were there for the taking.

Upon emerging for the second half, it was clear that the visitors had become jaded; however, that in no way should detract from the Poles' performance, which had only continued to grow stronger. Captain Szczepaniak brought a calmness to the team, while Ewald Dytko began to pull the strings in midfield, effectively controlling the course of the game. Poland then continued to test the Hungarian goal, with Piontek and Baran both attempting, but narrowly failing to hit the target. An equaliser suddenly seemed an inevitability. The fading Magyars gave their all just to try to weather the storm, but could last not even 20 minutes of the second half before the levee was breached once more. After winning the ball in his own half, Jabłoński searched a long pass forward to Piontek; he controlled, before laying off to the advancing Wilimowski, who in a fluid movement dribbled past two defenders and shot low into the corner past the advancing Sziklai. 2-2.

In less than an hour, the crowd's disappointment had turned into hope, then belief and, within another ten minutes, disbelief. When an attempted cross by Baran struck the outstretched arm of Hungary defender Sándor Bíró, the referee had no option but to point to the penalty spot, and up stepped Piontek to coolly slide the ball into the net. Then, with the crowd still deep in celebration, Wilimowski received the ball some way outside of the penalty area before beating two defenders and firing past the helpless Sziklai; completing his hat-trick, the 4-2 victory, and taking his international tally to 21 goals in 22 games.

Satisfied, the Polish defence clung on to their lead, and as the referee blew for full time the crowd were sent into raptures. Having just witnessed their country's greatest victory in its eighteen-year history, supporters walked away from Ulica Łazienkowska on that late summer's evening looking ahead in hope that, like their team's performance, the political situation would also offer improvement. Little did they know that their future had already been decided four days previously, many miles away in Moscow.

***

In the late hours of 23 August, Soviet Union foreign minister Vyacheslav Molotov and his Nazi German counterpart Joachim von Ribbentrop had met in the Russian capital to sign a non-aggression pact between the two nations. In addition to that agreement, secret plans were also made to carve up Central Europe—plans which would see Poland wiped completely off of the map. By the time that the country awoke on 1 September, Hitler's forces had already begun to attack the northern Polish defences at Westerplatte and *Luftwaffe* bombing had decimated the western town of Wieluń. The Second World War had begun.

Many of Kałuża's squad joined their compatriots in donning their uniforms, hoping to defend their motherland as they had done so resolutely against the Hungarians. Alas, they could not. By the middle of September the Soviet Red Army had joined the invasion from the east, crushing the tiring Poles.

Over the years, the victory against Hungary has become known in Poland as *'The Final Game'*—an apt title on many levels. As well as the final game before the outbreak of war, it would also prove to be the last time that Kałuża's charges would come together to represent their country. In the following years, each player was forced down their own individual path and emerged from the war with their own story to tell. Unfortunately, the story of how they tamed the team regarded by many as the best in the world—what should have been a story of great pride and joy—would become the one of least importance.

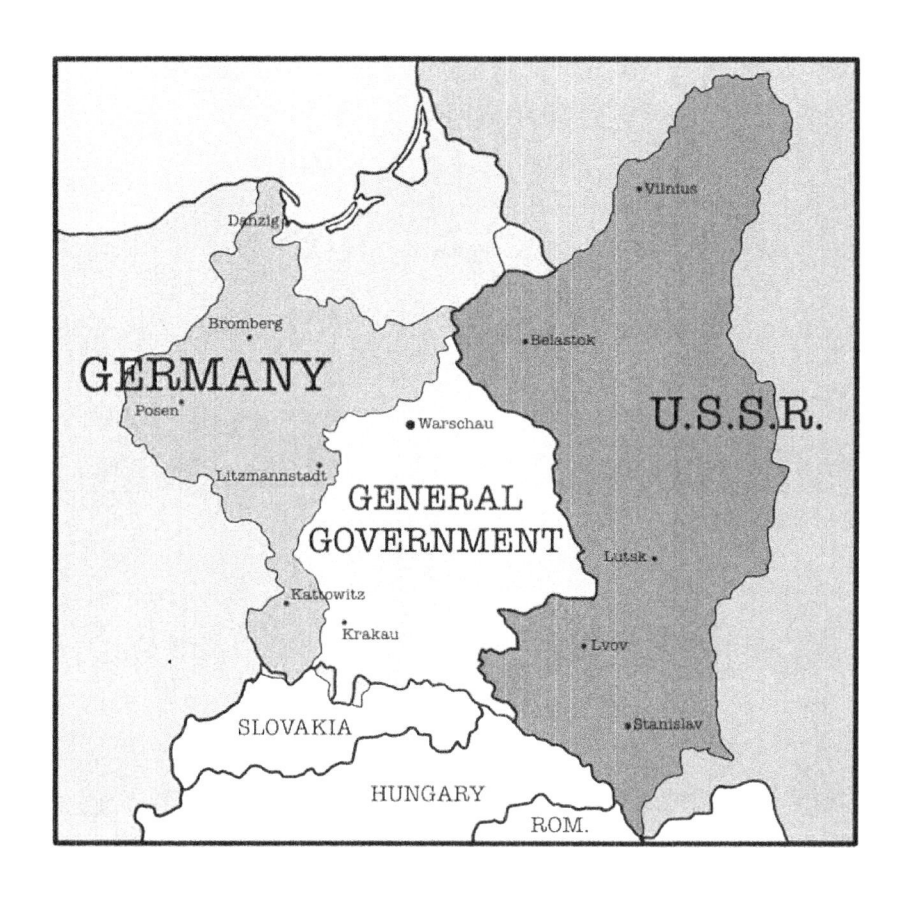

Act III
An Occupied Poland

CHAPTER ELEVEN
UNDERGROUND FOOTBALL

"It was dangerous, but we felt satisfaction because it showed us that, despite the terror, we were still here..."
- Leszek Rylski, clandestine player for Błysk Warszawa and recipient of the UEFA Order of Merit in Ruby

"Halt!"

As the SS officer's demand echoed across the field, for a moment the one-thousand-strong crowd froze to ponder their next move. That move was a straightforward one to make: run. As they did, shots were fired into the dispersing crowd, leaving two dead and many more injured.

The crime? In this instance, a game of football between two Warszawianin teams, Wir and Mirków, played fifteen kilometres south of the capital in the satellite village of Konstancin. It was a scene similarly played out many times across Poland during its six-year occupation.

The pitch had seemed the perfect place for a game: a suitably sized, partly grassy patch of land, sheltered by buildings, far enough away from the city as not to attract unwanted attention. However, it was seemingly not taken into account that Konstancin was also the home of the Nazi General of Warsaw, Ludwig Fischer, who upon hearing the cheers of the crowd in the distance sent officers to investigate. On this instance the 'watchers'—groups of men paid to keep an eye out for approaching Germans—were ineffective, and by the time the SS officers were finally spotted there was little time to make a getaway. The players were even forced to leave behind their belongings, and fled in their football kit.

***

From the very beginning of the German occupation in Western Poland, the Nazis were intent on eradicating all aspects of Polish culture; as a result Poles were forbidden to take part in any type of organised activity. This effectively meant that all sports competition was banned in Poland—the only country in which the Nazis implemented such a law. Football in particular had become so ingrained into Polish culture and society, and intertwined with patriotism and nationalism, that the occupiers offered strict punishment to those found flouting the rules. Naturally then, clubs were officially forced to cease operations almost immediately; not only for fear of punishment, but in many cases because their stadiums were accosted by the German Army for either the pleasure of its soldiers, or for the storage of machinery and ammunition.

Even so, despite being threatened with arrest, interment camps or even death, Poles continued to play football at every opportunity; however, their games were forced underground, away from the view of the occupying forces. Because of the risks involved, admission fees were collected and distributed amongst players, with a small amount of cash also being handed to the several men dotted around the ground who could quickly warn of any approaching Germans. This effectively made the players semi-professional—something which upon the outbreak of war had still been outlawed by the PZPN.

As a result of the new laws imposed upon them, Poles ceased to regard to football as just a game, but instead saw it as yet another way to rebel against the Nazis. For 90 minutes, both players and supporters were able to use their matches as a form of escapism from the tyranny and oppression being wreaked upon their country, effectively creating a temporary illusion of normality. Football also helped Poles to retain some sort of cultural identity, while even minor victories against the Germans—such as the fact that the players didn't pay any taxes on their earnings from the matches—were claimed and celebrated.

By early October 1939, Poland's army had caved in to the two-fronted attack by the Germans and Soviets, but despite the oppressive policies of both occupiers, football returned to the fields of Kraków before the month was over. In the suburb of Bronowice, Wisła defeated Krowodrza Kraków 3-1 in front of a several-hundred-strong crowd. According to many, including Wisła's young goalkeeper Jerzy Jurowicz, this was the game which made the German occupiers realise how much influence the sport could have on Polish society and ultimately led to its banning.

As the Germans clamped down on Polish freedoms, another half-a-year of inactivity passed before the resumption of any kind of organised football; this time well away from the watching eyes of the Nazi authorities. With the stadia of both Wisła and Cracovia commandeered by the *Wehrmacht* there were few places in-and-around the city which were suitable for clandestine competition; however, there was one which was almost perfect. Park Juvenia, the home of Juvenia Kraków, was a small, tree-lined patch of land on the south eastern edge of Park Błonia. Almost equidistant between the stadia of the city's two leading clubs, it was seen as the ideal place for the city's footballers to come together, while the trees around the perimeter of the pitch were able to comfortably conceal the activities in which Poles were partaking. The leaseholder of the ground, Aleksander Wódka, played an important role in bringing the game back to life in Kraków. Wódka had for many years been an activist of Juvenia, and is said to have even lived in an apartment at the facility. Towards the end of 1939 he was able to secure a lease from the city to use the facilities "at his own discretion"; so there he decided to implement the first 'Championship of Occupied Kraków'.

There are still many questions over how much the Germans were actually aware of the goings-on inside of Park Juvenia, but given the fact that the Sports Park contained a café frequented by Germans, and that

Wódka himself claimed that the authorities had consented to the activities, it is difficult to believe that the games were held in total secrecy. Still, players were advised to not wear the colours of their clubs outside of the sports park for fear of attracting unwanted attention. That is of course if they could even find club colours to wear; with equipment difficult to come by, players wore whatever they could get a hold of. On good days this would mean playing in mismatched colours, yet on the odd occasion, players would be forced to play without proper kit at all.

In total, eight teams came together for the 1940 championship, with Zwierzyniecki, Groble, Sparta, Juvenia and Bloki all joining teams put together by Wisła, Cracovia and Garbarnia. Many first team players, who had been fighting for the Polish championship twelve months earlier, took part, while there were even several Polish internationals—Artur Woźniak, Edward Jabłoński and Józef Korbas among them—who graced the Juvenia pitch.

Those three players all participated in Juvenia's opening match, in May 1940: the first *Święta Wojna*—'Holy War'— played during wartime, between Wisła and Cracovia. A symbolic meeting, as the last scheduled game between the two rivals had been among the first cancelled following the German invasion. The 3-0 friendly victory for Wisła proved to be a sign of things to come in the upcoming championship, as the Biała Gwiazda romped to a clear victory with seven wins from seven games. The inaugural clandestine competition proved so successful that eight more teams—Cracovia II, Wisła II, Wodociągi, AKS, Legia, Wawel, Prądniczanka and Dębnicki—joined for a 'Blitz' competition, in which games of two 15-minute halves were played, with Wisła again emerging victorious. Many also returned for the second *Okupacyjne Mistrzostwo* in 1941 where, once more, Wisła proved the strongest of the lot, even if they did require a play-off game to overcome a Cracovia side that had finished the season with an identical record.

1941 was also the year in which both Wisła and Cracovia celebrated their 35th anniversaries; but while Wisła marked theirs with a tournament at Juvenia, it was in a rather subdued manner. As noted in the diaries of Jurowicz, just a few days before the celebration, defender Władysław Szumilas was arrested by the Nazis for his alleged involvement in the Polish resistance movement. He later was sent to the Auschwitz concentration camp, where he met his untimely end at the hands of a German rifle. The arrests and round-ups of Polish intellectuals soon became commonplace, and was a part of the reason that the championship was abandoned in 1942. Aside from a few sporadic friendly games, football slipped far from the forefront of many Poles' minds, while the Nazi closure of Park Juvenia also left players with few safe places to play should they wish to indulge in their escapism.

The hiatus proved only temporary, and having been deprived of the sport for so long, 16 teams applied to compete in the revived championship in 1943—a number which increased to 22 within just a week. The decision was made to split the teams into three groups, with the top two from each going on to compete in a final round. Six pitches around the city were also sought to play the games; however, at many of these security was lax—in particular at the home of former Polish champions Garbarnia, which sat in a state of disrepair having seen its grandstands demolished by the Germans. These conditions invited a number of violent incidents, including one during the league's decisive match between the city's old foes Wisła and Cracovia. Incensed by a penalty decision given against his team, Wisła striker Mieczysław Gracz allegedly attacked the referee—former Cracovia player Tadeusz Mitusiński—before both sets of supporters stormed the pitch. The fighting quickly spilled out on to the streets, and into the nearby Rynek Podgórski, where sat the headquarters of both the SS and the local police. Luckily for the brawling supporters, the local military commandant was Hans Mitschke, a former player in Vienna. It was he who is reported to have brushed off the fighting by exclaiming that "football fans are the same everywhere—let them fight". Eventually Cracovia were handed a 3-0 walkover, and ultimately the championship; however, due to increased hostilities, it was a title they were unable to defend in 1944.

***

Like Kraków, Warsaw too had somewhere in which clandestine football was able to thrive. It was on Mokotów Fields—a public park in the south of the city—where in 1940, the first wartime competition in the occupied capital was initiated by former Cracovia, Polonia and Legia midfielder Józef Ciszewski. The venue was chosen, like Juvenia, because of the amount of foliage around the pitch, and additionally for patriotic reasons: it was there where the army said its goodbyes to Józef Piłsudski in 1935, before his body was sent to its final resting place at Krakow's Wawel Castle.

The inaugural *Mistrzostwo Pola Mokotowskiego* was contested by eight teams from across the city; playing each other twice—fourteen games in total—in a simple league structure. However, the facilities were also very basic, with strips of wood used as goalposts, which could quickly be removed should any Germans approach. Camouflage was also important for the teams, who initially took on names with little meaning, and therefore couldn't be linked to any pre-war entity. Continental, Berberys, Placówka and Błysk were amongst the entrants in the 1940 league, with the latter eventually emerging victorious.

> *"The tournament in Mokotów contributed to the revival of footballing life in the capital. It delivered energy and initiative to organise new teams in various districts of Warsaw, as well as in towns near to Warsaw".*
> - Leszek Rylski, Błysk Warszawa

The Mokotów tournament was not the only one to take place in Warsaw during 1940, as Polonia's stadium on Ulica Konwiktorska hosted a 13-team tournament during September, which included three teams created from the embers of Polonia itself. Two of them, Czarni and Bimber, contested the final, in which Czarni claimed victory. But while the tournament was largely a success, there was no chance of a second edition, as soon after the ground was confiscated by the Gestapo. Around the same time, the Wehrmacht commandeered Legia's stadium on Ulica Łazienkowska, while many other smaller stadia began to be used by other different departments of the German authorities. Any thoughts that Polish footballers had of returning from the shadows were quickly dashed, and once again the Mokotów competition became the pinnacle of Polish football in Warsaw.

As the games were forced underground, it only served to increase their popularity amongst Poles; before the 1941 competition, more than 30 teams registered their interest in competing. These included some familiar names from pre-war Warszawianin football: Marymont, Korona, Warszawianka and... a reformed Polonia. The latter even counted a number of pre-war Czarne Koszule among their ranks—most notably Poland captain Władysław Szczepaniak. Yet the increased popularity brought with it more problems, in particular that a game with over one thousand spectators would cease to remain a secret. That, coupled with the fact that more-and-more Germans had begun to frequent the fields in Mokotów, the 1941 competition would prove to be the last.

In response, several activists gathered at the apartment of former Legia midfielder Alfred Nowakowski on Christmas Eve, where a regional association was established. The aim of the Warszawskie Okręgowy Związek Piłki Nożnej was to bring structure, efficiency and organisation to wartime football, with games scheduled in various locations in order to help prevent detection by the Germans. As patrols around the city increased, these locations moved farther away from Warsaw itself, with matches taking place in smaller villages such as Piaseczno, Konstancin and Wołomin. Details of games were not publicised, with only word of mouth relied upon to attract crowds, yet from the outside still maintain a perception of spontaneity. However, the organisation continued to issue announcements and hold meetings right under the noses of the German occupiers, risking the lives of the activists and their families.

Both the 1942 and 1943 competitions were dominated by Polonia, whose nationalistic tendencies continued to make them the most attractive choice for supporters; but, as the team's popularity increased, so did the unwanted attention from German raids. In one reported incident before a game in Milanówek, a number of the Polonia team were surrounded by Gestapo at Warsaw's main station, with several rounded up and sent directly to labour camps. Still though, once the police had left, those who had fled managed to contact players from Polonia's second team and returned to the station to make the trip anyway.

However, not all Germans were hostile to the Poles, with at least one actively participating in the underground competitions. Henryk 'Milkowski' Milke was a Warszawiak of German heritage, who turned out for Korona during 1943; often using his nationality to help out troubled teammates. On one occasion in particular, a Korona activist was stopped by police close to Warsaw's Wschodnia railway station, and had all of the team's kit confiscated. Thanks to his *Volksdeutscher* status, Milke is said to have been able to show his identification at the police headquarters and retrieve the team's possessions.

Seeking the help of Germans was also occasionally seen as a survival tactic for Poles during the war, as was the case with many Polonia players in 1944. With police raids at their games becoming almost an inevitability, the Czarne Koszule chose to represent a team organised by German entrepreneur Walter Többens, who had been forced to employ Poles in his clothing factories after Warsaw's Jewish Ghetto was cleared. The team became known as WTC—Walter Többens' Club—but unofficially referred to themselves as '*Warszawskie Towarzystwo Czarnych*', maintaining a link to their heritage. As a result of their collaboration with Többens, the players were able to obtain work documents which helped them to avoid round-ups by the Germans. While clearly an act of self preservation, their closeness to the occupiers was seen by some teams as a betrayal and aroused suspicion from many others. Before long, they were prevented from entering the 1944 competition by the WOZPN.

By the middle of the year, fed up with being shunned by their compatriots, the club were prepared to sever ties with Többens and return to the name Polonia; however, they never had a chance to do so. At 5pm on the first day of August, men, women and children from across the city answered the Polish Underground Army's call-to-arms, and began to rise up against the city's occupiers.

The Warsaw Uprising had begun...

CHAPTER TWELVE
FROM THE BORDERLANDS TO THE FRONT LINES

—

On the extremity of the country's south western border, the slither of Upper Silesia belonging to Poland had been one of the first to come under attack from the invading Germans. As troops poured over the border, Polish units retreated eastwards in order to defend Kraków, leaving just a handful—mostly either veterans of the 1920s uprisings, or Boy and Girl Scouts—to defend the region's capital, Katowice. It was a handful that battled bravely, but when the Germans did gain control after three days of fighting, many were sent to their death.

Despite the resistance shown in the region, the German occupiers proved to be much more tolerant with the Silesians than they had been with the rest of the country—especially those who were of German heritage. Provided that they declared their loyalty to Nazi Germany, these Volksdeutscher would be allowed many of the freedoms afforded to German nationals, including the ability to participate in activities in which Poles were forbidden.

After seeking the advice of both Józef Kałuża and the Polish Government-in-exile, almost all of Silesia's Polish international players opted to sign the *Volksliste*, allowing them to continue playing football without the fear of persecution. Once they had done so, the majority were able to stay at their previous clubs, which had also been forced to declare themselves as German in order to continue operation. As a result, Ruch Chorzów became Bismarckhütter SV 99 and counted Teo (now 'Theodor') Peterek and Gerard ('Gerhard') Wodarz amongst their ranks, while across the city Leonard Piontek's AKS became known as Germania Königshütte. Elsewhere in Silesia, striker Edward Cebula continued at Śląsk Świętochłowice's successor TuS Schwientochlowitz, while brothers Ryszard and Wilhelm Piec ('Richard' and Wilhelm 'Pietz') remained with the rebranded Naprzód Lipiny, TuS Lipine.

At least one Upper Silesian club was spared the forced Germanisation process, as ethnic German side 1.FC Katowice were only too happy to revert back to their former name. Nazi leaders were also keen to promote 1.FC as the representatives of the region, and several players—notably Ernest Wilimowski ('Ernst Willimowski'), Edward Nyc ('Erwin Nytz') and Ewald Dytko—were plucked to play for the model club of occupied Upper Silesia, with the threat of being sent to concentration camps should they refuse.

While Erster may have been the authorities' favoured club, they were still far from the region's best. This was proved by their first season back in German competition, where a fourth-placed finish in their maiden *Gauliga Schlesien* campaign was the best that they could muster. As the Upper Silesian clubs were filtered into the new *Gauliga Oberschlesien* for the 1941/42 season, they began to slip even further off the pace. Instead, it was Germania who ascended to become the region's premier club, claiming the league's inaugural three championships. They were, however, unable to make a mark on the national play-offs, losing in the early rounds on all three attempts to teams from Vienna, Brieg (Brzeg) and Dresden.

Though the majority of players had signed the Volksliste largely in order to continue their football careers, once the ongoing war increased in intensity, their German nationality also brought with it the possibility of being drafted into the Wehrmacht. This was a fate which eventually befell many of the former Polish internationals: Peterek, Giemsa and Wodarz found themselves on the front lines in Northern France, Dytko ended up in Greece, and Nyc joined the Luftwaffe. Others did what they could to avoid being drafted, with a notable case being that of Wilimowski.

Ezi's decision to sign the Volksliste had been a gripe, not only for Poles, but also a handful of Germans who had been angered by his decision five years earlier to transfer from 1.FC to the pro-Polish Ruch. One local *Kreisleiter*, Georg Joschke, even claimed that Wilimowski should be forced to wear a letter 'P' on his clothes, signifying him as a Pole— something never once considered by the German authorities, who were only too aware of his talent on the football pitch and his status as a role model for Silesians, which in turn made him an excellent propaganda tool. However, foreshadowing the possibility of he and his teammates being drafted, Ezi's return to his former club was short lived. By February 1940 he took a job as a policeman in the Saxon town of Chemnitz, exempting him from the draft while also allowing him to continue playing football for the local force's team Polizei-Sportverein.

Wilimowski's new-found career in the police force soon proved to be supplemental to that as a footballer, as just a few months after his arrival in Saxony he was selected to play for the region's representative team as they embarked on their *Reichsbundpokal* (German regional cup) campaign. Seven goals in games against Sudetenland and Pomerania ensured him a guaranteed spot in the team for the Saxons' quarter-final game: a swift return to Katowice for Ezi, and a reunion with several of his former teammates who had been selected to play for their Silesian opposition. This occasion would prove to be the very last time that the Królewski Tercet shared a field, and Ezi marked it with yet another hat-trick to ensure passage to the semi-final with a 5-3 victory. Saxony would eventually go on to win the tournament, with Ezi scoring one of their two goals in the final against Bavaria.

Wilimowski's performances made an impression, not only in Saxony, but in the entirety of the Third Reich. His goalscoring exploits were noticed by the manager of the German national team Sepp Herberger, and in June he was appointed to his squad for a game against Romania in Bucharest. While Ezi's decision to retake German citizenship as a survival tactic may have been understood by some Poles, the decision to swap the white eagle on his chest for a black one was seen as a step too far, and many of the most sympathetic Polish fans now branded him a traitor. Yet, in Silesia, his image remained largely untarnished, and after moving from Chemnitz to 1860 München in the summer of 1942 he returned to his home region with the national team, helping to draw a crowd in excess of 50,000 to Beuthen for another friendly against Romania. Though Fritz Walter stole the headlines that day with a second-half hat-trick, the majority of the audience had been there for a chance to see their fellow Górnoślązak Ezi, and were sent home jubilant as he rounded off a 7-0 victory with just four minutes remaining.

Wilimowski collected yet more silverware in 1942, as 1860 München lifted the *Tschammerpokal* with a 2-0 victory over Schalke 04—again on target, scoring his side's second of the game to confirm the victory. But with the war only increasing in hostility, Ezi's draft into the Wehrmacht became an inevitability, and within a few months he had been deployed to occupied Kraków. Still, he was allowed to take time from his army duties to play football, turning out several times for Luftwaffe team PSV Mölders.

The call-to-arms, and particularly the link with the Luftwaffe, would eventually prove to be something of a blessing in disguise for Wilimowski. A friendship forged with legendary pilot Hermann Graf led to him being chosen to play for Rote Jäger—a military team created from serving German international players, and for a while led by Herberger, helping to spare them from the front lines. But more importantly for Ezi, his association with the German war hero was important in securing the release of his mother Paulina, who for a short period had been incarcerated in the Nazi concentration camp at Auschwitz.

The option to retake German citizenship had not only been limited to Silesians, but was also available for those of German descent from other areas which had previously been a part of Poland's Prussian partition. As the majority of the Wielkopolska region had been a part of the pre-war German state, many there who had taken Polish citizenship after the borders were redrawn opted to repatriate themselves once again.

One of these was Posen-born Fryderyk Scherfke, and his repatriation meant that in the space of just a few weeks, Poland had lost their only two World Cup goalscorers. Reverting back to his Germanic name 'Friedrich', Scherfke's draft into the Wehrmacht came quickly, and in 1940 he also obtained a supplementary role as the head of football in the newly formed region of Reichsgau Wartheland. While he only lasted a few months in this position, he later went on to both preside and captain over the Germanic 1.FC Posen, who were taken under the control of the Luftwaffe in October of that year. The takeover of the club encouraged Scherfke to relinquish both his roles, and he made the decision to retire from the game completely aged just 31.

In part due to his stature in the region, Scherfke was entrusted by the local authorities with a position outside of the sport working as a driver, transporting key officials from within the Gestapo. Despite having retired, his association with those from within the game—in particular his former Warta Poznań teammates—did not come to an end, as he often risked his life to use his position in order to help them when in need. Having been arrested for taking part in an illegal football match, forward Bolesław Gendera was released after Scherfke's intervention. On another occasion, Michał Fligier was also spared jail, despite being linked to the Polish resistance movement. Fritz later pulled September Campaign POW Marian Fontowicz from a train heading to a German labour camp after a chance meeting with the goalkeeper's wife, and was also able to prevent the wife of another goalkeeper, Zbigniew Szulc, from being sent to a similar fate.

But by 1942, Scherfke was forced to inform his friends he could help them no longer, as he felt as though he was being watched with suspicion. The following year he was sent to fight with the Wehrmacht on the eastern front, and in the dying throngs of the war was wounded in Yugoslavia and captured by British soldiers.

***

The east of Poland may initially have been spared the German onslaught, but the Soviet one which engulfed them just a few weeks into the conflict was hardly any better. Like in the rest of Poland, all Polish clubs were immediately forced to cease operations; however, under Soviet occupation, Poles were allowed to continue playing, but only for Soviet clubs.

The largest of these, unsurprisingly, appeared in the footballing cradle of Lwów, with both Dynamo Lvov and Spartak Lvov using the facilities left behind by Pogoń and Czarni. They also absorbed a number of their better players: Polish international Spirydion Albański was one of many Pogończycy who initially appeared for Dynamo with Wacław Kuchar as their coach, while Stanisław Szmyd and Piotr Dreher—the latter the scorer of Pogoń's final league goal—were among those who signed with Spartak. At the same time, several Leopolitan alumni wound up deeper inside the Soviet Union and plied their trade within top-flight Soviet clubs. One of the first was Aleksander Skoceń—an ethnic Ukrainian, and the star player of Ukraina Lwów—who went to play for Dynamo Kyiv. He was later followed by Pogoń's Polish international Michał Matyas and youth player Tadeusz Jedinak, while Adam Wolanin ventured even further to play for Spartak Moscow.

Former Wisła Kraków attacker Bolesław Habowski was another who made his way from Eastern Galicia to Moscow, turning out for both Dynamo and Spartak between 1940 and 1941; yet his journey did not come via one of the Leopolitan clubs, but rather Junak Drohobycz of the region's A-Klasa. Despite their relatively small stature, Junak had undergone a meteoric rise during the 1930s, climbing from the C-Klasa in just three years. Under the presidency of Polish Army Colonel Mieczysław Młotek the club set their sights on bringing top-level football to the small town, and were able to attract talented players such as Habowski in order to achieve their target. By the summer of 1939 they had reached the A-Klasa's play-off alongside Śląsk Świętochłowice, Legia Poznań and Śmigły Wilno, and in anticipation of their promotion (three of the four teams would go up) they had already planned the attempted coup of Ernest Wilimowski in order to make an immediate assault on the Polish championship in 1940. However, like for every other club in Galicia, the war put an end to Junak's plans and they were disbanded before Młotek's dream was realised.

While a handful of Junak's players were called into the Polish army for the defence against the Germans, a significant number were spared the immediate drafting. Many of these soon joined a regiment of the Polish Underground Army known as the *'Szare Szeregi'* (Grey Ranks), and from there a handful helped to establish the *'Biali Kurierzy'* (White Couriers)—a clandestine organisation which helped to smuggle people out of Galicia across the Hungarian border. By late September, the majority of these players had also taken the decision to cross the border themselves, where they joined up with a unit of soldiers made almost entirely from those evacuated through Romania and Hungary.

Although ultimately a fighting unit, the *Samodzielnej Brygadzie Strzelców Karpackich* (Carpathian Rifle Brigade) was filled with many highly literate Poles, who were keen to use any spare time to great effect. Among its ranks sat writers, actors, poets and singers, and with their help soldiers were able to express themselves creatively whilst not on duty. Some sang in choirs, while other put on shows and plays. Others gathered reading material for a mobile library which travelled alongside the men, while the Brigade even had its own publishing house to print newsletters, magazines and books.

Of course, they also played football.

Under the initiative of Colonel Młotek, the Junak players amongst the Brigade helped to create a representative team to play against teams of locals wherever they would pass. The squad was complimented by several top-flight players who had fled their occupied homes, including Pogoń Lwów attacker Antoni Komendo-Borowski, ŁKS Łódź defender Antoni Gałecki, and later, fresh from his adventure in the Soviet Union, Bolesław Habowski. Coached by former Junak striker Tadeusz Krasoń, the men played over 20 games from Budapest, through Yugoslavia, Syria and Palestine, and even as far as Egypt. They were good too, reportedly winning more than two-thirds of the games that they played. These included victories against the national teams of both Iran and Iraq (2-1 and 6-1 respectively), and also a team of English soldiers stationed in Baghdad.

The Carpathian Brigade remained in the Middle East until February 1944, when the entire unit was moved to Italy to fight alongside the Allied soldiers. As a part of Colonel Władysław Anders' Polish 2nd Corps they fought in several battles, notably those at Ancona, Bologna and Monte Cassino, and remained there until after the end of the war. Before being sent to the United Kingdom for their demobilisation in 1946, the team—now under the name of 'The Carpathians'—also played several games against Italian opposition. Prior to their games against Bologna, Lazio and Bari, the squad had also been joined by several Silesians—including former internationals Edmund Giemsa, Edward Cebula and Zygmunt Kulawik—who had earlier either deserted the Wehrmacht or been captured by the Allies.

But although the war had come to and end, returning home became fraught with difficulties; as the country's eastern Borderlands were gifted to the Soviet Union at the Yalta conference, many of those who had fought in the Carpathian Brigade—including the players from Drohobycz and Lwów—were left without a home. As a result, swathes of Poles eventually opted to start new lives in the UK rather than return to their now-Soviet-controlled homeland. Bolek Habowski settled in Buckinghamshire and Edmund Giemsa in Oxfordshire, before passing away in 1979 and 1994 respectively. Jan Wasiewicz even had a spell playing for Edinburgh club Hibernians towards the end of the war, before moving on to Argentina in 1949.

Another to stay put in the UK was ex-Junak goalkeeper and White Courier Stanisław Gerula. He was one of several who helped to continue The Carpathians' name by establishing a team of Poles in exile, who played a number of friendly games against established English clubs. In 1947 they entered the Berkshire and Buckinghamshire Senior Cup, and a year later the FA Amateur Cup—a trophy that Gerula went on to lift with Walthamstow Avenue FC in 1952, at the age of 38; in doing so becoming the first Polish player to play at Wembley Stadium.

But for those who instead opted to return to their homeland, they would quickly discover that it was a very different Poland to the one which they had left behind...

Act IV
An Oppressed Poland

CHAPTER THIRTEEN
EMERGING FROM CONFLICT

"I began to realise why the Poles were so dour and icy: they had been several times through hell, and war had steeled their hearts against everything. They had become so hard that nothing could now hurt them again."
- James Kirkup, "One Man's Russia", 1968

THE POLAND THAT EMERGED from the ashes of World War Two bore few similarities with the country which had been forced into the conflict. Physically, politically and mentally destroyed after six years of oppression and persecution, its borders revised and its population significantly reduced. The extent of damage caused by both the Nazi and Soviet occupations was not fully recognised until well after the Germans' surrender.

It continues to make for shocking reading. Approximately six million Polish citizens—one-fifth of the pre-war population—had perished, almost the entirety of the country's Jewish population among them. Many cities, towns and villages were razed to the ground as the Nazis retreated westwards, and others were snatched away as the Soviet border was readjusted. Even those who were left to lead the country into its new era would have struggled to recognise it as their own.

In an effort to rebuild as quickly as possible, Poles searched through the rubble for remnants of their past, only to be met with disappointment time and time again. The PZPN were no different, and as they searched it became clear that they too had lost many players, coaches and officials. Among countless others, former national team selector Adam Obrubański was among the many murdered by the Soviets in the Katyń massacre; both ex-Cracovia striker Leon Sperling and Legia Warsaw's Zygmunt Steuermann were killed in the Lwów Ghetto; and Józef Klotz, scorer of Poland's first international goal, was executed by the Nazis. Meanwhile, almost every single member of over 200 Jewish clubs which dotted across Poland had been either murdered or forced to flee Hitler's sickening acts of genocide.

Even surviving the war did not necessarily equate to acceptance from Poland's new communist government, with many Silesians treated suspiciously for having took German citizenship during the occupation. Players such as Leonard Piontek and Ewald Dytko were forced to sign a decree of loyalty to Poland and Polonise their names (to Leonard 'Piątek' and 'Edward' Dytko respectively). Erwin Nytz's name also returned to its Polish spelling, but only after he received references from former colleagues supporting the fact that he had never betrayed his country, and had actually helped resistance efforts against the Nazis. However, two of the Poland squad which faced Hungary just prior to the war, Ernest Wilimowski and Wilhelm Góra, were prevented from resuming their lives in Poland altogether. Having gone on to become a hero for the German national team, Wilimowski was immediately branded a traitor to the nation and forced to settle in West Germany. Góra—a veteran of Anders' Polish Army in-exile—was allowed to return, but within months had been arrested by the communist police for conversing in German, and was eventually forced to flee westwards to avoid further persecution.

Following the Potsdam Conference of August 1945, Poland's borders also moved westwards, with the Soviets annexing the eastern borderlands known as 'Kresy'. Culturally important cities such as Lwów and Wilno were suddenly lost, and with it their football teams too. Leopolitan football founders Pogoń, Czarni and Lechia, and former top-flight club Śmigły Wilno—all were completely erased from existence as the USSR gobbled-up Eastern Galicia and gifted other areas to their fellow socialist republic of Lithuania.

In total, Poland was stripped of close to 45 per cent of its pre-war territory, and while handed the majority of Silesia, Pomerania, the Free City of Danzig and a southern portion of East Prussia in compensation, the redesigned state was still significantly smaller than its predecessor. Germans were expelled from the newly recovered territories and replaced by those Poles forced from the east, while, just as Lwów and Wilno became 'L'viv' and 'Vilnius' respectively, cities now under Polish rule took on Polish names—Wrocław (Breslau), Szczecin (Stettin), Gdańsk (Danzig) and Olsztyn (Allenstein) among them.

As displaced Poles began to repopulate the recovered territories, football clubs inevitably formed—many taking on the characteristics of those that had been lost. Several teams incorporating the name 'Czarni' sprung up across the west of the country, while in 1946 Western Pomeranian club KS Biura Odbudowy Portów adopted green-and-white uniforms and rebranded themselves as Lechia Gdańsk, remembering the traditions of Lechia Lwów. Many Eastern Galicians also settled along the Odra river and its tributaries, and numerous clubs formed nearby paid tribute to the most-successful club lost during the conflict—Pogoń Lwów. Piast Gliwice, and a few years later Pogoń Szczecin, took on the blue-and-red hues synonymous with the Leopolitan giants, while Odra Opole did the same, and were even originally formed under the name 'Lwówianka' before being forced to change by the communist authorities.

However, the club regarded as Pogoń's true successors were a name that had been seen before. Having settled in Upper Silesia, several of the club's alumni—including Wacław Kuchar and Michał Matyas—decided, rather than to create a new club, they would help to reactivate one lost for over two decades: Polonia Bytom. The ex-Pogończycy joined several of Polonia's former activists with the intention of continuing the legacy of both clubs; and while keeping the Silesian club's name, the link to Pogoń was immediately evident with both Polonia's new colours and the almost-identical club crest.

With Warsaw in ruins, the first post-war gathering of the PZPN was held on 29 June 1945 in Kraków, and saw attendance from thirteen members of the so-called 'preparatory committee' and 22 delegates representing seven of the regional associations. Once Tadeusz Kuchar had been selected to lead the association on an interim basis and Kraków determined as its temporary headquarters, attention quickly turned to structuring the future of the Polish game.

The association needed to be quick—while rebuilding the country was of prime importance, teams had already begun to organise friendly games, and were eager to return to some sort of normality as soon as possible. Cracovia and Wisła had celebrated the country's liberation as early as January 1945 with the first post-occupation '*Święta Wojna*', while games in Warsaw and Łódź had also been organised by springtime.

A return to the pre-war league format may have been favoured by many, but with the country's infrastructure obliterated it was hardly considered. By the conclusion of the congress it was decided that a knock-out format would whittle 17 regional champions and three sub-divisional clubs down to a final four, who would then battle in a round-robin to determine the first champions of the Polish People's Republic.

Even before the national competition had begun, both Motor Białystok and Szombierki Bytom were forced into withdrawal—neither of them able to organise or fund cross-country jaunts. This left only eighteen to compete, with heavyweights such as Polonia Warsaw, Wisła Kraków, AKS Chorzów and Warta Poznań alongside some of Poland's newer clubs: KKS Olsztyn, Pocztowy KS Szczecin, Burza Wrocław and Tęcza Kielce. Also involved in Polish competition for the first time was Gedania Gdańsk—an ethnically Polish club formed in 1922, which had until the war spent much of its history playing in Germany's *Gauliga Ostpreußen*.

The pairings, by design, were largely favourable towards the big clubs, and AKS, Warta and ŁKS Łódź all progressed to the final stage with few obstacles. But while Polonia's path began with a 5-0 hammering of Ognisko Siedlce, they were dealt a much tougher hand in the last-eight, finally overcoming a strong Wisła Kraków side only by virtue of a last-minute winner.

Defeating the odds was something that this particular Czarne Koszule team had become accustomed to and, though war had weakened Polonia considerably, even the horrors faced during occupation had done little to weaken the city's support for Polonia. Under the initiative of their pre-war talisman Zenon Pieniążek, the club had reactivated in the early part of 1945, and had faced Okęcie Warszawa in the destroyed capital's first game following its liberation. Yet, uncomfortable that their historically rebellious and nationalistic club had been helped back to its feet by the oppressive Communist militia, Polonia's activists ensured it was an association which lasted merely a few months. Soon after, the battle-scarred stadium at Ulica Konwiktorska was gifted by the government to a youth soldiers' organisation and the club were forced to find refuge elsewhere.

Polonia began a nomadic period, taking up temporary residence in several different stadia around the capital, and while switching between the fields of Agrykola, Okęcie and Legia's Stadion Wojska Polskiego, they came within a whisker of lifting the first post-war Championship of Warsaw. Having dominated the regional groups with just a 1-0 defeat to Syrena Warszawa as the only blip on their record, they eventually came unstuck in a third game of the final against Radomiak Radom—not on the pitch where they collected a 4-3 victory, but off of it having played a player who at the time was still registered to Warszawianka.

Despite having six years of his career stolen, Pieniążek returned swiftly to the form displayed prior to the war when he had sat just behind Ezi Wilimowski in the goalscoring charts. As well as leading Polonia's front line into the 1946 Warsaw championships, he had also taken the role of the team's coach upon its re-emergence; however, just days after scoring in an early-June victory over Bzura Chodaków, the 33-year-old's career was brought to a premature end in a motorcycle crash which forced the amputation of a foot. The job of replacing Pieniążek on the sidelines fell to Stanisław Maszner, an activist of both Polonia and Warsaw's clandestine football association throughout occupation, while on the pitch Jerzy Szularz, Zygmunt Ochmański and Tadeusz Świcarz split goalscoring duties between them. Fortunately, the new setup continued as the old one left off: Polonia claiming the Warsaw championship comfortably ahead of Grochów Warszawa, and the attacking trio netting all of the team's eight goals against Ognisko and Wisła to progress to the final round of the national competition.

Polonia quickly took a commanding position in the final group; though suffering defeat to Warta Poznań in matchday two, a pair of victories against ŁKS, coupled with Warta's terrible away form, helped the capital club ascend to the summit. By the time that the Warciarze arrived in the capital in the penultimate round of games, their title aspirations hinged on the result. Ultimately a late brace from Szularz earned Polonia a share of the spoils, putting the Poznaniaks out of the running.

This left only AKS Chorzów within reaching distance of Polonia, but requiring victory in the capital on the first day of December to usurp them. Despite the freezing conditions gripping Warsaw, the crowd descended on Ulica Łazienkowska in excitement two hours before the game, and Polonia repaid their support with two goals in the opening quarter: the first after twelve minutes from left winger Stanisław Woźniak and then Świcarz's sixth of the campaign ten minutes later. Though Henryk Spodzieja pulled a goal back just before the break, the dismissal of AKS striker Stanisław Pytel six minutes into the second half, followed by Świcarz's second of the game with 20 minutes remaining, ensured Polonia were quickly back into a dominant position to claim the title. Given hope by the replacement of Polonia keeper Henryk Borucz through injury,

AKS did rally and were eventually able to score a second; however, another two goals proved to be a task much too difficult.

The referee's final whistle brought with it a wave of emotions: immediately relief and joy, but most prominently pride. As Władysław Szczepaniak lifted the first post-war championship amongst the backdrop of the still-smouldering capital, there was pride that Polonia had emerged from the ashes to attain such an honour, and it was this pride in their city which gave the Warszawianin people yet another reason to fight to rebuild it. There are many reasons for which Polonia fans refer to their club as *'Duma Stolica'*—The Pride of the Capital—and the 1946 championship victory is one of them.

***

While the PZPN's first post-war conference dealt with the recommencement of club competition, the association's primary goal following the war was the re-establishment of a Polish national team. Therefore, the very first item on the agenda was to appoint a new coach. While all twelve of the players who participated in the 1939 game against Hungary had survived the war, their coaches had not: Józef Kałuża succumbing to a potentially treatable illness in 1944 and his assistant Marian Spoida yet another of the many victims at Katyń.

One man fit the bill perfectly, and was selected for the vacancy with little opposition. Like his predecessor, Henryk Reyman was a legendary figure in Kraków. He was also well respected throughout the country, having risen to the rank of Major in the Polish Army after fighting in the Polish-Ukrainian War, Polish-Bolshevik War, the Silesian Uprisings, and more recently the September Campaign.

Reyman's new role was a tough one: hampered by an infrastructure which had been destroyed during six years of occupation, he and his assistant Wacław Kuchar were forced to start almost from scratch, compiling regular lists of players who would potentially be suitable for international football. To further exacerbate their problem, the lack of a single league system made it difficult for them to watch many of Poland's top players, while a shortage of usable roads and train lines meant that travelling across the country was an unenviable task, forcing them to often solely rely on the reports of a network of scouts.

To aid the coaches in assembling a core of players, several foreign teams were sought to take on unofficial representative teams across Poland. These included Swedish club IFK Norrkoping, who visited Kraków to face a team representing the city; Torpedo Moscow, the first Soviet club to travel to Poland, who duelled with an unofficial Polish team in the capital; and a team from the British Army on the Rhine, who played in Chorzów, Kraków and Warsaw. In addition, under the leadership of former internationals Tadeusz Synowiec and Stefan Kisieliński, a Silesian squad supplemented by several Cracovians also travelled to play games in Scotland. These types of meetings were preferred to full international matches immediately following the war, as Reyman believed that a Polish team would struggle to present themselves against national teams that had seen much less disruption.

It took almost two years for Poland to officially make their international return, with a trip to face Norway in the summer of 1947. With eight years having passed since the Poles' last game there was understandably little continuity between Kałuża's last squad and Reyman's first, and the former Wisła striker handed debuts to nine. Remarkably though, four players' international involvement was to traverse the war: Edward Jabłoński and Stanisław Baran called for their second caps after debuting against Hungary; Władysław Szczepaniak again captaining the team on his 32nd appearance and Walter Brom finally making his international bow having previously appeared as an unused replacement.

Ultimately, the journey proved a disappointment. Three second half goals quickly tilted the game in Norway's favour, and by the time that Jabłoński netted Poland's first post-war goal it was too late to make a difference. The squad had also been forced to travel to Oslo without their coach, who was denied a passport by Poland's communist government just a few days before the game, in fear that he would not return. Although Kuchar stood in his place, Reyman's tactics and team selections were still used, with left-sided defender Stanisław Flanek later recalling how Reyman even travelled with the squad to the airport, "took each of the players by the hand, discussed with them the tactics and told them how to play in the upcoming meeting".

Though Reyman was finally able to make his first appearance in the dugout in July 1947 as the Poles fell to defeat against Romania in Warsaw, still viewed with suspicion by the communist government it would prove to be the only time he would lead the team during his two-year reign. Just days before the squad travelled to Prague for a late-August friendly against Czechoslovakia, the coach was again denied permission to leave the country, and less than 24 hours before his team took to the field he announced his resignation, citing "forced difficulties and severe working conditions". Though he would eventually get another chance in the role a decade later, the problems he faced would soon become the norm for Poles, as communist influences grew and Stalinisation took a hold of their country.

CHAPTER FOURTEEN
DEFEATING THE OPPRESSORS

By the time that the 1940s became the 1950s, Communist policies had become entrenched into both Polish life and Polish sport. With pre-war sport described by the country's new government as "in the service of the bourgeoisie" and "used against the working class", there was an obvious eagerness to implement a similar structure to the one which had become the norm in the Soviet Union. After all, it was believed that "physical culture in the Soviet Union [was] one of the most-powerful means of a socialist education".

The government had the final say on the majority of sporting decisions as not to go against their communist ideals, but even so they regularly came up against stiff opposition from various governing associations. To aid the implementation of their centralised structure, the government oversaw the liquidation of all independent sporting associations in 1951, with the PZPN replaced by the 'Sekcja Piłki Nożnej' of the Główny Komitet Kultury Fizycznej (Main Committee of Physical Culture).

Prior to its disbanding, the PZPN had seen several successes: not only the reimplementation of the league structure which had served so well in the interwar years, but also the addition of a second tier in 1949 and the laying of the foundations for a returning national cup competition a year later. Still, it wasn't without influence from higher powers. The cup, for example, adopted the model used in the Soviet Union and was opened to even the country's smallest clubs—fitting well with socialist ideology. Communist propaganda claimed that around 7,500 teams, and over 100,000 players took part in the competition, while the decision to hand the title of Polish Champions to the inaugural cup winners in 1951 meant that practically any club in the country had the chance to become that season's Mistrz Polski.

One of the keys to implementing the new structure came with the government's assignment of a state-funded industry to each club, which was to become solely responsible for its financial needs. It was a trend that had started as early as 1948 with Wisłoka Dębica's fusion to the meat processing industry, in turn becoming the absurdly named 'Klub Sportowy Związku Zawodowego Pracowników Przetwórni Przemysłu Mięsnego' Dębica. By late-1950 almost every major Polish club had received similar treatment—some for better, some for worse.

Among those that thrived early in the era of socialism were the clubs linked to the military, and in particular Legia. Renamed as CWKS Warszawa (Centralna Wojskowi Klub Sportowy), they were quickly installed as the army's favoured club, and as a result were able to take their pick of the players called up for military service ahead of the regional OWKS clubs in cities such as Wrocław (Śląsk), Kraków (Wawel) and Bydgoszcz (Zawisza). Under the new name 'Gwardia', clubs linked to the militia also profited with the new system: Wisła Kraków, Olimpia Poznań and a new club founded in 1948, Gwardia Warszawa, the most notable. Meanwhile, the wealth linked to Upper Silesia's mining industry also ensured that several clubs in that region saw growth, in particular the swift rise of another club established just a few years after the war, Górnik Zabrze.

For every club which prospered there was another that suffered, and the communists were far from subtle in assigning the less-wealthy industries to clubs which were not in their favour. Punished in part for having spent the years of Nazi occupation as 'Germania', AKS Chorzów were placed under the patronage of the building industry and renamed as Budowlani Chorzów, while one of the symbols of Polishness, Cracovia, joined with the urban city services under the new moniker Ogniwo

Kraków. Still, the bastions of traditional Polish culture and values, Polonia Warsaw, were left in the worst situation of them all. If being linked to the destitute state railways and rebranded as Kolejorz Warszawa was not enough, they were then forced to watch as their sponsors chose to pump the majority of their limited funds into Kolejorz Poznań (formerly ZZK Poznań) instead. Unsurprisingly, all three of the former top-flight stalwarts had succumbed to relegation by 1954.

***

While the reorganisation of club football was ongoing, Henryk Reyman's resignation as national team coach had begun a period of instability at the PZPN. In three-and-a-half years, ten different men took on the role in some capacity, starting with the introduction of yet another 'Committee of Three' just days after the former Wisła striker's departure. Former Cracovia goalkeeper and incumbent PZPN Vice President Andrzej Przeworski was the experienced head of the group, leading the team with support from ex-referee Karol Bergtal and former trade union activist Czesław Krug. Their two-month reign towards the end of 1947 would give a brief glimpse of how the majority of the next decade would play out.

The Poles' September tour of Scandinavia had been a promising start for the trio: a high-scoring, narrow defeat to a Swedish side that would claim gold at the following year's Olympics, followed by a 4-1 mauling of Finland in Helsinki. Yet the honeymoon period was short-lived; with their first squad containing players mostly inherited from Reyman, the trio were accused of riding on the coat tails of their predecessor, and when they finally made their first proper selection for a Bergtal-led voyage to Belgrade in October things quickly unravelled. With seven goals shipped to their Yugoslavian hosts in just 35 first-half minutes, eventually falling to a record 7-1 defeat, and an uninspiring goalless draw with Romania just a week later, upon their return to Warsaw the committee were denied the chance to make another selection.

Returning solely to his position as vice president, Przeworski was involved in the selection of his own successor, Zygmunt Alfus. The 47-year-old had briefly played alongside Przeworski at Cracovia during the early twenties, and as a representative of the Śląski ZPN he had also worked closely with Reyman during his tenure. Aided by the reintroduction of league football in March 1948, Alfus made a handful of amendments to his predecessors' team and was rewarded with a fine 3-1 victory over Czechoslovakia in his second outing—by far the Reprezentacja's most impressive post-war result to date. But again a promising start was soon followed by heavy defeat, this time in Copenhagen against Denmark. Before the game Alfus had attempted to motivate his team by advising that "if [they] win this game, then [they] can go to the Olympics"; but having attempted to play the 'WM' formation without sufficient preparation, four Danish goals in the first half were followed by four more in the second, and the Poles' lack of reply meant that the defeat would surpass that against Yugoslavia as their worst ever.

"[Alfus' words] did not help us" quipped striker Gerard Cieślik several years later, "as the Danes were told the same thing!"; yet the defeat in Denmark was not the sole reason that the Poles missed the 1948 Olympics in London. With tightening relations between the east and west, and the creation of the so-called 'Iron Curtain', the communist governments in the Eastern Bloc were unwilling to allow teams to travel to the capitalist west. It was a decision that would not have come as a surprise for many within the PZPN, with both Mieczysław Gracz and Tadeusz Parpan already having been denied by the government the chance to travel to the British Isles in 1947 to take part in a 'Great Britain v. Rest of Europe' match at Hampden Park.

Despite having been the one to issue a statement declaring the Poles' impending absence, Przeworski still held feint hopes of sending a team to London. In his role as a representative of the Polish Olympic Committee, Przeworski was able to submit a Polish team to the competition, without consent from the authorities, in the hope that good results could convince them to change their minds. Three days before the Denmark game, Poland had been included in the Olympic draw at Arsenal's Highbury Stadium, where they were paired in the preliminary round with the United States of America. Yet reports of the draw never made it to Polish newspapers. Perhaps it was the 8-0 defeat which finally ended Przeworski's hopes of sending a team to London. Perhaps, however, it was the political implications of having to play against a country which was the epitome of capitalism, and everything that Poland's communist regime were against.

Alfus was able to take charge of a couple more games beyond his embarrassment in Denmark before an alleged, yet largely unexplained scandal engulfed both AKS Chorzów and the Śląski ZPN. Declared as an "enemy of the peoples' sport", Alfus was among several linked to the Silesian association who were handed lifetime disqualifications—disqualifications that would eventually be overturned after several years. It wasn't the first, or the last time that a Selekcjoner would become the subject of communist persecution either: Karol Bergtal spent several years in prison during the fifties on trumped-up charges, while in 1951 one of Alfus' successors, Stefan Kisieliński, was found hanged in a Warsaw hotel under extremely suspicious circumstances after a meeting with the secret police.

***

After the failed attempts of various committees of three, four and even five, Ruch Chorzów coach Ryszard Koncewicz was eventually appointed to the role of national team coach in 1950, having worked for several years alongside Wacław Kuchar as the team's trainer. While still maintaining his role with the Niebiescy, Koncewicz's aim was to prepare the team for the 1952 Olympics in Helsinki—the first which was to feature a team from the Soviet Union, and therefore would also see entries from its satellite nations.

Preparations initially ran far from smoothly, with the transfer of power from the PZPN to the GKKF in February 1951 causing severe upheaval within the Polish game. Ruch's rivalry with Wisła Kraków also led to the latter withdrawing several of their players from Koncewicz's national team squads in order to keep them fresh for their domestic campaign—a tactic with limited success for the Biała Gwiazda, who may have lifted the year's league trophy, but lost out on the newly implemented Polish Cup, and therefore the Polish championship, by virtue of a 2-0 defeat to Koncewicz's Ruch.

Club rivalries were required to be temporarily put aside early in the Olympic year as the GKKF sanctioned the establishment of three training centres around the country, from which the final Olympic team would be selected. The postponement of the domestic league until the Autumn freed up Koncewicz, Wisła boss Michał Matyas and Legia manager Wacław Kuchar to head the centres in Chorzów, Kraków and Warsaw respectively; though within a few months Koncewicz was moved on to replace Kuchar in the capital, and a Hungarian, Tivadar Király, filled the vacant position in Upper Silesia. The move proved a damaging one for Koncewicz as, with fifteen of the sixteen players selected to travel to Finland hailing from either the centres in Kraków or Chorzów, the decision was made to send only Matyas and Király to lead the squad.

Poland's stay in Scandinavia was shorter than hoped. Goals from Polonia Bytom's Kazimierz Trampisz and Szombierki Bytom's Jerzy Krasówka gave the Poles a 2-1 preliminary round victory over the French, but a 2-0 defeat to Denmark in the first round ended their involvement abruptly. Instead, the 1952 Olympics will always be remembered more for the situation off-the-field, and the unusual atmosphere created by the establishment of a separate athletes' village for Eastern Bloc countries in Otaniemi—several kilometres away from the main village, and demanded by the Soviets in order to keep athletes away from their western counterparts and "imperialistic propaganda".

"It was an extraordinary experience, all eclipsed by politics... At lunch, activists would even forbid us to pour ourselves juice in a bottle. They said that 'western imperialists would doctor photos, pasting a vodka label on the bottle, then write that 'the athletes from socialist countries drank alcohol at the Olympics.'"
- Kazimierz Trampisz; interview with Paweł Czado, Sport.pl, 2009

Often though, players would find ways to flout the rules imposed on them, such as when Trampisz and several other players were able to get their hands on a bottle of Coca-Cola before covertly drinking it behind a toilet. Even the coaching staff were not averse to defying the communists authorities: when asked by GKKF President and Soviet Secret Police Colonel Apolinary Minecki to hand back his Olympic clothing following the team's elimination, coach Király asked for a free hour, before hastily packing his bag and fleeing to the headquarters of his countrymen.

***

The death of Stalin in 1953 brought with it dramatic changes to the landscape of Eastern Europe. After a brief period which saw anything-and-everything—including even briefly the city of Katowice—named in remembrance of the deceased dictator, in February 1956 the incoming Soviet Premier Nikita Khrushchev finally denounced many of the actions of his predecessor. In turn, citizens of the satellite states demanded immediate political reform, while the death of Poland's communist leader Bolesław Bierut just a month later opened the door to that summer's worker protests in Poznań, and the eventual rise of the Polish United Workers Party's Reformers' faction led by Władysław Gomułka.

As the process of de-Stalinisation swept through the Eastern Bloc, the Soviets began to allow the Polish nation some political concessions—a temporary liberalisation and greater autonomy, in what would become known as the 'Polish October', or 'Gomułka's Thaw'. In reality though, little changed. Gomułka remained in power purely because the Soviets allowed him to remain in power. As historian Norman Davis wrote in *Heart of Europe: The Past in Poland's Present*, the country merely "ceased to be a puppet state, and became a client state".

While Poland was re-evaluating its relationship with the Soviet Union, the country's football clubs had begun to venture beyond the western periphery of the Iron Curtain for the very first time. Though the European Cup's originators, French newspaper *L'Equipe*, had originally deemed no Polish club worthy enough of a place in their inaugural competition, the GKKF took advantage of the English FA's decision to withdraw First Division champions Chelsea. But rather than send reigning league champions Polonia Bytom to fill the gap, 1954 cup winners Gwardia Warsaw were chosen instead to become Poland's first representative in continental competition. Though they battled to a hard-fought goalless draw away against Djurgårdens IF, in Warsaw the Swedish champions ran out comfortable 4-1 winners to progress with ease.

Off-the-field improvements to Polish sports infrastructure were also made during the fifties, with the building of two monolithic stadia—the likes of which had never been seen in the country before. The first was constructed in the capital, on the right bank of the Wisła, largely from rubble created by the city's wartime destruction. The 71,000-capacity Stadion Dziesięciolecia took just eleven months to build, and opened on 22 July 1955 alongside Stalin's 'gift to Warsaw', the colossal Palace of Culture and Science. The speed of construction proved an excellent piece of socialist propaganda, perfect for its first hosting duties: the Fifth World Festival of Youth and Students—a celebration designed purely to show the superiority of socialism over capitalism. Then exactly a year later, on the border between Katowice and Chorzów, the even larger Stadion Śląski saw its own inauguration. Unofficially capable of holding over 100,000 people, and in the centre of one of Europe's largest urban areas, it wasn't long before the arena became the de-facto home of the Polish national team, hosting many of the team's most important matches.

However, the Śląski's maiden game also coincided with the Reprezentacja falling to its lowest ebb. The 2-0 defeat to East Germany not only provided the GKKF with a great source of embarrassment, but it also left the national team with just one win in eleven attempts and confidence slipping to an all time low. Just a few weeks later coach Ryszard Koncewicz handed in a resignation letter, which the board accepted without the slightest hesitation.

Maybe the GKKF pressured the national team towards failure; in 1953 they had attempted to implement a three-year plan which would supposedly improve the level of the Polish national team to match that of their Hungarian counterparts. Ironically, this had come only a few months after the Polish team had been withdrawn from qualification for the 1954 World Cup, for fear of a heavy defeat after being paired against their oldest rivals. Even early on the unrealistic targets set were apparent, as while the Hungarians were scoring six goals at Wembley Stadium in what would become known as the 'Match of the Century', the Poles were on their way to Tirana, where they suffered a demoralising 2-0 defeat to Albania. Unsurprisingly, the GKKF's plan never came to fruition.

***

Though a first outing at the Dziesięciolecia—a 5-2 win over Norway in September 1956—saw Poland claim a first home victory in four years, the GKKF's rule over Polish football was rapidly weakening. By December 1956, the political thaw had allowed for the rebirth of the PZPN, and following the association's reinstatement, its conference of February 1957 was of great importance in bringing a sense of normality back to the Polish game. After almost a decade clubs began to return to their traditional names, while after a two-decade absence the Poles would once again enter into the qualification round for the World Cup. However, it was the return of Henryk Reyman, to the role which he had been forced to resign from eight-and-a-half years earlier, which came as the biggest surprise.

Several months prior to Reyman's return, his future charges had been drawn in a three-team group to qualify for the 1958 World Cup in Sweden—firstly with Finland, against whom Czesław Krug had recently led Poland to a 5-0 friendly victory, and most notably the Soviet Union. While nothing but victory was expected against the Finns, the ties against the latter were of intrigue for all Poles; not just because of the previous twelve years of hardships suffered under their proxy rule, but also due to the fact that it would actually be the first official meeting between the two countries. Ahead of the qualifying campaign, preparations were far from positive. Poland's only pre-qualification friendly, against Turkey at the Dziesięciolecia, ended in a narrow defeat—the fact it was the first ever international game to be shown on Polish television only added to the embarrassment. With just a month to go before their group opener in Moscow, Reyman and his assistants had their work truly cut out for them.

After much deliberation, the coach's solution was to make several changes to the side that failed to score against the Turks, handing international debuts to three, including Gwardia Warsaw captain Bolesław Lewandowski in the centre forward role, in place of Ernest Pol. In hindsight it proved not to be the tactical masterstroke that Reyman had hoped for: a 3-0 defeat left Poland's hopes of qualification already hanging in the balance. With the USSR expected to claim maximum points against Finland, it looked as though Poland would have to win all three of their remaining games to stand a chance of reaching the World Cup.

The first was passed with relative ease. As it had been in their friendly meeting two years earlier, Helsinki's Olympiastadion once again proved a happy hunting ground for Poland; a hat-trick for Górnik Zabrze forward Edward Jankowski giving the Białe-Orły a 3-1 victory and their first points of the campaign. Yet the difficulty of their second test, the return match against the USSR, was made clear by the fact that in August the Soviets had scored ten on their own trip to the Finnish capital.

With their penultimate qualifier planned for October, the game's importance led the PZPN to set aside time in late September for a pair of warm-up games. The second, a trip to Sofia to face Bulgaria, was nothing out of the ordinary; however, a jaunt to Catalonia to help to open Barcelona's Camp Nou stadium was something of an unexpected experience for the players. The Spanish club's invitation had originally been extended to 1956 league champions Legia, and advertisements for the inauguration had been made up to promote the fact. Nevertheless, the PZPN decided instead to send Reyman's charges under the guise of a Warsaw Representation XI, and they fell to a respectable 4-2 defeat against a team containing the likes of Antoni Ramallets and Laszlo Kubala. Just a few days later the Bulgarians also proved to be tough opposition for the Biało-Czerwoni, holding them to a 1-1 draw.

Despite the warm-up games and single round of league games scheduled for the first weekend of October, all that occupied Poles' minds was the first ever visit of their eastern neighbours. This hadn't passed the PZPN by either, and the squad was assembled in Upper Silesia a week-and-a-half prior to the game, during which time they would take on a Silesian XI to ensure preparations were of the highest standard. While the Silesians were soundly beaten, one man on their team stood head and shoulders above the rest. A ten-year veteran of the national team with 22 goals to his name, and twice the league's top scorer, Ruch Chorzów striker Gerard Cieślik was arguably the best post-war striker to date. Reyman didn't agree. He deemed Cieślik too slight and "lacking in militancy"; this was an opinion which one of the team's trainers, Ewald Cebula, strongly disagreed with.

> *"For me it was clear that this group had no right to play without Gerard. I argued with [fellow coach Tadeusz] Forys; I harassed Dyrda and Reyman, who were frequent visitors to the grouping, and finally I managed to persuade them. Gerard initially shied away; he regretted that the selectors accused his lack of militancy, but he never got rid of his ambition."*
> - Ewald Cebula

DEFEATING THE OPPRESSORS

***

Poland (v Soviet Union)
World Cup Qualifier; Stadion Śląski, Chorzów;
20 October 1957.

Goalkeeper: Edward Szymkowiak (Polonia Bytom).

Defenders: Stefan Florenski (Górnik Zabrze), Roman Korynt (Lechia Gdańsk), Jerzy Woźniak (Legia Warsaw).

Midfielders: Ginter Gawlik (Górnik Zabrze), Edmund Zientara (Legia Warsaw).

Attackers: Edward Jankowski (Górnik Zabrze), Lucjan Brychczy (Legia Warsaw), Henryk Kempny (Legia Warsaw), Gerard Cieślik (Ruch Chorzów), Roman Lentner (Górnik Zabrze).

Anticipation for the game had been huge and demand for tickets far outweighed supply; given the amount of applications, the 100,000-capacity Stadion Śląski could have sold out four times over. Many of those attending had grudges to bear with their oppressors; a feeling shared by several players including Edmund Zientara, who had been forced to spend time under a pseudonym to avoid persecution and Edward Szymkowiak, whose policeman father was murdered at Katyń. The atmosphere inside the Śląski was raucous. The noise could be heard all the way into the bowels of the stadium, where Stefan Florenski recalled that "the Russians had fear in their eyes" and that "the roar of the crowd had paralysed them". After the teams emerged on to the pitch, the spine-tingling pre-match rendition of *Mazurek Dąbrowskiego* could only have tipped the scales further into Polish hands.

On the pitch it showed...

From John Harold Clough's starting whistle Poland quickly went on the offensive, and within minutes Soviet keeper Lev Yashin was already forced into action. Having been able to edge in front of a defender, Cieślik managed to head a low cross goalwards which the 'Black Panther' pushed inches over the crossbar. Several other promising Polish efforts failed to test the keeper before the visitors were able to muster their first meaningful attack, and even then Szymkowiak was on hand to comfortably mop up any danger. As half-time approached the hosts continued to pile on the pressure; but just when it looked as though the teams would enter the break goalless, the Soviet defence was breached.

Cieślik's opener was not the prettiest, but the Silesian crowd could not have cared less. Good passing movement on the right-hand side between Ginter Gawlik, Lucjan Brychczy and Henryk Kempny allowed the latter space to cross into the Soviet box, and while Cieślik's shot was hit straight in the direction of Yashin, its power and downward trajectory deceived the Dynamo Moscow stopper, squirming over the line to send the Śląski into raptures.

The goal came at a crucial time for the visitors: the half-time interval either damaging their morale or giving them chance to recollect themselves. Just five minutes into the second half the former proved true, as Cieślik rose above the defence to head Brychczy's cross past an out-of-position Yashin, putting the game beyond almost any doubt. The Soviets did manage to make the scoreline more respectable when, with ten minutes remaining on the clock, Valentin Ivanov reduced the hosts' lead. But it was the Poles who finished the game stronger: Cieślik, Brychczy and Kempny all squandering late chances to reclaim the two-goal advantage.

Despite a 4-0 victory over Finland a fortnight later, qualification for the World Cup would prove to be a bridge too far for Reyman's men. Finishing level on points with the USSR, a play-off at a neutral venue was required to determine which of the two would advance; and while Polish proposals to play the game in either Belgrade or Vienna were swiftly refused by their opponents, a counter suggestion of East Germany's Leipzig—then home to several thousand Soviet troops—was suspiciously approved by the Polish government without input from the PZPN. With the partisan crowd behind them, a 3-0 victory for Gavriil Kachalin's side became just another example of the power held by the Soviet Union over its satellite states.

However, for many Poles, the game at the Śląski had been about more than just qualification. It had been about more than just football. As the players left the pitch on the shoulders of their adulating supporters, it was clear that it was rather a victory over their persecution. A victory over their unwanted ruler. In the grand scheme of things a minor victory it may have been, but against their oppressors the Poles believed there was no such thing as a minor victory.

CHAPTER FIFTEEN
A DECADE OF TWO CLUBS

VICTORY OVER THE USSR may have caused waves inside of Poland, yet beyond the Iron Curtain it had registered as barely a ripple. In the west, Polish footballing juggernauts such as Ruch Chorzów and Wisła Kraków remained largely unheard of, while names such as Brychczy and Szymkowiak were deemed as unremarkable as they were unpronounceable. It was a commonly held belief that success in the newly created European competitions would be the best way to promote Polish football to a wider audience, but achieving it would not be an easy task.

Polish clubs had got off to an inauspicious start in Europe, perhaps due to the fact that in the six seasons between 1956 and 1961 only two reigning league champions—Legia in 1956 and ŁKS Łódź in 1959—actually represented the country in UEFA's blooming European Cup. In opposition to the Autumn–Spring structure seen across the continent, Poland's Spring–Autumn league schedule was seen by the PZPN as to put their clubs at a disadvantage, and with this very much in mind they imposed a rule which meant that the reigning champions were not always selected to play in Europe: should the Mistrz Polski sit outside the league's top three at its summer break, the current league leaders would instead take their place.

The first club to suffer from the decision were Legia, who lost their place in the 1957/58 European Cup to fellow Varsovians Gwardia after dropping to 10th position by the time that summer arrived. Yet, while Gwardia's second appearance in the competition had started strongly, it was to end no differently than Polish clubs' previous outings. A 3-1 victory over Wismut Karl-Marx-Stadt in Warsaw was followed seven days later with defeat by the same scoreline in East Germany, and with the scores then level at one apiece in the deciding game, a power failure forced the referee to decide the game by alternative means. After 290 minutes of football the Polish club were finally eliminated by a coin toss.

First round elimination became a common theme for Polish clubs in Europe: Polonia Bytom suffered heavy defeat to MTK Budapest of Hungary in 1959, and Legia's campaign in 1960 resulted in elimination at the hands of Danish champions AGF Aarhus. On the occasion that the league champions did maintain a spot on the podium at the league's halfway stage, they too were embarrassed: first-time champions ŁKS defeated with ease by their Luxembourgish counterparts Jeunesse Esch. Górnik Zabrze did, for a short time at least, look as though they may break the duck in 1961, racing into a 4-0 home lead against Tottenham Hotspur before heavy-handed tactics from the English champions reduced the deficit to two goals and forced several of the Górnik side to complete the game whilst carrying injuries. Depleted, an 8-1 pummelling at White Hart Lane a week later left them the seventh straight Polish representative to be eliminated at the first hurdle.

Finally though, the PZPN's decision to align the country's league schedule with the rest of Europe by the summer of 1962 coincided with an almost instantaneous improvement in results. As they were beginning their very first Autumn–Spring season, winners of the truncated 1962 league competition, Polonia Bytom, became the first Polish club to advance in the European Cup, by virtue of a 6-2 aggregate victory over Greece's Panathinaikos. Though defeated by Galatasaray of Turkey in the second round, the Bytomianins' result not only raised the minimum expectation for their successors, it also lifted the pressure allowing Polish clubs to achieve much more. If a club could take advantage of the socio-political climate in order to dominate the domestic game, and in turn become regulars in Europe, then further progression would surely follow.

**

Though sustained domestic success would help to increase Polish clubs' chances of progressing in Europe, during the mid-fifties only one club was in a position to actually achieve it. By calling upon the league's best players for military service, Legia were able to build a talented squad with haste, profiting off the back of their rivals' success.

Legia's primacy amongst the military had become clear to see soon after the 1953 season when, after finishing above them, fellow army club Wawel Kraków were withdrawn from the league by their benefactors for the following campaign. Legia were then given the pick of Wawel's top players, with several making the move to the capital. The club then continued their policy of scouring smaller sides and cherry picking their better players—notably the Silesian duo of Ernest Pol and Edward Szymkowiak, who moved to Ulica Łazienkowska in 1953, and Lucjan Brychczy a year later. Established clubs were not exempt from being raided either, as goalkeeper Jan Bem, defender Horst Mahseli and top scorer Henryk Kempny made the switch from league champions Polonia Bytom before the start of the 1955 campaign; transfers which proved to be an immediate success, as the trio claimed back-to-back winner's medals while their former club suffered an embarrassing relegation.

Hungarian coach János Steiner had been the man to lead Legia to their maiden championship, and it was because of his influence that the likes of Pol, Szymkowiak and midfielder Edmund Kowal were convinced to stay at the club beyond the completion of their military service. Yet with military bosses unconvinced that a football coach could warrant a general's salary, soon after defeating Gwardia to claim the 1955 Puchar Polski they opted to replace him with ex-national team trainer Ryszard Koncewicz. While the decision initially looked to be justified with Koncewicz repeating Steiner's league and cup double, the coach sat on difficult terms with a handful of players and an exodus of the club's Silesian core soon followed.

Legia's ability to effectively pinch players from across the country had helped to propel them to the top, but it had begun to prove an unsustainable model for continued success. With more and more players deciding to return home after the completion of their service, they became reliant on finding a constant stream of talented conscripts and ultimately suffered from a lack of continuity. Yet, while Legia began to struggle, one club in particular began to thrive.

Due to the importance of having suitably trained staff working in an industry integral to the country's economy, coal mining was among several industries deemed by the Polish government as a 'reserved occupation'. This meant that miners were given exemption from the otherwise compulsory conscription to the army. The mining industry's leading club, Górnik Zabrze, began to take advantage of this loophole by offering players token jobs in the mines, meaning that when they stood in front of the Military Commission they were able to avoid both the draft and the forced transfer to Legia. These jobs were also offered to the likes of Pol and Kowal to tempt them away from the capital, both of whom happily accepted ahead of the 1957 season having been brought up amongst mining families nearby.

The experience of Pol and Kowal had undoubtedly made them Górnik's marquee signings, but they were by no means joining an inexperienced squad. Like the two former *Legioniści*, defender Henryk Hajduk also had a league title to his name from his time at Ruch. Marian Olejnik and Edward Jankowski had also both picked up several years of top-flight experience in the capital. It could also be argued that this experience was necessary for the club to claim its first league title, as when their nearest challengers Gwardia fell, Górnik held their composure. Dropping just three points in the final 13 games of their 1957 campaign, the Silesians finally climbed above Gwardia by virtue of a 3-1 victory over them in

September. The championship was then confirmed on the final day, with an emphatic 8-1 win against Odra Opole.

Still, many of Gornik's squad were veterans of their rise from the second tier, and after slipping to 3rd place in 1958 the management needed to refocus. It quickly became clear that the club's future success depended on the ability to combine it's experienced players with talented youngsters and, luckily for them, many young players saw neither the army nor Legia as their preferred route of choice. As such, the opportunity to join a club such as Górnik—especially for Silesians—was very welcoming.

Securing the signatures of Silesia's brightest young stars became Górnik's plan for sustained success, and around the turn of the decade they began to build a squad with the intention of dominating Polish football for years to come. 18-year-old striker Erwin Wilczek arrived from neighbouring Zryw Chorzów in 1959, while 20-year-old keeper Hubert Kostka joined from Unia Racibórz just over a year later. Following Poland's second-place finish in the Under-18's European Championship of 1961, the *Trójkolorowi* also secured the signatures of three of the side's top performers: Karol Kapciński, Jerzy Musiałek and Zygfryd Szołtysik; and though slightly older at 23, defender Stanisław Oślizło still had many of his best years ahead of him when he earned a "promotion" transfer to Zabrze, having already avoided the draft while playing at fellow mining club Górnik Radlin.

The squad building process was far from a quick one, and early on the club were only able to alternate between years of success and disappointment. Janos Steiner's appointment ahead of the 1959 season brought with it a second title to Ulica Roosevelta, but after he moved across Upper Silesia to Ruch Chorzów the following year, so did the trophy. The Zabrzanins did respond with a third title in 1961, while also coming close to a fourth in the shortened 1962 championship six months later. But defeat in a two-legged play-off handed Polonia Bytom their second title instead, and left Górnik looking for one final piece of their jigsaw.

"The offer from Górnik Zabrze was the most interesting as they approached my father's side—mining. They asked if he was working in the mines, suggesting he might have a better position if his son played in Zabrze, and invited him to a meeting with the minister of mining... It was a family decision, and as such an arrangement was made".
- Włodzimierz Lubański, „Życie jak dobry mecz"–Włodzimierz Lubański w rozmowie z Michałem Olszańskim

Towards the end of October 1962, the Polish national team fell to a 2-1 defeat against Czechoslovakia at the Tehelné Pole in Bratislava. Following the match, in celebration of his impending 30th birthday, Ernest Pol settled for a few rounds of drinks along with teammates Lucjan Brychczy and Jan Liberda; however, having banned the squad from drinking alcohol during the trip, when trainer Ryszard Koncewicz was made aware of the infraction, the trio came in for punishment. Despite some hard-line officials demanding long suspensions, Liberda and Brychczy managed to escape any punishment. Pol, however, was handed a three-month expulsion that ruled him out for a significant portion of Górnik's title push. Górnik managed to keep their challenge on track thanks to goals from their young contingent of Wilczek, Szołtysik and Musiałek, extending their lead to four points. However, both Pol's absence and his advancing years prompted Górnik to keep their eyes peeled for a potential replacement.

Just a short bus ride from Górnik's stadium, in the Sośnica suburb of Gliwice, a young attacker by the name of Włodzimierz Lubański had begun to attract the attention of some of Silesia's biggest clubs. Having garnered praise playing for nearby GKS Gliwice whilst still completing his education, league champions Polonia Bytom and cup winners Zagłębie Sosnowiec joined Górnik in pursuing a serious interest in the striker soon after his sixteenth birthday. All three used different tactics to try to procure the signature of young Lubański; but while Polonia's pitch of history and patriotism, and Zagłębie's offer of vast amounts of money were both tempting, Górnik's proposal—which included an improved position in the mines for Włodzimierz's foreman father—proved to be the most appealing option for the family.

After a few weeks of integration into his new team, Włodek made his first appearance in a Górnik shirt for an April cup clash against rivals Ruch Chorzów, while his league bow coincided with the return of Ernest Pol, at home to Arkonia Szczecin just a few days later. Within 30 minutes of his half-time introduction on the right wing, Lubański had rippled the net of Arkonia keeper Tadeusz Kwiatkowski, adding to goals from Pol and Joachim Czok in a 4-0 victory, and extending Górnik's lead at the top of the table to five points, ahead of the two clubs which he had turned down. It was a lead which never shortened as Górnik went on to lift the title with two games to spare—Włodek netting against Zagłębie, Wisła Kraków and Pogoń Szczecin to end the season with four goals. Within months the teenager's meteoric rise was confirmed, as he became both the national team's youngest-ever debutant and goalscorer following a 9-0 victory over Norway in Szczecin. Appearances and goals in European matches didn't have to wait much longer.

Yet winning a league title was far from enough to guarantee that a Górnik manager would keep his job, and over the next few years several managerial changes were made despite Górnik never relinquishing their crown. After a stuttering start to the 1963/64 season, a cup defeat to second-tier GKS Katowice was the final nail in the managerial coffin of Ewald Cebula. Hungarian Ferenc Farsang then brought with him a tactical revolution at the start of 1964: switching to a modern 4-2-4 formation like the one pioneered by both Belá Guttmann and the World Cup-winning Brazilian side of the late-fifties, and earning two league titles and the Puchar Polski for his troubles. Władysław Giergiel also had a chance to add the Puchar to his league title in 1966, but was asked to clear his desk before he could lead the team out in the final against Legia.

The reason for the last change soon became clear, as within a week another Hungarian, Géza Kalocsay, was placed in charge of Górnik. Kalocsay's acquisition was seen as something of a coup for the club: as a pre-war international for both Czechoslovakia and Hungary, and a part of the Czechoslovakian squad which finished second at the 1934 World Cup, Kalocsay had garnered a wealth of playing experience. Following his retirement he went on to earn similar honours in management, assisting Hungarian coach Gusztáv Sebes as the Mighty Magyars ended the 1954 World Cup as runners up, and also lifting domestic trophies with Partizan Belgrade, Standard Liege and Ujpest. Having led the latter to the semi-finals of the Cup Winners' Cup in 1962, Górnik activists believed that if there was any man who could help the club to progress in Europe, it would be Kalocsay.

Although his debut on the Górnik bench ended in defeat, Kalocsay's implementation of a 4-3-3 system soon yielded positive results in both the league and the European Cup. Górnik's fifth consecutive league title surpassed the previous record of four set by Ruch between 1933 and 1936, while progression to the second round proper of the European Cup was the furthest that any Polish club had advanced to date. However, the new coach's training methods had sparked rumours of disharmony in the Górnik ranks, and the switch to a modern, more-defensive tactic left some of the club's stalwart players with only bit parts to play. One of the most vocal critics, Ernest Pol, quickly fell out of favour with the Hungarian, and slipped down the pecking order as Kalocsay opted instead for Lubański to play in the central role up front.

The decision to reduce Pol's involvement may have proven unpopular amongst the Górnik faithful, but there was some justification: heading towards his 35th birthday, Pol's best years were certainly behind him, while the performances of Lubański and Szołtysik did not warrant anything other than a regular starting berth. Dismayed at seeing their hero cast aside, supporters became vociferous in their chants of *"Bez Pola, nie ma gola"* ("without Pol, there are no goals")—yet Kalocsay remained unswayed. As a spot in the starting eleven became increasingly rare, Pol made the decision to retire to America at the end of the season; his record-setting 186th league goal having already come in November's 2-0 victory at home to Zagłębie Sosnowiec. But with Lubański finishing as the league's top scorer for the second year in a row—a crown he would go on to keep for a further two seasons—Górnik fans had already bore witness to the emergence of their new hero.

***

While Górnik were consolidating their position as the strongest club in Poland, in the capital, Legia were struggling with their decline into mediocrity. Throughout the first half of the sixties, the Wojskowi failed to regain a footing amongst the country's top clubs; scraping into a top-half finish was the best that they could muster. But with the appointment of unyielding Czech coach Jaroslav Vejvoda in 1966, their fortunes finally began to turn for the better. Vejvoda arrived from Dukla Prague with title-winning experience, having lifted three Czechoslovakian championships with his hometown club. But, perhaps most encouragingly for Legia fans, he had experience of bettering Górnik, having twice progressed past them in European competition.

Vejvoda was first sounded out about the Legia job as the club celebrated its 50th anniversary with friendly games against Dukla and Tottenham Hotspur, and officially took charge of the side in the summer of 1966. Within the first two weeks of the season, he had doubled his win tally over Górnik—defeating them on the opening day of the league season and then twelve days later in the 1966 cup final, which had been delayed because of the national team's tour of South America. But while, for a sixth successive season Legia were unable to earn a spot on the podium, the 1966/67 campaign is forever remembered as an important one, with the acquisition of two players who would go on to become legends for both club and country.

The first was Robert Gadocha, a 20-year-old left winger from Kraków whose speed and ability to twist-and-turn with the ball had been developed whilst playing ice hockey as a youngster. Gadocha had been originally spotted by Lucjan Brychczy as a 17-year-old playing for Garbarnia, before being called to the city's army club, Wawel, two years later. Wawel did their utmost to hang on to the player, but as soon as Legia showed any serious interest, it was only a matter of time before his move to the capital. Vejvoda's faith in Brychczy's opinion became evident upon Gadocha's arrival as, within 24 hours of joining the club, he was thrust into the starting line-up for a league game at Zawisza Bydgoszcz; historian Andrzej Gowarszewski claiming that, with the winger's insertion into the starting eleven, "Legia's Achilles' heel had changed into a serious advantage".

Just a week after Gadocha, another young talent made his first appearance in Legia colours, yet his acquisition proved slightly more troublesome. Born in the Pomeranian town of Starogard Gdański, 19-year-old midfielder Kazimierz Deyna had been spotted by a Legia scout whilst playing for the local team Włókniarz; but while immediately sounded out for a transfer, by the time Legia officials arrived to complete the signing he was nowhere to be found. The teenager eventually surfaced in Łódź, turning out for ŁKS in a goalless draw with Górnik Zabrze, and when Legia's activists recognised his name in a copy of *Przegląd Sportowy* they quickly despatched men to Łódź to broker a deal. The military were able to secure the player's easy release by promising to postpone the military service of several other ŁKS players, and Deyna made his Legia debut in a November home draw with Ruch Chorzów.

From the outset, it was easy to see why the club were so eager to secure Deyna's signature: his ability to read and control a game were comparable to players several years his senior, while his vision and ability to pick a pass were better than that of any other player his age. He was also adept at advancing up the pitch and dangerous in sight of the opposition goal; a hat-trick against Śląsk Wrocław in just his tenth senior league game testifying to his goalscoring abilities.

The impact of the two arrivals was immediately noticeable: before, Legia had been languishing in the relegation zone with Vejvoda's position under threat, yet over the last sixteen games only champions-elect Górnik were able to maintain a better record. Legia finally got the better of their adversaries a year later, with their highest league finish since the turn of the decade, only to see the Trójkolorowi release their five-year-strong grip on the trophy to neighbouring Ruch by virtue of a 3-1 final day defeat to their Upper Silesian rivals—the legitimacy of which has long been debated by Legia fans due to the fact that Górnik went on to pummel Ruch 3-0 in the cup final just a few days later.

***

The 1968 Puchar Polski may have been Górnik's only piece of silverware of the season, yet it was far from their only achievement. Kalocsay's charges found distraction from their league form in the shape of the European Cup, and proceeded to reach heights that had never before been witnessed by Polish fans.

Górnik were drawn against Swedish club Djurgardens in the opening round of the competition, and sailed through with ease—a Lubański brace and a late Lentner strike at the Stadion Śląski ensuring the tie was practically over before the halfway point. The second leg in Stockholm then proved nothing more than a formality for the Polish champions, as Jerzy Musiałek's goal wrapped up the 4-0 aggregate scoreline. Next, the Trójkolorowi were handed a daunting trip east to face the conquerors of the reigning European champions, Celtic: Dynamo Kyiv. Despite their status as underdogs, and falling behind to a 12th-minute Alfred Olek own goal, a strike just minutes later from Szołtysik and a Lubański effort after an hour gave Górnik an unexpected advantage to take back to Silesia. Less than a fortnight later at the Śląski, another Szołtysik strike was enough to draw 1-1 on the night, and ultimately progress to the last sixteen. But there, the luck of the draw would not be on their side.

It had been six-and-a-half years since Augustyn Dziwisz had led his Górnik side to face Tottenham in their continental debut, and in that period the club had progressed from European novices to seasoned veterans. In Szołtysik and Lubański, they also possessed two players recently ranked in France Football's prestigious Ballon d'Or—Lubański tied in 16th position and Szołtysik 27th. However, the Champions of England, Matt Busby's Manchester United, were a different proposition to anything that any Polish club had faced before. Górnik's quarter-final opponents not only had former Ballon d'Or winners Bobby Charlton and Denis Law in their ranks, but also in Charlton and Nobby Stiles, two reigning World Champions; and that was before mentioning the likes of Paddy Crerand and George Best. Coupled with the strength of the opposition, Kalocsay was also forced to contend with the fact that their trip to Old Trafford was scheduled for the end of February, meaning that it would be his side's first competitive game in almost three months following the extended winter break.

Despite falling to defeat, Górnik's performance in Manchester was one they could return home proud of. Though suffering from the expected signs of rustiness and having been put under pressure for the majority of the game, a strong defensive display, and in particular a superb performance from Hubert Kostka in goal, frustrated the hosts. Górnik were finally broken after an hour with an unlucky Florenski own goal, while an unstoppable Brian Kidd effort just before full time ensured that Kalocsay and his squad left Old Trafford with nothing to show for their efforts. Nevertheless, Busby and his charges had learned that the return leg would not necessarily be a formality.

"But for goalkeeper Kostka, applauded off by every Manchester player, it was an agonising finale to a night when he had been both hero and villain.

"Kostka, yellow clad, brilliantly agile and always brave, had stood between United and the unassailable lead they sought to establish. And so the Polish keeper is entitled to feel that he was not beaten legitimately once in this match.
"Superbly disciplined. Skilfully drilled and fashioned into a unit of fighters, Górnik will give United problems in Poland."
- Ken Jones; Daily Mirror; February 29, 1968

Poland was still in the throngs of winter when Manchester United made the journey for the return leg, with futile attempts made to clear the Stadion Śląski pitch of ice and snow before kick off. In the lead up to the game Busby had attempted to convince the Italian referee to postpone, even offering to return to Katowice at a later date and at their own expense; but with their request denied, over 100,000 Silesians braved the freezing weather in hope that their Górnik side would be able to turn around their two-goal deficit.

Right from the first whistle it was clear that United were struggling to adapt to the conditions, and caused Górnik few problems. Busby had also taken the tactical decision to set up his team reasonably conservatively, believing that his back line was strong enough to withstand the expected Górnik onslaught; but this left his attackers—Best and Charlton in particular—mostly isolated, and when they did receive the ball they were easily snuffed out by Oślizło and Henryk Latocha in the heart of the Górnik defence. At the other end, the Red Devils' back line were holding strong despite a barrage of pressure from the Górnik frontmen, and as the half-time whistle sounded, the goalless scoreline played into the hands of the English champions.

By the time that the game recommenced, the freezing conditions had degraded even further, and almost immediately the visitors found themselves desperately clinging on to their lead. Having already been warned on more than one occasion for time wasting, United goalkeeper Alex Stepney was punished in the 68th minute for the same offence, and though Rainer Kuchta's effort from an indirect free kick failed to breach the entire United team lined across their own goal line, the prevailing sense was that a Górnik goal was now almost inevitable. Within 120 seconds, that inevitability had become reality; Kuchta sent a diagonal ball towards Lubański, who controlled, advanced forward, and fired a powerful shot off the underside of the bar into Stepney's net.

Alas, it would be too little too late. Though the Poles sensed blood, an injury to Erwin Wilczek left them unable to attack efficiently, and as the final twenty minutes ticked away on the Italian referee's watch, chance after chance fell by the wayside. With the elusive second goal failing to materialise, both the game and Górnik's European adventure came to an abrupt end. But while their season ultimately ended with the relinquishing of the league title they had held for the last half-a-decade, with United going on to claim their first ever European trophy, the Poles did at least become an interesting footnote in the Red Devils' history. As the English champions defeated Real Madrid in Manchester, drew in the Bernabeu, and then lifted the trophy after beating Benfica at Wembley, Górnik's narrow victory at the Śląski would be left as the only blemish of the champions' entire competition.

CHAPTER SIXTEEN
DOLLARS AND COINS

"[A]t first I didn't have any money, but after the first football matches we started to receive some rations; it was pennies, probably seventy five cents a day or something like that—money paid to us by the management... The [Polish] people living in the USA wanted to say hello to us—they put in our pockets various kinds of gifts and money. When, after the first such meeting with the Polish diaspora I returned to the hotel and started emptying my pockets, I found that I had picked up a few of these Dollars. I didn't know how to behave. I asked Staszek Oślizło, who looked after me and with whom I shared a room: 'Stasiu, what are they? What do I have to do with them?'. And he said, 'Hold on to them, Włodek, they are dollars, and you can buy some cool things with them'. For me it was amazing."
- Włodzimierz Lubański on Górnik Zabrze's trip to the USA, 1963; "Życie jak dobry mecz"—Włodzimierz Lubański w rozmowie z Michałem Olszańskim

ON THE EVENING OF 20 August 1968, four of the Warsaw Pact nations—the Soviet Union, Bulgaria, Hungary and Poland—began an invasion of Czechoslovakia, in order to halt the liberalisation reforms being led by newly elected leader Alexander Dubček. Over 250,000 soldiers streamed over the border that night, with a further 200,000 joining them in the coming days. More than 100 Czechoslovakian citizens lost their lives, with five times that number suffering injuries.

The international reaction was one of heavy condemnation, with even UEFA taking action against those countries involved. For the opening rounds of both the 1968/69 European Cup and Cup Winner's Cup, qualifying teams from the four nations were to be drawn against each other—a decision which the representatives were so unhappy with that they opted to withdraw from the tournaments altogether. For the second time, having won the league, Ruch Chorzów missed out on a place in the European Cup, while cup winners Górnik were left unable to build on their impressive European performance from the previous season. One Polish club did, however, take a place in Europe that season: Legia Warsaw, who participated in the Inter-Cities Fairs Cup, outside of UEFA jurisdiction.

Silesian domination in the league during the sixties had not prevented Legia from participating in European competition, twice representing Poland in the Cup Winner's Cup. On both occasions German opposition proved to be Legia's conquerors: the West's 1860 Munich at the quarter-final stage in 1964/65, and the East's Chemie Leipzig in the first round two years later. Though the Wojskowi did gain revenge against 1860 in the first round of the 1968/69 Fairs Cup before beating Belgians KSV Waregem in the second, Jaroslav Vejvoda's side eventually bowed out of the competition in the third stage to eventual finalists Ujpest. Worse still, their European exploits had proven to be a burden on their league form, and just weeks after their elimination a 2-1 home defeat to Górnik left them six points adrift of their rivals.

Yet with just nine games of the campaign remaining, few could have predicted the Trójkolorowi's spectacular collapse. Firstly, Geza Kalocsay's charges were beaten by relegation battlers Zagłębie Wałbrzych, and then in Wrocław by bottom-of-the-league Śląsk. Though they looked to have stopped the rot in the nick of time with a 3-1 win over Wisła, Górnik surrendered their lead in controversial circumstances just a week later; after an 81st minute Skowronek equaliser against GKS Katowice was disallowed for an infringement, the visiting players surrounded the referee.

> "I have been actively insulted. Górnik player Florenski hit me. Previously, I was [verbally] attacked by Oślizło and Wilczek—both, however, kept their hands to themselves."
> - Referee Bogdan Hirsch; Sport Vol. 58, 19 May 1969

With the match abandoned and GKS handed a 3-0 walkover, Legia claimed a 1-0 win over Stal Rzeszów to leapfrog Górnik and never looked back; Gadocha scoring once and Deyna twice during a 6-2 ceremonial passing of the torch against outgoing champions Ruch, and finishing as the side's two top scorers with 21 goals between them. Yet it would be the very last success of Vejvoda's three years at the helm, as he returned to Prague with the involvement of his employer—the Polish Army—in the invasion of his homeland very much in mind.

Legia did not need to worry; in Edmund Zientara they appointed a successor who knew the club inside out—not just from his nine years at Ulica Łazienkowska as a player, but also from several more as an assistant to both Vejvoda and his predecessor Longin Janeczek. The squad had also gained considerably in strength under the Czechoslovakian, with the players in their possession now arguably of just as high a standard as those which had won Górnik so many championships throughout the sixties. A strong defence marshalled by impressive goalkeeper Władysław Grotyński provided stability to the team, but it was further up the field where the true star quality lay: veteran Lucjan Brychczy and the more-defensive Bernard Blaut complimenting playmaker Deyna in midfield, and the pace of Gadocha and Janusz Żmijewski on the flanks supporting the predatory Jan Pieszko up front. The quality was evident as Legia began their 1969/70 league campaign unbeaten, with Gadocha and Pieszko netting ten goals between them in just six games.

To begin their first European Cup campaign in nine years, Legia were handed a potential banana-skin tie against Romanian champions UTA Arad. After falling behind in Romania, there was a huge sense of relief when Gadocha and Żmijewski finally gave them a narrow advantage to return home with. Back at Ulica Łazienkowska, Zientara's charges were frustrated with a nervous first-half performance, before eight unanswered goals in the second period—a brace for Gadocha, and one apiece for Blaut, Brychczy, Stachurski, Deyna, Żmijewski and Pieszko—

finally appeased the home fans and left them spending more time on their feet than on the stadium's wooden benches.

Legia's second round opposition, five-time French champions Saint-Étienne, would provide a much sterner test. *Les Verts* had been buoyed by a victory over Bayern Munich in the first round, and their two-goal hero from that game, the tricky striker Hervé Revelli, took advantage of slack marking to push them into a first-half lead in Warsaw. But again the Wojskowi fought back. Firstly, Pieszko slotted a neat shot past French international Georges Carnus, and then eight minutes from time the keeper failed to keep out a low Deyna drive. Legia then secured their progression a fortnight later in France, by virtue of another late Deyna goal: the midfielder finishing a counter attacking move with a beautifully curled, right-footed effort into the top corner.

The reward for defeating Saint-Étienne was a quarter-final against arguably one of the weaker remaining teams, Galatasaray of Turkey. Having perhaps learned from Górnik's rustiness against Manchester United, Legia's thorough preparation during the winter break included friendly matches against French and Belgian opposition, and they were able to get off to a great start by the Bosphorus with a strike from captain Lucjan Brychczy. Eventually leaving Istanbul with a 1-1 draw and an important away goal, the Turks were forced to attack in the second leg, allowing veteran Brychczy to twice more pick off the tiring defence in Warsaw. The 3-1 aggregate scoreline ensured that Legia surpassed Górnik's achievement two years earlier, becoming the first Polish club to reach the last four of the competition.

***

Drawn out of the hat to face Feyenoord, even the most optimistic of fans will have admitted that Legia were the underdogs for their European Cup semi-final. The Dutch club had defeated illustrious opposition to reach the last four, notably with a 2-1 win over cup holders AC Milan in the second round; while led by future coaching legend Ernst Happel, the team contained some of the greatest players ever to have graced the Eredivisie: Rinus Israel, Coen Moulijn, Wim Jansen and Ove Kindvall included.

 The Rotterdammers were welcomed to the Polish capital for the first leg on April Fools' Day with a pitch which in places was more suitable for use by pig farmers than footballers, and Legia used the conditions to their advantage, slowing the usually pacey Feyenoord attack. Also perturbed by the freezing rain, the visitors created little and were mostly limited to shots from distance. But while Legia were able to carve the better chances of the tie, they too were thwarted by the poor state of the penalty areas: Brychczy turning a shot wide as the ball stuck in the mud, and Żmijewski stumbling over his effort before deflecting the rebound off target. As the Italian referee's whistle blew to signal an end to the game, the Wojskowi players slumped off the pitch; their relief of a clean sheet overpowered by the frustration of the lead which they could have had.

 With two weeks until the second leg in the Netherlands, the team would have time to collect their thoughts, and ensure that their preparations were of the highest standard. Besides a single league game, Legia's schedule between the first and second legs was relatively clear, so it was decided that on the way to Rotterdam the team would stop in East Germany for a warm-up game against Vorwarts Berlin—the team which Feyenoord had defeated in the previous round. Soon after defeating GKS Katowice at Ulica Łazienkowska, the squad headed to Warsaw's Okęcie airport to begin their journey. It was there that their hopes of reaching the final began to crumble.

> *"Even that day at Okęcie we were warned of 'unannounced customs checks'. Someone got a tip and we were told that there might be a raid. Usually they didn't 'comb' us, because they didn't want a scandal with athletes representing the country."*
> - Lucjan Brychczy, "Kici"

For the handful of Poles exposed to western culture, it had become common practice to return from trips abroad with "luxury items"—jewellery, cosmetics, designer clothes—which could not be purchased east of the Iron Curtain. As the demand for the fruits of capitalism increased, some of those who travelled west were able supplement their income by smuggling such goods back to Poland, which could later be sold on the black market. There was a large risk involved: products had to be bought with western currencies, which were illegal to possess in Poland; so when Władysław Grotyński and Janusz Żmijewski were pulled aside at Okęcie and found to be carrying around $2,500 in cash, a hefty punishment was inevitable.

Grotyński had become well known around Warsaw during the late sixties: driving through the city in his beloved white Ford Mustang, gambling on the horse racing at Służewiec, and drinking at the upmarket Adria restaurant. Given that wages at Legia were significantly lower than at Górnik and Ruch, it was hardly surprising that the goalkeeper had been resorting to underhand activities to fund such a lifestyle. According to Legia basketball player Włodzimierz Trams, it wasn't Żmijewski's first involvement in illegal activities either. Looking to earn a reduction of his own punishment for smuggling gold from Italy, he told authorities that the he had co-conspired with the two footballers to sneak jewellery back from Istanbul a couple of months earlier.

The pair had reportedly been singled out at Okęcie after a tip-off from one of the underground money changers from which Żmijewski had bought his currency, and were grilled by officials as their teammates waited on the plane. Eventually the players were allowed to travel, but only under the supervision of Legia president and Warsaw military commander General Zygmunt Huszcza. With a fear that the two may possibly look to defect to the west, two coach loads of soldiers masquerading as supporters were also sent with the team to ensure that they returned to Poland after the game.

"Instead of focusing on the most important match of our lives, we talked about what would happen to Władek and Janusz" remembers Brychczy, while the players themselves were focused solely on the punishment which could be expected on their return home. Unfortunately the weight on the players' minds showed in their performance at De Kuip, where after just three minutes they were 1-0 down—Willem van Hanegem rising above full-back Władysław Stachurski to loop a header over Grotyński. Within half-an-hour Legia's hard work in Warsaw was rendered meaningless, and the tie put beyond any doubt by Franz Hasil's thundering 20-yard volley.

The team returned to Poland amidst eagerness from the military to cover up the entire affair, yet Grotyński and Żmijewski were punished with hefty fines reaching into the tens-of-thousands-of złotys for their misdemeanours. Żmijewski was later given a suspension by the PZPN, before being cast out to Ruch Chorzów in 1972 with his reputation in tatters. Grotyński too was on borrowed time, and not just at Legia; a suspect in several other cases involving smuggling and fraud, he was eventually sentenced to four years in prison in 1971.

***

"Rzuczona moneta... Polska!!!! Górnik!!!! Brawo!!!! Brawo!!!! Proszę państwa, a więc sprawiedliwości stało się zadość!!!!"
- *Jan Ciszewski; Stade de la Meinau, Strasbourg; 22 April 1970*

Jan Ciszewski was not considered a learned man: he did not know foreign languages, and by his own admission barely even knew Polish; yet in front of a microphone there was no one better. As the lead sports commentator for TVP Katowice it was he who had relayed information of Górnik Zabrze's European Cup run back from Stockholm, Kiev and Manchester; his gravelly tones becoming almost as synonymous with the club's successes as the players themselves. His grammar may not have always been perfect, but he was loved by viewers due to his simple, yet emotive use of language to portray the scene in front of him to those watching on their black-and-white TV sets. It is said that, even when they weren't looking at the television screen, he had the ability to make viewers feel as if they were beside him in the stadium.

Janek was also an avid gambler, and prior to Górnik's Cup Winner's Cup Second Round Second Leg against Rangers in 1969, he entered a Glasgow bookmakers looking for odds on the Poles to secure victory at Ibrox. "More than 20 to one", Włodek Lubański recalled that the commentator was offered—an astronomical price considering Górnik had stuck seven past Olympiakos in the first round, and had already beaten the Scots 3-1 back in Chorzów. "I took a big risk" Ciszewski admitted to the Górnik players before the game. "My whole allowance, all of my savings, everything… everything I put on you. Tomorrow you have to win".

Inevitably, with seventeen minutes of the game played, Górnik fell behind; a thunderbolt from midfielder Jim Baxter leaving Kostka grasping at thin air. As the first half wore on, multiple chances to equalise were squandered, leaving Ciszewski an animated and anguished figure in the gantry; while just one more Rangers goal would give the hosts an advantage on away goals. But with a tactical change from Kalocsay, Górnik stepped up in the second half: Alfred Olek, Włodek Lubański and Hubert Skowronek putting them through with comfort. "Well… Finally…" stuttered the out-of-breath Ciszewski as he stormed into the locker room after finishing his commentary duties; "Finally you thought about me… I won…".

The victory at Ibrox was one of Kalocsay's final acts as coach; in early December he returned to Budapest to take the reins at Ferencvaros, leaving Górnik, as he had often promised, capable of defeating any opposition. To replace the Hungarian, Górnik moved swiftly to appoint former Polish international midfielder and coach Michał Matyas; and after taking the squad on a five-week winter tour of South America, *Myszka* led them to Bulgaria to take on their quarter-final opponents Levski Sofia.

Having won three of their four previous outings in the competition by four goals, the Bulgarian supporters were confident of a repeat success against Górnik, and though after just five minutes Szołtysik plundered the first goal that Levski had conceded during the tournament, by half-time the hosts' dominance ensured that they had taken the lead. A Jan Banaś equaliser soon after the break only resulted in more pressure being piled upon the Polish back line, but just when Górnik looked as though they would escape back to Poland with a draw, their battle-scarred defence allowed Georgi Asparuhov to slip free and divert a Kostov free kick past Kostka, with the referee still waiting for an opportune moment to blow the final whistle.

Defeat in such a manner had been disappointing, yet the Trójkolorowi returned to Poland the happier of the two teams; with two away goals in the bag just a narrow, low-scoring victory would be enough to progress, while the hostile Silesian crowd was certain to tip the scales further in Górnik's direction. Matyas reaffirmed faith in his squad by naming an unchanged outfield for the second leg. The only change came in goal, where Jan Gomola replaced the injured Kostka.

Górnik began to show nerves early on at the Śląski, yet largely thanks to the imposing presence of centre-back Jerzy Gorgoń and intelligence of his partner Staszek Oślizło they never looked like falling further behind in the tie. Then on the stroke of half-time, much-needed relief from the ever-reliable Lubański: he raced on to a loose ball and coolly placed a left-footed shot under the outstretched arms of the Bulgarian keeper. Jan Banaś doubled Górnik's lead eleven minutes into the second half, converting a Szołtysik cross to leave Levski needing two goals to progress. The Poles continued to defend with vigour and resolve, and Kirilov's scrambled goal on the hour was all that they could muster.

Levski had provided Górnik's toughest test of the competition so far, yet semi-final adversaries AS Roma would prove to be a significantly sterner proposition. Though *I Giallorossi* had struggled through the 1969/70 season—out of the Coppa Italia, and settling for a mid-table finish in Serie A—under the legendary coach Helenio Herrera, with his trusted *Catenaccio* tactic, Górnik would still need to be at the top of their game to secure a place in the final. That they were when Herrera travelled to Zabrze on a scouting expedition following the draw, demolishing GKS Katowice 4-1 and leading the Argentine to declare that he had miscalculated: "I thought fate had been kind to Roma, but I have since found out that Górnik are a good team".

Perhaps the biggest compliment that Roma paid Górnik was their use of mind games to try to unsettle them: firstly there being no delegation from the Italian club to meet the team at the airport, and then the Romans denying Górnik permission to train on the Stadio Olimpico pitch. Rather than showing his annoyance, Matyas instead led a session on one of the city's parks in front of groups of surprised children.

Once Górnik were allowed inside the Olimpico, their rich vein of form did not falter; but although the better chances fell their way, they had to settle for just a low-scoring draw. Banaś put the Poles ahead after 28 minutes, nipping in front of the defender to fire past Alberto Ginulfi from Lubański's low cross. Lubański himself uncharacteristically squandered several golden opportunities, before Górnik were made to pay for his wastefulness in the second half, as Elvio Salvori slotted between Kostka's legs to equalise. With time running out, Lubański was thwarted once again—this time by the woodwork after skilfully rounding the goalkeeper.

Even before the result in Rome, the rematch at the Stadion Śląski had been built to be one of the most-anticipated matches in Polish history. Over 200,000 people applied for tickets, with buses laid on for supporters from as far away as Szczecin and Białystok. The 90,000 who made it inside the stadium were rewarded with one of the most dramatic nights in European football history.

With nerves in abundance, the game didn't start positively for Górnik; just nine minutes in, they fell behind. A clumsy challenge from Rainer Kuchta on Salvori saw the visitors gifted a penalty, and though Kostka dived correctly to parry Fabio Capello's initial effort, the striker reacted quickest on the rebound to put Roma ahead in the tie. Almost immediately Herrera tinkered with his tactics, signalling for his charges to focus on defence. Leaving Cappellini alone in attack, the remaining ten players settled behind the ball and were able to nullify Górnik's attack with great effect; even with the second-half introduction of Władysław Szaryński in place of Deja, the stubborn Italian back line refused to budge. Resigned to their elimination, the crowds slowly began to vacate the terraces as full time ticked closer.

But as the game entered its concluding moments, drama struck; with Górnik pushing men forward in desperation, centre-back Gorgoń was felled by Salvori just yard-or-two from the spot in which the Italian had been tripped almost an hour-and-a-half earlier. The offence was unquestionable and the Spanish referee immediately blew his whistle, yet at first glance the positioning of it did not seem to be so clear. The Italians proclaimed the challenge was "outside the box", the Poles proclaimed "inside"—perhaps even the official himself was not entirely sure. As the entire stadium waited with bated breath for his decision, the quick-thinking Erwin Wilczek motioned the arbitrator towards the goal area, leaving only one decision for him to make...

Penalty!

The ferocious roar from inside the emptying Śląski enticed those already on their way out to turn around with a renewed sense of hope. After a brief discussion amongst teammates, Lubański, his heart undoubtedly pounding, yet seemingly without a single drip of sweat on his brow, carried the ball towards the spot. Upon realising the enormity of the situation, the crowd suddenly fell deathly silent; and all over the stadium men put their heads in their hands, unable to watch for fear that their little glimmer of hope may be extinguished completely. The striker took five steps back and waited for the Roma players to finish their protests before inhaling, and beginning his run…

The dream wasn't over. Not yet.

As Włodek's shot flew powerfully into the roof of the net, the Górnik players wheeled away in euphoria, while their Roman counterparts fell to the ground in exasperation. Almost immediately, the referee's whistle sounded; but rather than it signalling a Roma victory, it was now a precursor to a further 30 minutes of play. It had taken Górnik over 80 minutes of toil to retain just a lifeline in the tie, but with just one kick, momentum had swung dramatically in their favour.

The turn of events left the Italians shell shocked, and the usually cocksure Herrera—himself now utterly demoralised—was dealt the unenviable task of trying to reinvigorate his players during the short break. It didn't work as he had hoped, as within just three minutes they conceded once more: Lubański sneaking past the fatigued Roma defence and firing beyond the dejected Ginulfi at his near post, from the very tightest of angles.

Górnik battled away for the remaining 27 minutes, but rather than press for a third, Matyas opted to cut down on their attacking efficiency and attempted to retain possession in order to tire out the chasing Italians. Yet, with the Poles just mere seconds from securing a place in the final, the Chorzowianin night took in its final breathtaking twist: from almost nowhere, Francesco Scaratti's 20-yard thunderbolt flew into the top right-hand corner of the Górnik net, leaving Kostka rooted to the ground and Silesian hearts devastated.

As the Italians embraced in the centre of the pitch, the Górnik players slunk down the long tunnel. Some wiped away tears, others cursed furiously. Kostka, who could have done little to prevent the goal, lay broken on a dressing room bench.

"Why do you have such grave faces?" an entering journalist quizzed to the annoyance of the devastated players.

"You don't have any smarter questions?" retorted Szołtysik on behalf of the whole team.

"Smarter?!" answered the shocked journalist. "What do you mean 'smarter'?! Well, guys, where are we playing the third match?"

Still adjusting to UEFA's recently introduced away goals rule, the players had not realised that goals scored in extra time were not weighted as they were in the regular 90 minutes, and incorrectly assumed that Scaratti's strike had eliminated them. It was a rule which had even escaped the stadium announcer, who delivered his commiserations to the dissipating crowd upon the final whistle.

With just fourteen days between the second leg at the Śląski and the final, the deciding match was hastily arranged by UEFA for the Wednesday in-between. Prior to the second leg, Roma had offered money to Górnik to agree to play any decisive match in Italy. Górnik refused, and ultimately the sides settled on the French city of Strasbourg—the site of Silesian heroism in 1938, with Ezi Wilimowski's four goals against Brazil. However, as a naturalised Frenchman, Helenio Herrera was happier with the choice of venue, and Górnik arrived in the country to be greeted by numerous newspaper interviews with *Il Mago*, most of which claimed that he had finally figured out how to defeat the Poles.

Herrera's plan turned out to be designed, not to beat Górnik on the pitch, but rather to defeat them before the game had even kicked off, by disrupting their preparations on the day of the match. Firstly, with the two teams having been given just a single coach between them to ferry the two squads from their hotel to the stadium, Herrera reportedly told the driver to delay the pickup of the Górnik squad, forcing them to rush to the ground at the last minute in whatever vehicle was available. Górnik's players were then prevented from using the stadium's warm-up room as the doors had been locked by the occupying Italian squad, forcing them to prepare in the corridors of the stadium. By the time that kick off arrived, the Poles were dishevelled and completely unprepared.

But, in a twist of fate, after just three minutes a floodlight failure brought the game to a sudden halt. After a lengthy delay the game resumed, but only for a further five minutes as the lights went out once more. When the game finally recommenced after a break of almost half an hour, Roma had become sluggish, and any advantage that Herrera's antics had earned for his side had been completely lost.

Górnik dominated the first period, but for all of their possession, their attack—particularly Lubański—was kept reasonably contained. The striker was regularly forced to come deep in search of the ball, and often then found himself crowded out before being able to do anything with it. But in the 40th minute he broke free: receiving the ball close to the halfway line, Włodek advanced forward, skipped past the outstretched leg of Luciano Spinosi and from outside the area placed a shot with both precision and power that clattered off of Ginulfi's left-hand post, before coming to rest in the back of the net.

Herrera had previously predicted that the team which scored the first goal would be the team to progress to the final, yet with his Roma now trailing, it was not a prediction he was willing to stick to. With ten minutes passed in the second half, a collision just inside the Górnik 18-yard box resulted in the referee handing the Italians a controversial penalty, to be duly converted by Capello.

Górnik responded by exerting more pressure, but ultimately with little reward, and as the clock ticked firstly over 90 minutes, and then over the additional 30, for the third week in a row the teams could not be separated. After more than five-and-a-half hours of football, a place in the 1969/70 Cup Winner's Cup Final would ultimately need to be decided by other means.

The French referee Roger Machin beckoned over the two captains Oślizło and Capello, while a crowd quickly began to assemble around them. Machin then pulled out a coin, or rather a token—green on one side and red on the other—and asked Oślizło to choose between the two. The Górnik captain chose green—"the colour of hope" he would later claim, as opposed to the red which represented the communist influence over Poland—and waited for it to be thrown in the air...

"All of his colleagues, besides Stefan Florenski, didn't watch the draw. They were too nervous. Helenio Herrera ominously chastised the falling coin; however, fate chose the Poles. Stanisław Oślizło jumped with joy; while reporting on the meeting, Jan Ciszewski in a hoarse voice shouted 'Poland!!!! Górnik!!!!... Justice has been done.'"
- Andrzej Gowarszewski, Encyklopedia Piłkarska: Koleckja Klubów – Górnik Zabrze, 2009

***

Górnik Zabrze (v Manchester City)

European Cup Winner's Cup Final; Praterstadion, Vienna;

29 April 1970.

Hubert Kostka – Stefan Florenski (Alojzy Deja, 85'), Jerzy Gorgoń, Stanisław Oślizło (c), Henryk Latocha – Zygfryd Szołtysik, Erwin Wilczek (Hubert Skowronek, 75'), Alfred Olek – Jan Banaś, Włodzimierz Lubański, Władysław Szaryński.

Victory against Roma had taken its toll on Górnik. Having returned from Strasbourg to a heroes' welcome, the players were back at Pyrzowice Airport just a few days later, heading to Vienna, where FA Cup Winners Manchester City awaited them in the final. The Citizens had defeated Schalke 04 in the semi-final, but unlike their Polish counterparts had not required the inconvenience of a third game to do so; the English side therefore arrived in Austria fresh, while Górnik were in dire need of a rest.

The difference in fitness was noticeable immediately, with tricky striker Francis Lee in particular causing havoc in the wearied Polish defence. Lee was involved heavily during the opening exchanges, and could have put his team ahead after ten minutes: flicking the ball spectacularly over the head of Alfred Olek inside the box, he aimed a volley into the top corner which Kostka was forced to acrobatically punch away. Just two minutes later he was again integral in City's play, but this time they did take the lead: fizzing a low shot from distance, the usually reliable Kostka bundled the slippery ball straight into the path of Lee's strike partner Neil Young, who accepted the simple tap-in gratefully.

Though Górnik were allowed more time in possession following the goal, the Englishmen went on to double their lead just a few minutes before the break. Young caught Oślizło in possession before being upended clumsily by the rushing Kostka. Lee then smashed the resulting penalty so hard towards the middle of the goal that the keeper's legs could not prevent it from crossing the line.

During the break a heavy downpour transformed the Praterstadion pitch into a swamp, descending the game to a scrappy contest amidst which Górnik finally seemed to develop a modicum of momentum. Halfway through the second period they were finally able to take advantage: City failing to clear a free kick which then allowed Oślizło to poke a shot past goalkeeper Corrigan on the turn. Ultimately it would turn out to be nothing more than a consolation for the Trójkolorowi, as the remaining quarter of the game ticked by with little incident, to a backdrop of English fans singing *"You'll Never Walk Alone"*.

"As we drove to the final with Manchester City in Vienna," Stefan Florenski told Przegląd Sportowy in 2010, "we were told that we had achieved more than anyone could have expected and that even a high defeat would not be a tragedy. To this day I regret it, because if we went to the final with a different attitude, then maybe we would have won." Florenski was not alone, with many players recalling an air of complacency after their win against Roma. Some talked of how they had been made to feel like stars following the semi-final, while for most of the team their pre-match preparations had been spent waiting for the opening of a Viennese department store in order to buy gifts for family and friends.

Nevertheless, even without the trophy, Górnik once again returned to Poland as national heroes; and while Legia's European Cup semi-final berth would later be matched, Górnik's final appearance remains to this day the highest achievement in Europe by a Polish club. It could even be argued that, without the rivalry that built between the two clubs during the sixties, neither would have reached the heights that they did.

The Wojskowi went on to win a fourth title in 1970, the Trójkolorowi a fourth cup; and while their individual successes were duly celebrated, their biggest achievement was finally securing Poland's place on the European football map. Those achievements would build a platform for the country's game to progress into the coming decade—the 'golden era' of Polish football.

CHAPTER SEVENTEEN
GOLDEN EAGLES

"Football is a simple game. You can win, you can lose, you can also draw."
- Kazimierz Górski

THOUGH THE POLITICAL THAW of the mid-fifties had helped to pave a supposed "Polish way to Socialism", during the following decade the country's economy underwent a long period of stagnation. In December 1970 this, coinciding with a poor harvest, led Władysław Gomułka's government to suddenly increase prices on basic foodstuffs; and when protests broke out in several northern cities, the government ordered the army to respond with force, leaving over 40 people dead and thousands more injured. Gomułka's position, along with those of his closest associates, was ultimately left untenable; forced to resign before the end of the month, he was replaced as First Secretary by the leader of the Katowice Voivodeship, Edward Gierek.

Gierek had presided over great industrial progression during his 13-year reign in Upper Silesia, and as a result garnered strong praise from the Muscovite hierarchy. He was well trusted by Soviet premier Leonid Brezhnev, but at the same time, crucially also by much of Poland's working class. As a former miner himself, he was able to apply a common touch which appealed to workers, and after cancelling the price increases put in place by his predecessor, he began to experience a period of considerable popularity throughout the country.

Gierek was also considered by Poles as relatively westernised, having spent a large portion of his early life in France and Belgium. He soon used this footing to stretch Poland westwards, establishing good relationships with France, West Germany and the USA; even going as far to secure multi-billion dollar loans from western banks, with the intention of increasing the country's industrial output. Before long, signs of Poland's new relationship with the west became visible in everyday life: Fiat cars were driven on roads, Coca-Cola could be bought in shops, and even the restrictions on travel to the other side of the Iron Curtain were significantly relaxed. Gierek's approach to government was hugely different to that of the old 'apparatchiks' of the communist elite, and thanks to his new approach, Poland suddenly began to herald a new era of prosperity.

Almost concurrently, Poland's national team began a revolution of its own. Having failed to qualify for successive World Cups, Ryszard Koncewicz's third spell as Selekcjoner was brought to an end, and in his place the PZPN asked youth team boss Kazimierz Górski to make the step up. Górski's relationship with the national team stretched as far back as 1948, when he made his one and only playing appearance in the infamous 8-0 defeat to Denmark in Copenhagen. *Sarenka*—meaning 'Roe-Deer', and nicknamed as such due to his speed and nimbleness—had played just the opening 34 minutes of the game, before being carted off with the Poles still only a single goal down, allegedly unable to handle the pace and physicality of the game. The attacker's call up had come at the insistence of his fellow Leopolitan, Wacław Kuchar, then working as coach Alfus' lead trainer. Kuchar knew Górski well, having coached him in a pre-war Lwów representation team, and also several years later at Soviet-backed Dynamo Lvov. The pair later reunited in 1949 as Kuchar took the head coaching job at Górski's club Legia; eventually bringing his protégé into the coaching fold at Ulica Łazienkowska in the years preceding his retirement.

By the time of his appointment, Górski had built up an impressive reputation within the PZPN; as well as having looked after the junior national team for four years during his early managerial career, and the youth team since 1966, he had also briefly co-operated with Antoni Brzeżańczyk and Klemenz Nowak to lead the seniors for a pair of

European Championship qualifiers in 1966. The 49-year-old was known for his modesty and a mild, liberal approach to discipline, which in postwar Poland was revolutionary. Previously, coaches were seen as a separate entity to the playing squad; Górski changed attitudes, and instead saw his players as friends or colleagues, which helped to create a tighter-knit community within his squad.

> *"For him [Górski] it was like going to work. If you have a bad boss, you do not want to; but if he is cool, warm, open, then you come in positively. It was in that mood the players came to Kaziu's groupings."*
> - Paweł Zarzeczny, Journalist

Just as important as the appointment of the coach himself was that of his two assistants, Jacek Gmoch and Andrzej Strejlau. Gmoch was a former midfielder whose career was ended abruptly by a multiple leg fracture in 1968. While later coaching at Legia, his mathematical and methodical approach led him to create the 'Information Bank'—in-depth analysis carefully collected to provide the coach and his team with as much information on their opponents as possible. It was a tool significantly more advanced than anything seen in Poland before, and one that the PZPN were keen to take advantage of with his appointment in 1971. Strejlau joined the following year, and was regarded as a great talent finder. As a youth coach alongside Górski, he had helped the progression of a number of talented young players; while, as well as assisting the senior team, Strejlau was to continue his work with the nation's young players, taking on the role that Górski had vacated. However, the relationship between Gmoch and Strejlau was at times extremely frictional, with the pair often disagreeing on tactical and team selection issues. Górski often used this to his advantage, letting the pair argue their points furiously before making his final decisions. The process would quickly lead to positive results.

Though Poland ultimately failed in qualification for UEFA's European Championships in 1972, accession to the Olympic tournament of the same year was treated with equal, if not greater importance. The Olympics remained a huge propaganda exercise for the Socialist Bloc of countries, and with their quasi-professional players—'Shamateurs', as they became known—they continued to dominate the football competition ahead of western nations.

Still, reaching the Olympics was far from a formality: a 3-1 defeat in Bulgaria, in which Lubański was sent off after mouthing obscenities at the Romanian referee, leaving Poland to play catch-up from the get go. Even after a pair of two-goal wins against Spain and a 3-0 revenge victory over the Bulgarians, the Poles' hopes of qualification to a first tournament in over a decade hinged on the Spanish amateurs taking an unlikely point from Bulgaria in their final game. Miraculously, they did—twice taking the lead, and finally equalising with ten minutes to go, in an enthralling 3-3 draw.

Despite only qualifying by the skin of their teeth, there had been signs that Poland could medal in Munich. On their last visit to West Germany, in their qualifying group for Euro '72, they had earned an impressive goalless draw against the *Nationalelf*, and similar levels of performance would make them dark horses for the tournament. A place on the podium would be a considerable justification of Górski's appointment.

POLAND SQUAD

1972 Olympics; Munich, West Germany.

Goalkeepers: 1. Hubert Kostka (Górnik Zabrze), 18. Marian Szeja (Zagłębie Wałbrzych).

Defenders: 2. Antoni Szymanowski (Wisła Kraków), 3. Jerzy Gorgoń (Górnik Zabrze), 4. Zygmunt Anczok (Górnik Zabrze), 13. Jerzy Kraska (Gwardia Warsaw), 14. Marian Ostafiński (Ruch Chorzów), 19. Zbigniew Gut (Odra Opole).

Midfielders: 5. Lesław Ćmikiewicz (Legia Warsaw), 6. Zygmunt Maszczyk (Ruch Chorzów), 7. Ryszard Szymczak (Gwardia Warsaw), 8. Zygfryd Szołtysik (Górnik Zabrze), 9. Kazimierz Deyna (Legia Warsaw), 17. Andrzej Jarosik (Zagłębie Sosnowiec).

Forwards: 10. Włodzimierz Lubański (captain, Górnik Zabrze), 11. Robert Gadocha (Legia Warsaw), 12. Kazimierz Kmiecik (Wisła Kraków), 15. Grzegorz Lato (Stal Mielec), 16. Joachim Marx (Ruch Chorzów).

The core of players left behind by Koncewicz—many of whom had plied their trade in continental competition with either Legia or Górnik—were undoubtedly a talented group of individuals, but it took some work for Górski to mould the team into his own vision. During the first 18 months of his reign, the coach called upon a total of 38 different men and quickly came to the conclusion that he was better not to always choose the best individuals, but rather those who fit his concept. With only seven of Poland's 19-strong Olympic squad being veterans of Górski's first selection just 15 months earlier, the changes were easy to see.

The Olympic draw itself had presented some minor problems for Poland: though Gmoch's Information Bank was well stocked with reports on their East German neighbours, knowledge on Colombia was limited to titbits remembered by the Górnik players who had toured there during the sixties, while Ghana were still an unknown quantity to the majority of nations outside of Africa. Luckily the gulf in quality between Górski's team and their non-European opposition was vast, and the Białe-Orły's navigation was assured with high-scoring victories over both, with plenty of room for improvement.

The final group game against East Germany would then determine who took first place in the group, with the Poles trailing only on goal difference. Poland had a point to prove, having been beaten soundly by Georg Buschner's team when they met in Rostock two years earlier. The date of the game had historical significance too: 1 September—33 years to the day after Nazi Germany had invaded Poland. Górski's Eagles were in need of little more motivation ahead of the game.

Gadocha and Deyna had so far been in stunning form with five and three goals respectively, but in Nuremberg, Poland's opener after six minutes came from a less-expected source. Whether Lubański's header had crossed the line before being cleared is still debatable, but when the ball fell to Jerzy Gorgoń, the defender thundered the return into the roof of the net from six yards for his first ever international goal. Joachim Streich levelled for the East Germans on the stroke of half-time with a back-post header, but after an hour Poland's lead was restored—again through Gorgoń, who rifled an outwardly curling, forty-yard stunner into the stanchion of Jürgen Croy's goal. Judging by his celebration, perhaps no one on the field was more surprised than the centre-half himself.

The Biało-Czerwoni took control from there on in, and should have extended their lead five minutes from time when Gadocha slid a penalty wide of the post. Luckily it didn't matter; Poland claimed victory in both the game and the group, and as a result were kept apart from both their West German hosts and the reigning Olympic champions Hungary in the second stage. Instead they were grouped with Denmark, Morocco and the Soviet Union, knowing that defeat against any of them would most likely end their chances of reaching the final.

The Danes were Poland's first opponents in the second round, and had the benefit of a day's extra rest compared to Górski's side. They were also eager to make amends for the 2-0 defeat suffered to Hungary in their last outing and arrived in Regensburg fired up, while the Poles' start to the competition had left them slightly fatigued and possibly with an air of complacency too. Subsequently the first half was one of Scandinavian domination, but their only goal came after half-an-hour: Gorgoń giving away a free kick which Kostka spilled, leaving Heino Hansen to thump into the net. Deyna equalised with a curled shot from 18 yards minutes later, after a neat lay off from Lubański, but it could not mask the lacklustre performance. As arguments broke out in the dressing room during the break, Poland's future in the competition hinged on the team's reaction.

> "Kazimierz [Górski] arrived to the locker room during our argument. He saw what was going on... And what did he do? He left the locker room quietly and stood under the shower, not showing us his eyes, while we continued with a sharp, very strong criticism of each other... After about five minutes the struggle began to calm down. Then, when the tension had eased a little, Kazimierz entered the locker room, looked at us and said: 'Gentlemen; I listened to you, I heard what you said. Enough is enough—now please go and win this match.'"
> - Włodzimierz Lubański, „Życie jak dobry mecz"—Włodzimierz Lubański w rozmowie z Michałem Olszańskim

Górski may have only spoken a few words, but their impact was huge; with them, any tiredness or complacency was seemingly forgotten as soon as captain Lubański led the team back over the white line. The Poles immediately switched from a position of subordination to one of complete control, and though they were unable to find a winner, they never looked like losing either. The change perhaps even saved their entire tournament.

***

Four days later, the Polish squad awoke with all attentions focused on that evening's game in Augsburg; meetings between Poland and the USSR were typically highly charged, but none had ever had as much riding on it as their clash at the Rosenaustadion. The Soviets were heavy favourites to defeat Denmark in their final group game three days later, while Poland had the luxury of a head-to-head with the group's whipping boys, Morocco; whoever would emerge victorious in the meeting between the two socialist neighbours, would likely earn the right to fight for the gold medal.

But upon heading to breakfast in the Olympic Village, swathes of armed police would form the most terrifying of distractions. During the night a group of Palestinian terrorists had forced their way into the apartments of a number of Israeli athletes, murdering two and taking another nine as hostages. As Górski's men began their preparations for the game, there were serious doubts over whether the Olympics would continue.

It was quickly decided by Górski that the best course of action would be to continue as planned—at least until advised otherwise. The squad ate, returned to their apartments, and around noon boarded a train for the short journey north west. At the stadium their routines continued until, during the warm up, a representative for the International Olympic Committee informed both sides that the games would not continue. Less than half-an-hour after the teams had slunk back to the locker rooms the IOC returned to say that the game would go ahead before, minutes later, again word was passed down of the game's cancellation. Finally, as would controversially be reiterated by IOC President Avery Brundage during the following day's memorial service for the victims, it was confirmed that "the games must go on", and just a few minutes late of the scheduled start time the Norwegian referee began proceedings.

Of course the uncertainties had affected both teams equally; however, the Soviets were able to adapt to the situation better. Immediately following the kick off, wave-after-wave of attack seemingly pummelled towards Kostka's goal before Dynamo Kiev forward Oleh Blokhin finally converted a cross from the right-hand side, giving the USSR a well-deserved lead after 29 minutes. When Gorgoń—the pillar of the Polish defence so far—was forced to leave the pitch due to injury just a few minutes later, the Poles found themselves on the brink of elimination.

The half-time break could not come soon enough; however, this time Górski's team talk did not have the same impact as it had against the Danes, and the Soviets began the second half just as they had ended the first. As attacks continued to hammer the Polish goal, Górski looked to make his final change with 25 minutes remaining, bringing on attacker Andrzej Jarosik for the tiring full-back Zbigniew Gut; yet as Górski summoned the Zagłębie Sosnowiec frontman to warm up, he was met with refusal. Shocked, the coach instead turned to Zygfryd Szołtysik, and hoped that the midfielder's chemistry with Górnik team mate Lubański would be enough to spur his men.

Instantaneously the captain's effectiveness improved, and after two quick attempts at goal he was brought down clumsily in the penalty area by defender Khurtsilava. As the referee pointed to the spot, regular penalty taker Lubański instead handed the ball to Deyna, later claiming the onset of an unusual sudden lack of confidence. Deyna too later admitted his nerves in the situation, yet his perfectly executed shot was far too powerful and accurate to be stopped by the outstretched arms of Soviet keeper Rudakov. With 11 minutes remaining the Białe-Orły had given themselves a lifeline, but still needed a winning goal to keep their hopes of a gold medal alive.

The equaliser invigorated Poland and suddenly they had become the dominant team, soaking pressure in the back line and surging forward with pace on the counter attack; the only thing now seemingly against them being the rapidly ticking clock. With eight minutes remaining, Maszczyk and Lubański combined right from the Polish half only to see the alert Rudakov thwart the latter before he could fire off his effort. With five minutes left, Ćmikiewicz forced a corner kick which was easily cleared by the Soviet defence. Time was quickly expiring.

"The last minute of the match. The referee has apparently added time for interruptions in the game—so probably about three minutes until the end. Robert Gadocha, Lubański, Szołtysik!!! Wonderful shot!! And Ladies and

Gentlemen, a goal! Zygfryd Szołtysik, making his fiftieth appearance in our national team, with a wonderful goal that gives us the lead."
- Jan Ciszewski

It was a goal deserving of winning any match; Szołtysik accepting Lubański's lay-off and curling a right-footed shot beyond the fully stretched Rudakov. Minutes later, the closing whistle blew and Poland had set one foot in the Olympic final, only the team from Morocco—goalless in three of their five games so far—standing in their way.

In Nuremberg, the Africans offered little resistance: Kmiecik, Lubański, Gadocha and a Deyna brace ensuring Poland passage into the gold medal match with a 5-0 rout. Rather importantly, the Poles didn't even need to progress into the higher gears, allowing them to conserve energy for their final game of the tournament, just two days later. Unfortunately, the result came at a cost: frustrated, the Moroccans compensated their lack of ability with aggression, causing injury to full-back Antoni Szymanowski and ending his Olympics a game earlier than hoped.

***

Poland (v Hungary)

Olympic Gold Medal Match; Olympiastadion, Munich;

10 September 1972.

Hubert Kostka – Zbigniew Gut, Lesław Ćmikiewicz, Jerzy Gorgoń, Zygmunt Anczok – Zygfryd Szołtysik, Kazimierz Deyna, Zygmunt Maszczyk, Jerzy Kraska – Włodzimierz Lubański (c), Robert Gadocha.

The final match was set up to be one of the most intriguing of the entire tournament: on one side stood the Poles who had been, and perhaps continued to be underestimated, while on the other were the Hungarians, who had so far been able to maintain their position as favourites to collect a second successive Olympic title. It would also be the battleground for Antal Dunai and Kazimierz Deyna, with seven goals apiece, in their race to claim the tournament's golden boot.

Ujpest striker Dunai was one of only four Hungarians to have been involved with their gold medal-winning team in 1968, yet the new blood had continued the rich vein of form of their predecessors throughout their stay in West Germany. Like Górski's men, the Magyars dropped only a single point en-route to the final, defeating Denmark in the first round, and both East and West Germany in the second, on the way. Crucially though, their experience of tournament football set them apart from the Poles, and while Poland had shown a tremendous account of themselves so far, they remained as underdogs. History also did not fall on the side of the Białe-Orły, having lost ten of the previous eleven meetings against their oldest adversaries. In fact, not a single member of Poland's 19-man squad had been born to witness their country's last victory over Hungary —the much-reminisced 'Final Game' before the war, more than three decades earlier.

Around 60,000 fans took their places in Munich's brand new Olympiastadion on the penultimate day of the games, mere hours after the USSR and East Germany had, in true socialist style, shared the bronze medal with a 2-2 draw on the very same field. Just prior to kick off the heavens opened and would not subside until well after the final whistle, soaking the third of the stadium not covered by its iconic translucent canopy and slowing the pitch enough to hamper both sides' effective use of their pacey attacks.

As he had done against both the USSR and East Germany, Górski set up his team as a 4-4-2 in an attempt to stifle the Hungarian midfield, and while both teams showed attacking intent from the first whistle, in the early stages István Géczi found himself the busier of the two goalkeepers. But as the first half bore on the Magyars began to gain a foothold in the game, and 41 minutes in created the best chance so far: Dunai, bloodied and bandaged after an earlier clash with a Polish defender, managing to force an acrobatic save from Kostka, despite a tame header.

Though the game now looked to be heading into the break without goals, within seconds the deadlock was broken: Polish hero Deyna involved, yet not as he'd have liked. Looking to start a quick counter attack, Deyna received the ball in the right-back position usually occupied by Zbyszek Gut. Attempting to play the ball to the Odra defender, he was dispossessed by Béla Várady, who was then afforded time to bear down unopposed on Kostka's goal from an acute angle. Not knowing whether to expect either a pass or a shot, Kostka found himself caught in two minds, while Várady opted for the latter into the now-loosely guarded net. With just three minutes until half-time, it was a sucker punch for Poland.

The mistake could have quite easily forced Deyna to retreat into the shadows, yet coming so close to the break, Górski was able to exert his influence before the damage could increase further. Focusing on the positive aspects of the first half, he praised his team, and in particular Deyna, heavily. The midfielder began the second period like a man possessed; within two minutes dragging the Poles back on to level terms, twisting-and-turning two Hungarian defenders and hitting a shot from distance that had enough power to deceive the flailing Géczi.

Buoyed, Górski's men began a further spell of dominance, and fewer than twenty minutes later Deyna pounced once more to turn the game on its head. Robert Gadocha won the ball back after haranguing the Hungarian right-back, Zygmunt Anczok punted a long ball into the box, and with the defence unable to clear their lines the ball fell to Deyna, whose first touch took him around the goalkeeper and allowed him to bury his second into the unattended goal.

Deyna was withdrawn thirteen minutes from the end, complaining of a groin injury, but by that point his work was done. His brace had ensured both Poland's seventh and final gold medal of the Olympics, and his own status as the tournament's top scorer with nine goals. The German referee's final whistle was greeted by an eruption of joy from the players—a scene repeated in front of the TV sets of an entire nation.

> *"It's over, Ladies and Gentlemen! The match is over! Ladies and Gentlemen... Well... My God... What am I supposed to say?! I have waited twenty years for this moment. Polish football has waited over fifty...".*
> - Jan Ciszewski

The awards would continue for Górski's Eagles, long after they had stood atop the podium to recite *Mazurek Dąbrowskiego* and collect their good medals. On their return home, the team was invited to a reception with First Secretary Gierek, where state awards were dished out: 16 of them collecting the Gold Cross of Merit (*Złoto Krzyż Zasługi*), and Górski, Lubański and Kostka awarded the more-prestigious Knight's Cross of the Order of Polonia Restituta (*Krzyż Kawalerski Order Odrodzenia Polski*). Of the playing squad, only Andrzej Jarosik missed out, after his refusal to play against the Soviets—a fact kept from Gierek due to the First Secretary's support of Jarosik's club, Zagłębie Sosnowiec.

As deserved as they may have been, the state honours bestowed upon the Olympic squad were laced with propaganda, designed to show that the country's new direction was better than the old; but carefully, in his words of congratulations, Gierek made little mention of attributing their success to the socialist ideology. Whether it was a conscious choice or not, the perceived distancing of sport and politics perhaps even helped to increase Gierek's popularity further, and did more to enhance the feelings among Poles that his new brand of socialism was more desirable than that of their conservative neighbours. In addition, the increased emphasis placed upon the architects of sporting successes—notably the athletes and coaches—gave rise to the first embers of superstardom within Polish sport.

CHAPTER EIGHTEEN
MUNDIAL

"Środkiem Gorgoń... i Hockey, ucieka Yorath. Yorath, Hockey; Tomaszewski przed Hockey'em... Gol! Dwa-Zero, proszę państwa. W Cardiff, a Trevor Hockey chyba do końca życia nie będzie się golił gdyż miał tu olbrzymie szczęście."
- Jan Ciszewski; Wales v Poland, Cardiff, 28 March 1973

DEFEAT IN CARDIFF was a wake up call. Still buoyant from their heroics in Munich six months earlier, the Poles were comfortably overturned by a Welsh side which considered the Olympic football competition as only a second-rate tournament, and saw Poland's success in it as almost meaningless. The Red Dragons were not even considered the strongest in the three-team group, having only earned one point from two games against England. Playing against amateurs from Colombia and Ghana had been one thing, but now against teams full of professional players, the Poles were expected to struggle.

Górski had been well aware of the challenges which lay ahead, and he continued to scour Polish football for players who could add something to his squad. Some of those he looked towards were new to the national team setup: Henryk Kasperczak, a midfielder who had been heavily involved in Stal Mielec's strong start to the 1972/73 league season and Mirosław Bulzacki, a six-foot-tall centre-back from ŁKS Łódź. Others, such as Wisła left-back Adam Musiał and ŁKS keeper Jan Tomaszewski, returned to the fold after being left out of the Olympic squad. By the time of the next qualifier against England at the Śląski, all four were in contention for a starting berth.

Still, Górski wasn't without problems before the early-June meeting, having been handed doubts over the fitness of his captain Włodek Lubański. In the week prior to the game, the striker had opened a deep cut on his right knee in a training ground clash with Górnik teammate Jerzy Gorgoń. Unsure whether he would recover in time, Stal's Jan Domarski was drafted in as his likely replacement. But while doctors were hesitant to declare him fit, Lubański had no intention of missing the game, and went as far as disguising the injury so that the opposition wouldn't know where to kick him.

By 5:30pm on 6 June, the late-afternoon sun and smoke from the nearby Baildon steelworks had combined to create an orange haze which bathed the Stadion Śląski. As the teams emerged from the bowels of the arena, this combined with the fans' raucous chanting to create the most intimidating of atmospheres; the assembled English journalists in turn bestowing upon the stadium its lasting nickname: *Kocioł Czarownic*—the 'Witches' Cauldron'.

Just as the Soviets had been 16 years earlier, the English—dressed in their exotic yellow third strip—were overcome by the incessant Silesian crowd, and just seven minutes after kick off had fallen behind. Gadocha sprinted away claiming that his free kick from the left-hand side had given Poland the advantage, but a clear deflection on its way through showed otherwise. Whether the lunging Jan Banaś or the desperate Bobby Moore got the final touch is to this day still debated, but to the 90,000-strong crowd, the only statistic that mattered was the 1-0 scoreline.

For the Poles' second goal, which came only two minutes after the half-time break, there was no ambiguity at all. Heeding pre-match advice from Jacek Gmoch, who had noticed in his analysis that Moore had a habit of holding onto the ball, Lubański was able to dispossess the English captain, bear down unopposed on Peter Shilton's goal and calmly slot the ball into the net off of the right-hand post. Górski's squad had shown in Chorzów every quality that they hadn't in Cardiff: they were physically strong, quick and clinical, and the shell-shocked Three Lions did not have an answer.

Though no further goals would be surrendered at either end, what was possibly Poland's finest-ever victory was to end on a sour note—one that would shape the national team for several years to come. Hoping to capitalise on a long ball forward to further extend Poland's lead, Lubański skipped over a late tackle from Roy MacFarland, only to catch his weakened knee on the full-back's flailing leg. As the striker crumbled to the floor, he immediately screamed out in agony, and after being dragged off of the pitch by the doctors, he was unceremoniously bundled into the back of a Fiat 125p, to be taken to the nearby hospital. As inconspicuous as the challenge may have been, ongoing complications to the subsequent surgeries meant that it would be over three years until Lubański would once again wear the White Eagle on his chest. Meanwhile, at what had now become a crucial period in qualifying, Górski would have to find a new man to lead his squad.

Kaziu Deyna was the obvious choice to take the armband; already one of the key figures in the dressing room and arguably the most-talented player in the squad, the Legia captain led the Reprezentacja for five of a six-game North American tour in preparation for the return leg against the Welsh. Górski was also in search of a right-sided forward that could play alongside Domarski and Gadocha, and settled on Grzegorz Lato—Domarski's strike partner at Stal Mielec and the league's top scorer during the club's unexpected title-winning campaign. Though his receding hairline gave the impression of a man much older than his 23 years, Lato's youthfulness was evident in the way that he could run full-backs ragged with boundless enthusiasm. This he did in a mid-August friendly against Bulgaria when, eager to prove Górski wrong after being left out of the trip across the Atlantic, he turned in a man-of-the-match performance and scored both goals in a two-nil win.

To combat the brutalist tactics used by the Welsh during their first meeting, Gmoch had encouraged the Poles to be equally as assertive at the

Śląski. Surprised by their opponents' new-found aggression, Dave Bowen's team immediately fell onto the back foot and became intimidated into making simple errors. In the 30th minute, Gadocha capitalised on one of them—a stray, weak backpass—to fire the hosts into the lead. Less than five minutes later he turned provider, sending an inch-perfect cross in the direction of five-foot nine-inch Lato, who rose above the defence to head into Gary Sprake's net. Trevor Hockey's red card just before the break, and a third goal from Domarski just after it, secured the result and left the Welshmen unable to qualify. At Wembley, where Andrzej Strejlau was watching England put seven goals past a hapless Austria, the result was met with jubilance by the English fans.

> "At the end of the match, on the screen, the result of the parallel match in Chorzów was shown, where Poland won 3-0 with Wales. I remember that all of [the fans] then got up from their seats rejoicing, and they started to sing the national anthem, because to decide qualification they were going to play in their own stadium, with Poland."
> - Andrzej Strejlau

***

The Polish team flew into London a few days prior to their group decider at Wembley, and were greeted by newspaper reports predicting a comfortable victory for Alf Ramsay's Three Lions. The consensus was that the defeat in Chorzów had been all down to England's failure to perform, and at Wembley, with a place at the World Cup on the line, there could only be one outcome. England were the founders of the game, had never failed in qualification for a World Cup, and had won it only seven years earlier—the idea that they might not reach the tournament at all was seen as utterly absurd.

> *"...I don't just look for the England victory I confidently expect anyway. I look for us to run away with it, win easily, qualify gloriously."*
> *- Frank McGhee; Daily Mirror; 17 October 1973*

The British press were also far from kind towards Górski's men, with one newspaper even going as far as to make jibes about the players' appearance. Likely in an attempt to undermine the task ahead of Alf Ramsay—a man whose job he was after for himself—Derby County manager Brian Clough singled out Tomaszewski for criticism on television, labelling him a "circus clown in goalkeeper gloves", while his assistant Peter Taylor referred to the Poles as "donkeys". Ramsay too showed signs of arrogance when, having been offered a recording of Poland's 1-1 draw against the Netherlands by ITV, he reportedly snapped: "We know how to beat Poland—we don't need any films!". He also told the *Daily Mirror* prior to the game that his players "know they are better than the Polish team" and "know they are good enough to win". However, the England coach had been concerned enough to travel to Rotterdam to watch the game in person; having played as a right-back during the infamous 6-3 defeat against Hungary 20 years earlier, he knew all too well about the consequences of underestimating teams from Eastern Europe.

> *"Walking onto the pitch at Wembley, I had legs of jelly. I was thinking: 'Please, don't let it be another 7-0!'".*
> *- Jan Tomaszewski*

The Polish team may have been acquainted to the vociferous supporting roar of the Śląski, but at Wembley, with the noise now directed towards them, it was nothing short of intimidating. The shrieking, whistling and chants of "animals" continued for the duration of the Polish national anthem, and as the teams lined up for kick off there was no respite. The Poles' nervousness could have proved costly almost straight away: just 45 seconds were on the clock when Tomaszewski rolled the ball on the floor, blindly unaware that Allan Clarke was standing nearby. As the Leeds United striker pounced, Tomaszewski was able to react quickly enough, diving on top of the loose ball—but not before Clarke had begun to swing his right foot, making contact with the keeper's left hand. It was later revealed that Tomaszewski had broken bones in his fingers, and had been forced to rely on copious amounts of painkilling spray to see him through to the final whistle. The challenge woke him from his stupor too, and he went on to produce one of the finest goalkeeping displays ever seen under Wembley's iconic Twin Towers.

That isn't to say Tomaszewski's performance was perfect; several times, with a rush of blood to the head he found himself out of position, only to have his blushes spared by either a crucial defensive block or wayward English shooting. But the saves he did make were bordering on the sublime, and spurred on by their custodian's self-inflicted need for bravery, on the occasions that Tomek found himself in trouble the Polish defence were willing to throw themselves in front of everything that the English attack could muster. The hosts could, and probably should have been at least three goals up at the break. Despite the onslaught, they entered the dressing rooms at half-time on level terms.

Ramsay was by far the happier manager of the two at the break, and although his players had begun to show signs of frustration, he encouraged them to continue as they were—for all of their domination, surely a goal would eventually come. Meanwhile, Górski told his team to remain resilient in defence, and predicted that as the game wore on the English would become frustrated and begin to panic—then maybe his forwards could capitalise and perhaps even put them in front.

Twelve minutes after the restart, it was Górski's prediction that was proven correct. Lato was the architect, gambling on a punted ball forward by Kasperczak which should have been cleared with ease. But rather than hoof into the stands, Norman Hunter elected instead to keep the ball in play to start another attack, and found himself dispossessed by the rampaging Lato before he'd even had a chance to take a second touch. Lato continued to bomb forward, and in space created by Gadocha's decoy run he found Domarski, who hit a first-time shot that squirmed past Shilton's feeble dive, to give the Biało-Czerwoni the unlikeliest of leads—a fifteen-second counter attack which left Wembley in stunned silence.

England responded to falling behind by continuing in the manner that they had played the entire game and were handed a chance to equalise from twelve yards moments later, when Adam Musiał was adjudged to have felled Martin Peters just inside the box. Peters later admitted to tumbling a little easily, but considering that they had made over 20 unsuccessful attempts at Tomaszewski's goal so far, even a penalty kick wasn't met with much confidence. Clarke, though, was the most confident man in the stadium, and sent the ŁKS stopper the wrong way to level the scores.

Though finally beaten, Tomaszewski was not in the mood to give up, and produced a string of stunning saves throughout the final half-an-hour to keep the English attack at bay. The finest of the night was saved for last: with just minutes remaining, Clarke sent a right-footed thunderbolt from seven yards towards the top corner of the net; but whilst wheeling away in celebration of almost certainly sending his country to the finals, he was left aghast to see Tomaszewski's yellow-sleeved arm appear from almost nowhere to miraculously parry the ball away from goal. "I knew then that they would not score again", remembers Tomaszewski; however, in the final embers he would still be reliant on Antoni Szymanowski's perfect positioning on the line to deny substitute Kevin Hector a dramatic winner.

> "The end, Ladies and Gentlemen! The end! Poland are in the World Cup Finals! Ladies and Gentlemen, this is the truth! This is the truth!"
> - Jan Ciszewski

***

"After the group draw, when it was known that we would play most of the matches in Stuttgart, German coach Max Merkel came up to us and said, 'I want to propose a great resort to you... This is a hotel that is not on the list of the Organizing Committee, but it was there that the German team prepared for the World Cup in Switzerland, where they won the world championship.' I listened in disbelief. I was convinced that there was some self interest in this, but, surprisingly, the then president of the union, Stanisław Nowosielski, bought it. Górski, with some concern said 'We'll go, we'll see.' We arrived, and we saw the beautiful little town of Murrhardt, the hotel called "Sonne Post" and the owners, the Bofingers, who knew football very well. Our doubts were resolved."
- Henryk Loska, national team attaché, 1974; Mundial '74: Dogrywka, Karolina Apiecionek

The World Cup of 1974 is for many reasons considered as the first of the modern era: it was the first to be televised across the world entirely in colour, the first to be played for the new Silvio Gazzaniga-designed trophy, and the first to see kit manufacturers advertise with their trademarks on the participants' shirts. It then seems fitting that the now more westerly leaning Poland, with its new-found love for consumerism, should use the tournament as its return to the international stage.

The Poland squad arrived in West Germany to their new Adidas kit, with the now-iconic three stripes running along the sleeves, but without the squad numbers which the players had originally requested. Due to a clerical error by a PZPN official, the 22 players were listed by position, meaning that captain Deyna was denied his favoured number '9' shirt, Gadocha missed out on his usual '11' and first-choice keeper Tomaszewski was given neither the number '1' jersey or his preferred '20'; instead the trio were handed '12', '18' and '2' respectively.

The tournament draw in Munich pitted the Poles against two of the pre-tournament favourites: an Argentinian team which had progressed through qualifying without losing a game, and an Italian one who had done similar, but also had the added distinction of having reached the final in Mexico four years earlier. While Gmoch's Information Bank was crammed with analysis of those two, there was next-to-nothing on the Poles' other Group Four opponents, Haiti. For that reason, while Górski led his first team to Belgium for a mid-April warm up, Strejlau had been dispatched to the Caribbean with a squad of fringe players, for what was a scouting mission as much as it was an audition. In total, seven of those who made the trip to Port-au-Prince were eventually called upon by Górski for the World Cup, supplementing 12 who went to Liège. As well as Tomaszewski and Gorgoń, who were both recovering from injury, the only other player in Górski's 22-man squad to have made neither trip was Lech Poznań midfielder Roman Jakóbczak. He was a late choice ahead of Zygmunt Garłowski, allegedly at the behest of the PZPN, who wished to ensure that all corners of the country were represented.

POLAND SQUAD

1974 FIFA World Cup; West Germany.

Goalkeepers: 1. Andrzej Fischer (Górnik Zabrze), 2. Jan Tomaszewski (ŁKS Łódź), 3. Zygmunt Kalinowski (Śląsk Wrocław).

Defenders: 4. Antoni Szymanowski (Wisła Kraków), 5. Zbigniew Gut (Odra Opole), 6. Jerzy Gorgoń (Górnik Zabrze), 7. Henryk Wieczorek (Górnik Zabrze), 8. Mirosław Bulzacki (ŁKS Łódź), 9. Władysław Żmuda (Gwardia Warszawa), 10. Adam Musiał (Wisła Kraków).

Midfielders: 11. Lesław Ćmikiewicz (Legia Warszawa), 12. Kazimierz Deyna (capt., Legia Warszawa), 13. Henryk Kasperczak (Stal Mielec), 14. Zygmunt Maszczyk (Ruch Chorzów), 15. Roman Jakóbczak (Lech Poznań).

Attackers: 16. Grzegorz Lato (Stal Mielec), 17. Andrzej Szarmach (Górnik Zabrze), 18. Robert Gadocha (Legia Warszawa), 19. Jan Domarski (Stal Mielec), 20. Zdzisław Kapka (Wisła Kraków), 21. Kazimierz Kmiecik (Wisła Kraków), 22. Marek Kusto (Wisła Kraków).

Coach: Kazimierz Górski.

Assistants: Andrzej Strejlau, Jacek Gmoch.

Though many fans and journalists believed that Górski would stick with the same eleven that had earned Poland the right to play at the World Cup, the coach himself was constantly looking for areas where the team could be improved. The night before they took to the field to face Argentina, Górski informed the players of three changes: Zygmunt Maszczyk would replace Ćmikiewicz for his first competitive appearance since the defeat in Cardiff; Andrzej Szarmach, Lubański's replacement at Górnik, would come in for London goalscoring hero Domarski and, perhaps most surprising of all, 20-year-old centre-back Władysław Żmuda would take the place of Bulzacki.

The latter was considered as Górski's riskiest move: not only was Żmuda largely inexperienced at international level, he would also be tasked with marking Argentina's teenage prodigy Mario Kempes. Indeed, within just a few minutes of kicking off, the Rosario forward escaped Żmuda, before failing to test Tomaszewski. Almost immediately the miss would prove costly for the South Americans, as before the clock reached the 10th minute, the Poles raced into a two-goal lead.

Lato scored the first, tapping into the unguarded net after Carnevali fumbled a Gadocha corner kick. Within two minutes of the restart, Lato had intercepted a searching Argentine ball forward and played in Szarmach, who clinically doubled the lead. Both Gadocha and Szarmach had chances to further extend Poland's advantage either side of the break, yet were denied by the woodwork. La Albiceleste were able to show signs of recovery in the second half, but Lato's second of the game, sandwiched between Helenia's perfectly placed curling effort and Babington's scrambled finish, was enough to claim Poland's first-ever World Cup victory.

The squad's celebrations were short lived, as they woke up the following morning to speculative headlines in the *Bild Zeitung* tabloid newspaper declaring that two of their players had failed drug tests following the game. The players in question, right-back Szymanowski and second-half substitute Domarski, vehemently denied the accusations aimed at them, but were forced to wait for three days before their names were eventually cleared—severely hampering preparations for their meeting with Haiti in Munich. When the Biało-Czerwoni were informed that the allegations should in fact have been aimed at two Haitian players, Górski's charges were handed the perfect motivation to negate the effects of the previous few days' disruptions.

Haiti had already provided one of the early shocks of the tournament, having ended Italian keeper Dino Zoff's record of 1142 minutes without conceding in international football, before they eventually succumbed to a 3-1 defeat. Poland's released frustrations afforded *Le Rouge et Bleu* no repeat joy, plundering seven goals in a thoroughly dominant performance; Lato again netting twice, Szarmach thrice, Deyna scoring a header and Gorgoń another now-trademark 40-yard screamer. With Italy and Argentina sharing the points from their meeting in Stuttgart, Poland's qualification to the second stage was secured with a game to spare.

That final game, back in Stuttgart against the Italians, presented Górski with the opportunity to rest players ahead of the second round. Cynically, it also presented both teams with the opportunity to manufacture a result—a draw of any score—which would see both teams progress. Górski was not interested in doing either, and again fielded a full-strength team to keep momentum heading into the next round. Though the *Azzurri* began the game brightly, by half time, goals from Szarmach and Deyna had put Poland into a commanding lead. As the teams made their way to the locker room at the break, several were temporarily distracted by a scuffle in the corridor. "[T]hey offered us money", recalled substitute Bulzacki; "they wanted to buy a draw"—a testimony backed up by several others in the Polish camp. Though the amounts allegedly proffered to the Polish players were astronomically high, if anything it served only to motivate them, and Fabio Capello's 86th minute strike was not enough to extend the Italians' stay in West Germany any longer.

Though Górski's starting eleven had remained consistent throughout the first round, for their second stage opener against Sweden, Adam Musiał was replaced by Zbigniew Gut—but due to neither tactical reasons or injury. Along with several others, Musiał had been to celebrate the win over Italy with a movie, but arrived back at the hotel 20 minutes late. While the others managed to avoid detection, the Wisła full-back was stopped by Górski in the lobby, and at one point even came close to being sent home for breaking his curfew. Several senior players protested that the punishment was much too strong, and though Górski did reduce it, he still gave his players an ultimatum: if they didn't win against the Swedes without him, Musiał would be sent back to Poland.

Górski's actions seemed very uncharacteristic—until then there had been a relaxed atmosphere around the squad, and with results going their way the players saw no reason for the strictness. But that is where Górski's genius came into effect: he knew that things had been going too well for his team, and like in the fourth match of the Olympics two years earlier—the 1-1 draw with Denmark—he knew there was a big risk of complacency setting in. The players needed to be shocked into a reaction.

It worked. Just. Lato's 40th minute header was enough to give Poland a 1-0 victory and their first two points of the second round. They did, however, have Tomaszewski to thank; the keeper diving to his right to palm away Staffan Tapper's second half penalty. As promised, Musiał returned to the starting line up against Yugoslavia four days later; there Deyna and Lato gave Poland a 2-1 victory, setting up a clash with West Germany—a winner-takes-all play-off to decide who would contest the final.

***

Ahead of their trip to Frankfurt, there were nerves amongst the Polish camp; during their stay in Murrhardt, every need had been taken care of, and even with the impending crucial meeting against the hosts, the locals had come out in numbers to wave off the Poles—German flags in one hand and Polish in the other. But away from their base, there was a worry of how they would be treated, even to the point where the backroom staff considered taking their own food and water on the 200km journey. Ultimately though, Górski decided to put his trust in the host nation who had so far been nothing but warm to his team.

The squad arrived at the Waldstadion to bright sunshine—some of the most beautiful weather seen during a tournament which had until then been plagued by terrible conditions. Yet, as the players warmed up on the field, once again grey clouds gathered, this time to produce the worst rainstorm seen so far. The drainage on the pitch—which already had large patches of destroyed turf after hosting the opening ceremony three weeks earlier—could not cope. It was not fit to host any game of football, let alone what had effectively become a World Cup semi-final. Yet, with so many VIPs and dignitaries in attendance, the organisers were adamant that the game must go ahead, and once the rain had subsided, firefighters were sent to pump water from the field and volunteers were deployed with rollers.

The long delay forced the Polish team to break a superstition of not returning to the dressing room, and in doing so, captain Deyna had not seen that the efforts of clearing water had been largely focused on one half of the pitch. After winning the toss, Deyna opted to take the ball, leaving his opposite number Franz Beckenbauer able to choose to defend the saturated end of the pitch for the first half. With the ball frequently held up in the mud, the Polish attack—already missing Szarmach through a quadriceps injury picked up against the Yugoslavians—was unable to take advantage of its far superior pace. Nevertheless, they still worried German keeper Sepp Maier, albeit mostly from distance: Deyna and Lato both going close to giving Poland the lead they needed to progress, having headed into the match trailing their opponents on goal difference.

Attacking in a swamp for the opening 45 minutes took its toll on the Poles, and having been able to conserve energy, following the break the Germans soon found themselves in the ascendency. After just eight minutes, the tiring Żmuda felled Bernd Hölzenbein with a lunging tackle inside the box; and though Tomaszewski was able to keep out Uli Hoeness' weak penalty (in doing so becoming the first goalkeeper to save twice from the spot during a World Cup), a winning German goal was becoming an increasingly likely. That goal eventually arrived 14 minutes from the end: Gerd Müller given enough freedom in the penalty area to break both the deadlock and Polish hearts.

Even now, the '*Mecz na Wodzie*' is still remembered in Poland with both great pride and great incredulity: satisfaction that their heroes performed so competitively against the eventual World Champions, yet frustration of what could have and, had the match taken place in better conditions, perhaps even should have been. Meanwhile, in Germany, the memories somewhat pale in comparison to those of a few days later, when their side defeated the Johan Cruyff-led Dutch team in Munich to lift their second World Cup. Still, those that are able to vividly recall the '*Wasserschlacht von Frankfurt*' will point to how, against an arguably better team, fortune favoured them that day; and, like the Poles, how things may have turned out very differently.

"I do not know whether we would have won on a dry field, but we would have stood a better chance."
- Kazimierz Górski

FROM PARTITION TO SOLIDARITY

"I'm sure we would not have beaten the Poles had the weather been different."
- Paul Breitner, West Germany full-back

***

Though Lato had not been able to use his blistering speed to its full effect against the German defence, the Munich crowd were treated to one last glimpse during the third-place play-off against outgoing champions Brazil. In the 76th minute, Grzesiu left the Canarinhos' defence for dust and advanced on goalkeeper Leâo, before sliding the ball past him to secure, not only Poland's status as the third best team in the world, but also his own position as the tournament's top scorer with seven goals to his name. In addition to collecting their medals at the post-tournament banquet (silver in colour, after Germany's gold and the Netherlands' gold plated), there came even more individual successes: Kazimierz Deyna as the tournament's third-best player behind Beckenbauer and Cruyff, and Żmuda, who beat off stiff competition for the title of the competition's top young player; both clearly showing how much of an impression Górski's Eagles had made.

Unsurprisingly, back at home, Gierek's government attempted to use the successes to fuel their propaganda-laden agenda, with a televised reception for the squad at the Workers' Party headquarters. But while Gierek's popularity among the Polish public remained high, dark times had already begun to descend upon him. The day prior to Poland's 1-1 draw at Wembley, petroleum companies in several Arab countries had raised their oil prices by almost 70 per cent in response to the USA's support for Israel in the Yom Kippur War; and with Poland's entire economy still dependent on loans from America, France and West Germany, the ensuing financial crisis in the west had dire consequences for the Polish government. Gierek's economic plan had been reliant on increased exports to the west, but hindered by inefficient industry and inferior products, these exports did not increase in line with initial projections. Ultimately, between 1971 and 1976, the country's foreign debt increased tenfold, and as the Polish economy began to falter, the price rises on food that had been deferred six years earlier were now seen as essential.

Within hours of the June 1976 announcement by Prime Minister Piotr Jaroszewicz, police mobilised in the major cities to quash the inevitable protests; but factory workers in the smaller cities of Radom and Płock, and the Warsaw suburb of Ursus, managed to take the authorities by surprise. Attacking local government offices, protesters quickly overran the underprepared police forces, and by the time that these forces were strengthened hundreds-of-millions of złotys damage had already been caused. Protesters were savagely beaten, with three killed and almost two hundred wounded in Radom alone. Hundreds were arrested, while thousands more eventually lost their jobs. Gierek desperately clung onto his by eventually cancelling the rises; however this only served to make his government look both economically inept and politically weak.

The 1976 Olympic Games in Montreal took place just a few months after the unrest, and was a chance for Poles to take their minds off of the situation at home. But while Poland increased their medal count on the 1972 games and climbed the medal table in doing so, the football team were not able to defend their title from Munich. Three straight victories in Canada—against Iran, North Korea and Brazil—earned them an expected place in the Olympic final, however their status as favourites meant little as they were defeated 3-1 by an unfancied East German team.

The game was Górski's last in charge of the Reprezentacja; having been inundated with job offers from around the globe, he plumped for the head coaching position at Greek club Panathinaikos, leaving the national team in a significantly higher position than when he had arrived.

The same, however, could not be said for Gierek. Though the early part of his time in charge is, in hindsight, seen as the most-prosperous spell of the Communist period, the decline during the end of the decade ultimately left the country no better off than when Gomułka was ousted. With the most positive nationally uniting events of the decade being football-related, it can be of no wonder that, for a certain demographic, the 1970s are now remembered as Górski's era rather than Gierek's.

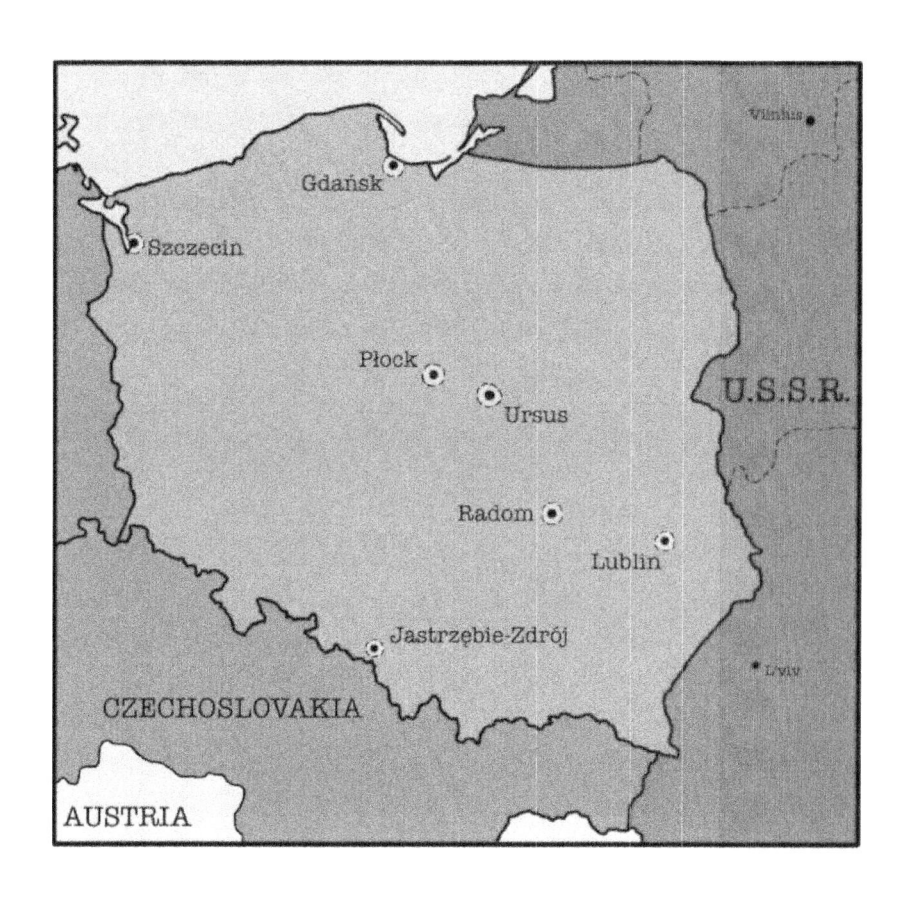

Act V
A Rebellious Poland

CHAPTER NINETEEN
OKĘCIE

"When we returned to Poland, [coach, Jacek] Gmoch did not talk to anyone. In London, where we had a stopover, he sat in a corner away from us, threw his hood over his head and growled whenever someone wanted to ask something."
- Andrzej Szarmach, "Diabeł, nie Anioł", 2006

WHOEVER HAD TAKEN CHARGE of the national team following Górski's departure would have been able to select from what can perhaps be considered as Poland's finest generation. There were the likes of Tomaszewski, Gorgoń, Żmuda, Deyna, Szarmach and Lato, who all reprised their roles from West Germany; even Włodek Lubański had returned, now fit again and plying his trade in the west with Belgian side Lokeren, if not quite at the levels he had previously attained. In addition, some of the brightest young talents to have emerged for several years were now forcing their way into contention: notably Wisła Kraków midfielder Adam Nawałka, who collected *Piłka Nożna*'s award for the Newcomer of the Year in 1977, and both ŁKS attacker Stanisław Terlecki and Widzew midfielder Zbigniew Boniek, who had shared the same title a year earlier.

Preparations for the 1978 World Cup in Argentina had looked optimistic from the start; five wins and a draw from their six qualifiers seeming to reinforce those beliefs. Yet, by the time that Poland's qualification was secured, the atmosphere among the squad had already begun to deteriorate, and the values instilled by Górski had become almost non-existent. Much of the blame for that was put at the feet of one man: Górski's replacement, Jacek Gmoch.

Andrzej Strejlau had long been considered as Górski's natural successor by both the players and the fans, so the appointment of Gmoch—who had resigned from the coaching setup following the '74 World Cup in frustration that he had not been given the credit that he felt he deserved—was a big surprise. Gmoch's use of reports and statistics soon shaped almost every aspect of how he coached the squad; introducing high-intensity training methods picked up in the USA, bringing in doctors and dieticians to monitor players' health, and even using psychologists' assessments to determine whether players were compatible with each other on the pitch. His new methods were perhaps twenty-or-thirty years ahead of the time; however, the problem wasn't necessarily that these new tools were utilised, but more the fact that Gmoch was stubbornly reliant on them.

Performances at the tournament were far below expectations; still, Gmoch's charges progressed to the second round as group winners. A goalless opener in Buenos Aires against reigning champions West Germany came despite the Poles having carved many of the better chances, while 1-0 and 3-1 victories in Rosario could have been worse had either the Tunisian or Mexican attackers been slightly more effective in front of goal. Poland finally came unstuck in the second phase, despite beginning it with arguably their strongest showing in a 2-0 loss to hosts Argentina. A narrow victory over Peru gave the Biało-Czerwoni hope going into their final game against Brazil, however a 3-1 defeat sent them home, with Gmoch unable to match his predecessor's achievement four years earlier.

That said, Poland's disappointing second-round exit in Argentina cannot be solely attributed to the coach and his methods, with several other factors causing distractions to the players. Disputes with the PZPN over bonuses were a headache that had not been a factor four years earlier, while the GKKF had also spent money allocated for the team's Adidas equipment in order to kit out those representing Poland in other sports. Many of the team were now also approaching their 30s, and primarily concerned with attracting potential suitors in the west for a lucrative transfer. Szarmach later said that the team had played in the tournament "without faith, without passion, without conviction" and, even before Gmoch's inevitable departure in late 1978, that the national team was in desperate need of "new people, new ideas and new orders".

Those new ideas and orders came from within Gmoch's setup as Ryszard Kulesza, who had also replaced Gmoch as Górski's assistant during the 1976 Olympics, stepped in to fill the void. Kulesza was well liked by the players, in part due to the fact that his management style was far removed from the authoritarianism of his predecessor. Kind, gentle and approachable, his constant smile was infectious; Stanisław Terlecki remarking in his book that Kulesza "loved people and [was] optimistic about life". It was an impressive attitude to possess considering some of the horrors seen as a teenage boy—during the Warsaw Uprising he had been forced to watch as his father was shot dead, and was even lucky to escape alive himself after being thrown in front of a passing German tank.

The new people, meanwhile, came as a result of several of Górski's Eagles flying the nest for the final time. Gorgoń removed himself from selection following the World Cup, while both Deyna and Kasperczak effectively announced their retirements from the national team by transferring to Manchester City and Metz respectively. Tomaszewski and Lubański also saw their international careers peter out, returning only to properly say goodbye in front of their own Łodzianin and Silesian crowds during the early 80s. In their place a new generation, spearheaded by the likes of Boniek and Terlecki, had already begun to fill the voids.

***

"Let the spirit descend and renew the face of the earth, the face of this land."
- Pope John Paul II; Kraków; 12 October 1979.

Though the 1976 protests had damaged Gierek considerably, he was persuaded to stay in his position by several senior politicians within the Workers' Party. Interference from Soviet leader Brezhnev, who advised the First Secretary to forget about further price manipulation, was intended to quell the dissenters; but Gierek's response of introducing rationing for basic commodities meant that the frustrations of the Polish public would continue further.

For the first time in decades Poles had also become invigorated by religion, with the election of a Polish Pope, John Paul II, in the Vatican. One of his first state visits, in the autumn of 1979, was a return to his homeland—reluctantly agreed to by the communist government. Head of the KGB, Yuri Andropov, had already concluded that a Polish Pope would serve to "destabilise Poland and undermine Soviet authority in the Eastern Bloc". US President Ronald Reagan believed similar, stating that religion "may turn out to be the Soviets' Achilles' heel".

In his speeches on Warsaw's Plac Zwycięstwa and Kraków's Park Błonia, at which he spoke to over five million people, the Holy Father stressed the need for his compatriots to bring God back into both family life and education. Having seen religion suppressed for decades by the atheist Communists, pushing Catholicism back into Poles' minds served also to expand their thoughts of freedoms, and the gargantuan crowds hanging on the Pope's every word highlighted to the aggrieved Polish public that it was they, not the ruling elite, who were in the majority. The final signs that Gierek's interminable demise was coming to an end appeared in August 1980, by which time the country's economy had shrank for the first time since the war, the national debt had reached $18 billion and living conditions had plummeted dramatically.

Once again strikes broke out across Poland, with the most vocal being in the economically important shipyards of Gdańsk. Originally the dockers' protest had been ignited by the firing of Anna Walentynowicz, a 50-year-old crane operator who had been involved with illegal trade union groups fighting for better conditions for those on the docks; however, led by electrician and former shipyard employee Lech Wałęsa, it soon transformed into a protest over nationwide issues such as labour reform, civil rights and freedom of expression. Despite attempts to prevent news spreading, the strikes garnered widespread support across the country and the decision not to use military force against the workers can be considered as one of the government's first signs of concession.

After seven days of non-violent protest and further strikes breaking out across the country, from the north western port city of Szczecin to the Upper Silesian mining town of Jastrzębie-Zdrój, Gierek sent in officials to meet with the workers, with the aim of agreeing a deal. The resulting Gdańsk Agreement was signed on 31 August, becoming one of the first examples of allowing citizens to bring democratic change within a communist political structure.

Among the activists' 21 demands, which were all met, the first two points allowed workers the right to establish trade union groups independent of communist control and the right to strike without fear of retribution. Less than three weeks after the agreement, Wałęsa led the formation of *Solidarność* ('Solidarity')—the first independent trade union established in a Warsaw Pact country. Within its first year it would attract nine-and-a-half million members—over one third of Poland's working population—and amassed a power which would eventually allow it to directly influence Polish politics. Yet its influence had already been felt in the crippled Worker's Party where, just three days after the trade union's birth, Gierek was finally ousted as First Secretary and replaced with Stanisław Kania. The cracks in Polish communism had begun to appear.

***

"What time did you leave the hotel on 29 November?"
"08:00."
"Are you sure it was 08:00? Are you sure it wasn't 08:02?"

"No. Maybe it was even 08:03. I don't know the time exactly, because I have one of your Russian watches."
- Interrogation of Stanisław Terlecki by General Marian Ryba, December 1980

It wasn't just in the shipyards, mines and factories where Poles had begun to revolt against the authorities; on the streets, in the bars and even on the football terraces, it was no longer a challenge to find someone with an audible distaste for the communists. International footballers, however, were hardly in a position to go against the regime—under the current system they reaped benefits which the general public could only have dreamed of. There were no long waiting lists for cars or apartments, luxury goods were easily obtainable, and foreign travel was a regular occurrence. On top of that, the vast majority of players continued to earn a wage for their token jobs, despite never setting foot in a factory or a mine. This was something that Solidarność latched on to, and before long the tide of goodwill towards the footballers began to slow.

Stanisław Terlecki was one of the exceptions within the Polish game; the son of two university lecturers, he himself had begun studying for a degree in history from the University of Łódź whilst continuing to forge a successful footballing career at ŁKS. Off the field, Terlecki was gaining notoriety for his staunch anti-communist views; known by his teammates to shun the usual sports magazines for western news journals, they often joked to him that his nose was "growing upwards". However, having attempted to establish a footballers' union during the late 70s, Stasiek gained a reputation amongst the authorities as a troublemaker, and eventually earned the wrath of the PZPN, who banned him from the game for six months.

Even with his suspension, and an injury limiting his participation in the 1978 World Cup to a role as a television pundit, Terlecki returned to the national team under Kulesza's stewardship. By 1979 he was scoring in Poland's unsuccessful Euro '80 qualifying campaign, and the following year was a shoe-in for the squad to square off in a three-team World Cup qualifying group alongside Malta and East Germany.

Ahead of their group opener against Malta in December 1980, Kulesza gathered his squad in Warsaw's Hotel Vera, ten days before the game, in order to prepare. With the Mediterranean climate of Valetta in complete contrast to the Polish winter, the coaching team had organised a warm weather training camp in Rome and a practice match against Perugia, before making the short hop to the island nation just over a week later.

The evening before the team were due to leave for the Italian capital, goalkeeper Józef Młynarczyk and attacker Włodzimierz Smolarek left the Vera in defiance of the coaches' orders. Later claimed by Smolarek that they were unhappy with the food in the hotel, the pair headed to the upmarket Adria restaurant and met up with Wojciech Zieliński—a sports commentator for Polish network TVP, and friend of Młynarczyk. Both Smolarek and Młynarczyk had not long returned from England, where their Widzew Łódź side had been crushed 5-0 by Ipswich Town in their UEFA Cup third round clash. Zieliński, however, was more interested in their trip to Turin in the previous round, where Widzew had beaten Juventus on penalties. More specifically, he was looking for news on his estranged wife—a lady well known around Warsaw—who had recently travelled to the Italian city.

While Smolarek headed back to the Vera at around 2am, Młynarczyk stayed alongside Zieliński at the Adria, being plied with drink until the early morning. When the goalkeeper returned to the hotel at approximately 7am—just one hour before the team were due to depart for Okęcie Airport—he was tired and in fear of the wrath of the national team coaches.

As the team boarded their coach for the four-and-a-half mile journey, it was impossible for Młynarczyk to hide the effects of the night before. Seemingly too fatigued to even carry his own bags, Smolarek was forced to aid him; yet reaching the front of the bus, the Widzew midfielder was confronted by Bernard Blaut, one of Kulesza's assistants, who informed him that the goalkeeper would not be travelling with the team. Upon hearing the decision, an angry Terlecki rushed to the front of the coach to join Smolarek in protest. Another two of Młynarczyk's Widzew teammates, Boniek and Żmuda, also stood in defence of their colleague—the argument becoming so heated that, at times, the players were forced to be held back. But while the situation was eventually diffused and Młynarczyk was left behind, it was far from the end of the incident. The fired-up Terlecki decided to stay back too, and with his own car conveniently to hand, he drove Młynarczyk to Okęcie to confront the management.

Having spent the night at his own home, Kulesza was due to meet the squad at the airport; and immediately upon their arrival, and in front of the assembled national media, Boniek and Żmuda approached the manager in support of their colleague. The pair were able to calmly convince Kulesza to change his decision, informing him that Młynarczyk was struggling with personal problems—particularly the recent death of his father and subsequent ill health of his mother. However, arriving himself minutes later, Terlecki began to cause havoc. In an attempt to distract the journalists from the worse-for-wear goalkeeper, he began to knock microphones and cameras to the ground, and pulled plugs out of their sockets whilst shouting "*nie filmujecie, nie filmujecie!*". Fellow teammate Andrzej Iwan later said that "[Terlecki] made so much commotion that it was impossible to sweep everything under the carpet".

As the team arrived in Italy, news of the incident at Okęcie had already spread like wildfire. The next morning almost every national newspaper had run the story, with *Przegląd Sportowy* calling for the PZPN to show "No mercy for those guilty of the scandal at Okęcie", and *Tempo* proclaiming that such subordination "cannot be tolerated". It would not be: just days later, PZPN president and Polish Army General Marian Ryba arrived to escort the so-called *banda czworga* ('band of four')—Boniek, Terlecki, Młynarczyk and Żmuda—back to Poland; but not before the team had further gone against the PZPN's orders not to associate themselves with the Vatican whilst in Rome, by spending an hour-and-a-half with the Pope himself.

Kulesza eventually led the remainder of the team to Malta where, whilst the Poles led 2-0, Maltese supporters forced the abandonment of the game by pelting the players with rocks. However, the reception given to the four players back home in Poland, especially by the state-influenced media, was perhaps even worse.

> "We felt like bandits who had killed millions of people. And we were just players, one of whom drank a little too much, and three others, who when a colleague was ruthlessly attacked by activists, stood in his defence."
> - Stanisław Terlecki; "Pele, Boniek i Ja"

**

Both the PZPN and the Workers' Party were keen to make examples of the four; the football association in order to prevent future player rebellions, and the government to distract the public from the ongoing political crisis. Within weeks, the PZPN had organised a public trial for the four players—a trial with an outcome seemingly pre-determined from the start, and solely designed to turn the public against the players by highlighting how much better off they were compared to the average Pole. Boniek later described the interrogation as a "cabaret", and Terlecki treated his own questioning as such with his provocative and occasionally humorous responses.

Though the majority of the statements given—including that of Kulesza—had been in support of the players, almost all of them were dismissed by the authorities. The only versions of events accepted were those of coach Kulesza and Blaut, with the former's knowledge of the events at the hotel being second-hand, and the latter having also accused Boniek and Żmuda of emotional blackmail. Within a week of the trial, the verdicts were handed down: both Boniek and Terlecki were banned from football for one year, Żmuda and Młynarczyk for eight months, while for his own supporting part Smolarek received a two-month suspended sentence.

Before Christmas, Kulesza too was gone; resigning in protest at the harsh punishments handed to the quartet. Both Widzew and ŁKS were also angered, and even briefly considered withdrawing from the PZPN in a protest of their own. Widzew, who at the time sat four points clear of army club Legia at the top of the league, were particularly aggrieved at losing three of their most influential players for the second half of the season—especially as the sentences had been dished out by a former military prosecutor in Ryba, on the testimony of former Legia player Blaut.

With the help of Kulesza's successor, Antoni Piechniczek, Żmuda was able to have his ban overturned quickly, and returned to the Widzew squad in time for the resumption of their ultimately successful league campaign in March 1981. Boniek and Młynarczyk were not available to help their teammates capture the title, but did also receive reductions on their sentences at Piechniczek's behest—both returning during the summer break, ahead of Widzew's first appearance in the European Cup.

Terlecki, however, was not as fortunate. Despite several appeals to overturn his suspension, the authorities' contempt for him ensured he was never successful; and in the Spring of 1981, ŁKS called time early on his contract with the club. With no other Polish team willing to risk signing the outspoken attacker, Terlecki was forced abroad and signed with American Indoor Soccer's Pittsburgh Spirit in the summer. Despite a later, reasonably successful stint with New York Cosmos, and then a return to Poland with both ŁKS and Legia in the second half of the 80s, his history of insubordination ensured he would never again be selected to wear the White Eagle on his chest.

CHAPTER TWENTY
NINETEEN EIGHTY-TWO

"...before the World Cup in Spain we were with the Polish team in a private audience with [Pope] John Paul II, and we asked him to pray for our success at the championships. 'I wish you all the best, but... the Pope does not pray for such matters', replied the Holy Father..."
- Zbigniew Boniek

GAMES AGAINST FELLOW SOCIALIST BLOC COUNTRIES were, on paper, friendly; however, in reality they were wars. Poland's World Cup qualifier against East Germany in October 1981 was no exception. Piechniczek's men had already defeated the Germans several months earlier at the Stadion Śląski, meaning that victory in the return game would assure their progression to the tournament in Spain. Even a draw would be enough for the Poles, provided that they could avoid defeat against the group's whipping boys, the Maltese, a month later. However, the Poles knew from experience just how tricky a trip to Leipzig's Zentralstadion could be; two years earlier they had been defeated there in a Euro '80 qualifier, with several of the squad believing that the water they had consumed at half-time may have been poisoned. The Polish staff took no chances this time and travelled with their own supplies, despite a protest lodged by the Germans to the Polish Ministry of Foreign Affairs, which only strengthened the Poles' suspicions.

On the field, Poland's start could hardly have been any better: Andrzej Szarmach's second-minute header being followed 180 seconds later by a skilful rounding of the keeper by Włodzimierz Smolarek. An ill-gotten penalty brought the GDR back into the game shortly after the break; however, Smolarek's second of the game—a solo run from the halfway line, finished from an acute angle—ultimately rendered a second from the hosts as a mere consolation. Poland's fourth World Cup appearance had been assured with a game to spare, and to celebrate, following their destruction of Malta in Wrocław, the team were whisked away for a mid-December trip to Hungary.

***

> "Today I address myself to you as a soldier, and as the head of the Polish government. I address you concerning extraordinarily important questions. Our homeland is at the edge of an abyss. The achievements of many generations and the Polish home that has been built up from the dust are about to turn into ruins. State structures are ceasing to function. Each day delivers new blows to the waning economy...
> "Citizens; the load of responsibility that falls on me in this dramatic moment of Polish history is huge...
> "I declare, that today the Military Council of National Salvation has been formed. In accordance with the Constitution, the State Council has imposed martial law all over the country...
> "This is the ultimate way to bring the country out of the crisis, to save the country from collapse...
> "I appeal to all the citizens. A time of heavy trials has arrived; we have to stand those in order to prove that we are worthy of Poland.
> "Before all the Polish people and the whole world, I would like to repeat the immortal words: 'Poland has not yet perished, so long as we still live!'"
> - General Wojciech Jaruzelski, 13 December 1981

Stanisław Kania's reign as Polish First Secretary was short-lived. In October 1981, just thirteen months after succeeding Gierek, he too was removed from power after being caught on tape criticising the Soviet leadership. His replacement came in the form of General Wojciech Jaruzelski, the Chairman of the Council of Ministers and Minister of National Defence. A staunch anti-religion Communist despite his Roman Catholic upbringing, Jaruzelski was in many ways the antithesis of Kania; where his predecessor had looked to build bridges with both the Catholic Church and Solidarność, he instead looked to burn them.

The declaration of martial law on 13 December 1981—under the misleading premise that it was necessary to prevent a Soviet invasion—was designed to do just that. The following days saw thousands of pro-democracy activists incarcerated, strict curfews imposed, the country's borders sealed and military units become a constant presence on the streets of major cities. Nationwide strikes were inevitable, and were quashed with force; Jaruzelski reneging on an 11-year-old promise made following the 1970 troubles, to ensure that the military was never again used to suppress protesters. The worst single act of the First Secretary's betrayal occurred at the Wujek Coal Mine in Katowice, where nine miners—including Rozwój Katowice defender Zbigniew Wilk—were killed, and almost two dozen more injured. With their leaders and activists in detainment, Solidarność were unable to fight back, and the government quickly set about erasing all symbols of the democratic trade union.

Understandably, as the country was plunged into turmoil, Polish sport suffered immeasurably. The national football team, who had been left stranded in Hungary as Jaruzelski sent the army on to the streets, were suddenly handed the task of preparing for a World Cup in which their participation was now in doubt. However, the Government had no intention of stopping the Polish team from travelling to the tournament; in fact, they saw it as a necessity. In their minds, they hoped that Polish success on the pitch would help to calm the social unrest back at home, and as such used vast sums of the country's dwindling foreign currency reserves to pay for the rights to broadcast the tournament on state television. This did, though, leave many Poles in a quandary, as since the introduction of martial law, the number of television viewers had dropped significantly in response to the government-run, propaganda-laden broadcasts. Some even believed that, if people lent their backing to the national team, they would be inadvertently showing support for the communist regime's propaganda machine.

But attitudes towards footballers in general had changed since the incident at Okęcie; Poles had become more rebellious towards the authorities, and footballers were now seen as representative of society as a whole. Unlike many other sportsmen and women, footballers generally would never court the regime. Not wanting to provoke the authorities, yet unwilling to show support for them, when probed by journalists the players instead looked to avoid discussing political issues altogether; they could, after all, still be prevented from travelling to the World Cup. A seat on the flight to Spain represented the chance for a player to change the future for both himself and his family; strong performances during the tournament could attract suitors from abroad, and ultimately earn a ticket away from the problems they had begun to face back at home.

One player was not prepared to wait for that chance: Jacek Jarecki, Poland's young fourth-choice goalkeeper from army club Śląsk Wrocław, who made a break for freedom a month before the start of the tournament. Doubting that he would be able to usurp either Piotr Mowlik or Jacek Kazimierski to gain a place in Piechniczek's 22-man squad, and with his long-time girlfriend having already managed to escape Poland with her family just a few months before the imposition of martial law, Jarecki saw his inclusion in a pre-tournament training camp in Murrhardt as an opportunity to forge a new life in the west. The evening before flying back to Warsaw, several senior players caught the flustered 23-year-old struggling to squeeze through a half-open hotel window, outside of which his equally panicked partner was waiting. Grzegorz Lato—who had been entrusted with the keys to the Sonne Post hotel having stayed there with

Górski's squad eight years earlier—was one of those players, and after a brief discussion he opened the door to allow Jarecki his freedom. The rest of the Polish-based squad, however, were not tempted; many had family back at home, and had no intention of leaving them to fend for themselves.

***

POLAND SQUAD
1982 FIFA World Cup; Spain.

Goalkeepers: 1. Józef Młynarczyk (Widzew Łódź), 21. Jacek Kazimierski (Legia Warsaw), 22. Piotr Mowlik (Lech Poznań).

Defenders: 2. Marek Dziuba (ŁKS Łódź), 3. Janusz Kupcewicz (Arka Gdynia), 4. Tadeusz Dolny (Górnik Zabrze), 5. Paweł Janas (Legia Warsaw), 6. Piotr Skrobowski (Wisła Kraków), 7. Jan Jałocha (Wisła Kraków), 9. Władysław Żmuda (captain, Widzew Łódź), 10. Stefan Majewski (Legia Warsaw), 12. Roman Wójcicki (Śląsk Wrocław).

Midfielders: 8. Waldemar Matysik (Górnik Zabrze), 13. Andrzej Buncol (Legia Warsaw), 14. Andrzej Pałasz (Górnik Zabrze), 20. Zbigniew Boniek (Widzew Łódź).

Forwards: 11. Włodzimierz Smolarek (Widzew Łódź), 15. Włodzimierz Ciołek (Stal Mielec), 16. Grzegorz Lato (Lokeren, BEL), 17. Andrzej Szarmach (Auxerre, FRA), 18. Marek Kusto (Legia Warsaw), 19. Andrzej Iwan (Wisła Kraków).

Coach: Antoni Piechniczek

The Polish squad arrived in Spain at a much lower level of preparation than they had hoped. With several national football associations refusing the PZPN's invitations to play friendly matches in the build up to the competition, the team's only pre-tournament tests had come against lower-league clubs and reserve teams during training camps in Spain and

West Germany. It was unsurprising then to see the Poles start their tournament slowly. A goalless draw against an Italian team which had finished fourth in their last two major tournaments appeared a decent result; however, the cagey performance still drew frustrations and criticisms from many within the Polish media. These feelings were exacerbated by a second goalless draw, five days later against Cameroon; a much-more dominating performance, but having been expected to win the game comfortably, it was considered almost as bad as a defeat.

Much of the country's press had directed their ire at one man in particular: Zbigniew Boniek, who had signed a contract with Italian giants Juventus before the tournament. "Now he has his money, he doesn't care", scapegoated one Workers' Party-supporting newspaper—failing to see the irony of throwing their country's best player under the bus, despite the government having received a hefty portion of the 28-year-old's transfer fee in order to allow him to leave the country. Instructed to portray Boniek's move to the west as a form of betrayal to the socialist state, several journalists commented in articles that his performances warranted him being dropped to the bench for the win-or-bust game against Peru. Some even suggested that the midfielder should sit in the stands instead. Piechniczek had no such intention, instead opting to move Boniek into an attacking position to replace the injured Andrzej Iwan. "Luckily, I decide" the coach told Jan Ciszewski over a glass of whiskey in his Spanish hotel room. "If we win with Peru, you will see that everything will change."

The media had also failed to acknowledge its own role in Poland's performances. By aiding the government's narrative that the players held the hopes of the nation squarely on their shoulders, they were partly complicit in placing an insurmountable pressure upon them. When, on the morning of their final group game, government activists reminded the squad of how it was their responsibility to bring joy to their families and friends who were struggling back at home with ration queues and curfews, frustrations finally began to boil over. From the moment the team stepped over the white line at the Estadio Riazor, nervousness and a lack of motivation were immediately visible, and another lacklustre Polish performance was almost foreordained.

While Piechniczek's charges did not have to be at their best to dominate their South American opponents, wastefulness in front of goal meant that their anxieties only continued to grow. In a first half characterised by many missed opportunities, the closest Poland came to breaking their goalscoring duck was through Boniek, who scooped the ball over the stranded keeper only to see the effort ruled out by the Mexican referee. Goalless at the break for the third game in a row, and now 225 minutes without a goal in the tournament, elimination from the World Cup had now become a serious concern.

As the team returned to the locker room, several of the activists who had tried to motivate the team earlier that day attempted to offer their further encouragement, only to be denied by the hastily locked door. Piechniczek instead proffered his own advice: "Play for both the fans and yourselves", he stated, trying to remove some of the pressure from the shoulders of his weary players. "Playing football should be fun; if it isn't, well, then you shouldn't play football."

It was then left to Boniek, who until that point had been uncharacteristically quiet, to rally the troops: "This is our 45 minutes... We have to score that goal!"

> *"Here's a chance: Kupcewicz, ladies and gentlemen. Smolarek pressing on his own... He scores! A goal, ladies and gentlemen, at last!"*
> *- Jan Ciszewski*

Włodzimierz Smolarek's left-footed drive into the bottom corner of the net wasn't the only goal of the game; over the next twenty-one minutes, the Poles plundered the Peruvian net a further four times. Lato slotted under the marauding keeper and into the empty goal, Boniek turned in a low ball across the six-yard box, Buncol drilled a shot into the bottom corner and substitute Ciołek thundered into the roof of the net. With each goal came an outpouring of Polish joy; Polish relief. Even a late consolation from the South Americans failed to dampen the newly discovered Polish spirit. Boniek's goal in particular saw an emotional response from the midfielder, gesticulating furiously towards the journalists in the press box who had criticised him.

Not only did the victory assure Poland qualification to the second round, but following Italy's draw with Cameroon, they did so as group winners. First place also meant relocation, from the cooler climes of the Spanish north west to the Mediterranean heat of the Catalan capital, Barcelona—something that the PZPN had not completely prepared for. Having failed to pay a deposit for their preferred hotel, the association were forced to find another after Argentina's national team secured the reservation. The replacement, some 50km away from the city in the foothills of Montserrat, was far from suitable. With no air-conditioning to help the players acclimatise to the temperature difference, several developed a fever in the build up to their second round clash with Belgium.

One of those affected was Boniek, who struggled to train in the two days leading up to the game. Yet, with Piechniczek's unwillingness to change a winning side, Boniek would continue alongside Lato and Smolarek in the attacking role. After only four minutes his decision was justified; collecting a backwards pass from the energetic Lato, Boniek thundered the ball from the edge of the penalty area, off of the underside of the bar and into the Belgian net.

The goal was the first major action of what would later be described as "the game of Boniek's life". The second came 22 minutes later; Kupcewicz's searching cross-field ball, nodded back into the box by Buncol, with Boniek's own header looped to perfection over the stranded custodian Theo Custers. It was a goal that immaculately displayed Poland's almost-telepathic teamwork, and exemplified the fact that they were far from purely a one-man display. Boniek, however, was the team's orchestrator: Steve Powell's famous photograph of Diego Maradona terrorising six Belgian defenders will forever remain as one of the iconic images of the 1982 World Cup, yet those Belgian defenders undoubtedly recall the movement and skill of Zibi as their toughest test of the tournament. Poland's third goal of the game, just eight minutes after the break, was further evidence of Boniek's brilliance; following sublime footwork from Lato, the moustachioed midfielder rounded the keeper and tucked calmly into the empty net—securing not only his hat-trick and the 3-0 victory, but also pole position at the top of Group A.

> *"The Belgians wanted to play cautiously; but all alone, Boniek was going to take charge of all their plans."*
> - Onze Magazine, July 1982

***

With the victories against Peru and Belgium, World Cup fever had begun to proliferate back in Poland—suddenly, almost the entire country wanted to show support for their team. As a result, television broadcasts had become popular again, and for Poland's final group game against their great rivals the USSR, audiences were expected to be at an all-time high.

While the increase in viewership was exactly what the government had hoped for, it also exacerbated a problem that they had so far been coping with. Since the imposition of martial law, across the world support for Solidarność had begun to grow, and symbols of the trade union—which were now illegal to display in Poland—were steadily becoming visible in the stadiums during Poland's games. This wasn't an issue in TVP's Warsaw studio, where the output was easily controlled; however, with the live feed from the official broadcaster in Spain, additional measures were put in place to provide censorship. At the touch of a button, the live feed could be replaced with pre-recorded videos of supporters during other matches—effectively erasing all signs of support for Solidarność.

Poland's first round games in Vigo and A Coruña had seen only minor displays in support of the exiled trade union, but in Catalonia their activists were afforded more freedom. Particularly under General Franco's oppressive rule, which had ended only seven years earlier, many Catalans had yearned for independence from the rest of Spain. Many also sympathised with, and related to the Polish peoples' plight. Therefore Poland's game in the Nou Camp, against the Soviets, was seen as the perfect place to make a statement—to show everyone that Solidarność was still alive despite the communists' attempts to destroy it. Suddenly the match was no longer just a de-facto World Cup quarter-final, but also a game against both the communists and martial law; one in which defeat was not an option.

Prior to kick off, Solidarność supporters—some of whom were Polish expatriates that had managed to escape the country before the imposition of martial law—had distributed approximately 5,000 small red-and-white flags, emblazoned with the union's logo, inside the stadium. In addition, 15-metre-long banners of a similar design were held aloft at either end of the pitch, providing a red-and-white, anti-communist backdrop to every piece of attacking play—Soviet or Polish.

In Warsaw, the television editors frantically began their attempts to censor: each time the ball approached one of the goals, a shot of another team's fans was inserted, or the feed was hit with temporary interference. It was an absurd practice that, after a short period of time had to be abandoned completely. Meanwhile, in the stadium, Polish government officials were equally as exasperated, and early in the second half they eventually managed to persuade the Guardia Civil to confiscate the banners. As they did, Polish supporters screamed for help from the Catalans—to which the 65,000 in attendance responded loud and clear: "*Solidaridad! Polonia!*"

Listening to the chants, the Polish players' motivation increased, and while Piechniczek's men had set out to ensure they didn't concede, they actually forged the better chances themselves. Still, unable to find a breakthrough, the Poles' fatigue allowed their opposition to finish the game strongly; in small spells the defensive line of Żmuda, Janas, Majewski and Dziuba had to be at their very best to soak up the Soviet pressure. They were, however, afforded an outlet: amongst a tiring Polish team, the tireless Smolarek continued to irritate the Soviet defence. On several occasions during the closing stages he sought security close to the corner flag and danced teasingly over the Adidas Tango, each time wasting a few precious seconds.

As the Scottish referee's final whistle eventually signalled Poland's third goalless draw of the tournament, rather than disappointment or frustration as per the previous two, it was instead met with a sense of victory. Reaching the semi-final once again—especially at the expense of their fiercest rival—was more than any Pole had imagined, and brought with it scenes of ecstasy on the pitch. Players and coaches embraced, Ciszewski exclaimed that the players had "proudly represented the country", and Boniek even appeared on Polish television wearing the pinstriped shirt of defender Sergei Baltacha as a war trophy—delighted, even though a clumsy first-half foul on Volodymyr Bezsonov had earned him a second yellow card of the tournament and an automatic suspension for the last-four game against Italy.

The following day, the story of the game adorned both the front and back pages of newspapers all across the world—as much for the happenings off of the pitch than on it. Many western outlets opted to illustrate their coverage with a photograph of the Soviet team lined up in front of the Solidarność banner, while one even supplemented it with the headline: "Poland – Russia, 0-0. Solidarność – Soviet Union, 1-0."

***

Though still buoyant from their exploits four days earlier, reaching the final proved to be a step too far for Piechniczek's wearied charges. In the running for the Golden Boot and Golden Ball awards (of which he would eventually win both), Boniek's new Juventus team mate Paolo Rossi put an end to Poland's World Cup dream. The Poles' exhaustion was evident throughout, as *Il Torero* twice evaded slack marking to score from close range. Meanwhile, Boniek's leadership was sorely missed as he watched on from the stands; he sat next to Andrzej Szarmach, who controversially had seen little playing time during the tournament and was dropped from the semi-final squad altogether, despite an excellent record against the Italians.

Both Boniek and Szarmach were reinstated to the starting eleven for the third-place play-off against France in Alicante, and the pair combined four minutes before the break to cancel out René Girard's opener. A delightful chip by Boniek was hit first time on the half-volley by Szarmach, and crossed the line via a rebound off of the post. However, the 31-year-old's celebrations were muted—before the game he had been informed by Piechniczek that it would be the last of his nine-year international career.

There were no mixed emotions for defender Stefan Majewski though, who, moments before half-time rose highest to meet a Kupcewicz corner, giving Poland the lead. Within two minutes of the restart Kupcewicz scored one himself, beating the French keeper at his near post with a well-placed free kick. *Les Bleus*, already battered, bruise and depleted from their highly physical encounter with West Germany in the semi-final, were now rattled too. Though Alain Couriol's strike, with eighteen minutes left on the clock, gave them a lifeline, it was the only time during the second half they were able to breach the stubborn Polish defence.

The Białe-Orły collected their second silver medal in eight years on the Alicante pitch, not from FIFA President Joao Havelange, but rather their own captain Władek Żmuda. In an awkward exchange, the Brazilian handed Żmuda the tray of medals to dish out to his teammates himself, with many misinterpreting the incident as a political protest against martial law. However, the truth is that Havelange didn't distribute medals to either team; the Poles were actually supposed to be given their awards by PZPN President Włodzimierz Reczek, who was struggling to walk on the day of the game having suffered severe burns in the Spanish sun.

For the third time in a decade, the Polish squad arrived back at Okęcie to a heroes' welcome. The following morning they were whisked to the Workers' Party headquarters, where Jaruzelski and key members of his government bestowed upon them further honours and expressed the country's gratitude for their unexpected success. While the team's exploits had, as the First Secretary had hoped, distracted the public, many looked for the players to perhaps make a gesture of some kind, in protest at the regime's actions and martial law in general. In reality though, they couldn't—they were footballers not political activists, either playing abroad or harbouring dreams of doing so. As well as Boniek, Lato and Szarmach, Żmuda had agreed a move to Hellas Verona, Marek Kusto was set to sign for Beveren and Paweł Janas was to join Szarmach at Auxerre. Neither they, nor any of the other players, could risk having their passports taken from them.

"...Sometime after the World Cup I was in the Vatican again, this time with the Juventus team. The Holy Father picked me out of the group, called me to him and whispered in my ear: 'You see, if I knew you would get a medal in Spain, I would have definitely prayed for you.'"
- Zbigniew Boniek

CHAPTER TWENTY-ONE
THE OLD LADY AND THE NIGHT THAT CHANGED POLAND

THE RISE OF WIDZEW ŁÓDŹ during the 1970s was nothing short of extraordinary. Having begun the decade battling their way out of Poland's fourth tier, the *Czerwono-Biało-Czerwoni* ended it in the first, both challenging for the Polish championship and already versed in European competition. Back-to-back league titles in 1981 and 1982 became the crowning glory for, not only the team now referred to as '*Wielki Widzew*' ('The Great Widzew'), but also for the man that was ever present during their ascent to the summit of the Polish game: Ludwik Sobolewski.

Former military officer Sobolewski had joined Widzew as their Head of Football in 1970, and like the club itself he quickly rose up the ranks. Having ascended to the presidency in 1977, Sobolewski projected his vision for Widzew to match the achievements of both Legia and Górnik. Their start was promising: UEFA Cup progression past Manchester City in 1977, and then Manchester United in 1980, meant that by the time of their maiden league title they had already claimed two scalps which had evaded Górnik a decade earlier.

These strong European showings, followed by an impressive two-legged victory over Italians Juventus, had repercussions for Widzew: clubs from abroad soon began to take notice of their star players. In addition to the departures of Italy-bound duo Boniek and Żmuda, fellow Mistrz Polski Jan Jeżewski and Andrzej Możejko were tempted by moves to Finland, while several others transferred elsewhere within Poland. Ahead of a second defence of their title, the rapid dissection of Wielki Widzew began to look as though it may curtail their success.

However, the outgoing transfers provided the club with a financial windfall, and now operating on a model closer resembling that of western clubs rather than their Polish exemplars, Widzew reinvested in young, uncapped talent to fill the gaping holes in their squad. Future internationals Wiesław Wraga, Tadeusz Świątek and Krzysztof Kajrys were supplemented by a current one in Śląsk Wrocław's World Cup medal-winning defender Roman Wójcicki. Despite the extensive personnel changes, Władysław Żmuda (the club's coach since 1981, as opposed to their former captain of the same name) was still able to lead his rebuilt team into the winter break just a point behind leaders Śląsk.

Still, Widzew's two domestic titles alone were not enough to match the feats of either Legia or Górnik; in order to do that they would have to also go the distance in European competition. Żmuda's charges had unsuccessfully made their debut in the European Cup in 1981, with defeat to their Belgian counterparts Anderlecht. However, their sophomore attempt a year later showed a significant improvement; a 7-2 demolition of Maltese champions Hibernians helping to boost the young team's confidence, prior to the inevitable meetings with more-established opposition.

Widzew's second round foes, Rapid Vienna, were one of those teams. They too had started their tournament strongly, with a heavy first-round victory over Avenir Beggen—forcing the Luxembourgish goalkeeper to collect the ball from his net on thirteen occasions. But while Henryk Bolesta was made to do the same twice in the Austrian capital, and Józef Młynarczyk three times in Łódź, goals from Mirosław Tłokiński in the first leg, and then Zdzisław Rozborski, Krzysztof Surlit, Wiesław Wraga and a Paweł Woźniak brace in the second, gave the Poles a 6-5 aggregate victory and a place in the quarter-finals.

If Rapid were a difficult obstacle to overcome, then Widzew's next challengers—three-time European champions Liverpool—were possibly as tough a draw as they could have been handed. The Reds approached the last-eight tie unbeaten in eleven First Division games and fourteen points clear of their closest rivals, and if that wasn't enough for the Poles, days before their first meeting a flu pandemic had swept through the Widzew locker room. But, though the odds were stacked in the English club's favour, in front of the Łodzianin supporters their star-studded squad—Bruce Grobbelaar, Kenny Dalglish, Graeme Sounness and Ian Rush among them—were humbled. Two second half goals gave Widzew an unexpected advantage to take to England: Tłokiński pouncing on a Grobbelaar howler, and Wraga thundering a header from 18 yards.

Despite trailing, and failing even to score an away goal, the Liverpool players were still highly confident of achieving both victory and progression in front of their own hostile supporters. An early period of dominance suggested this too; so when Phil Neal converted from 12 yards after Marek Filipczak was correctly adjudged to have handled the ball, the Anfield wolves sensed the blood of their wounded prey.

Yet, six minutes before the break, the Liverpudlian crowd was silenced; at his skilful best, Włodek Smolarek teased Grobbelaar before being clattered to the ground by the Zimbabwean. Tłokiński expertly placed his own spot kick to both re-establish Widzew's two-goal lead and net an important away goal of their own. Then, on the other side of the half, the three goals that the English champions needed became four, with Smolarek himself afforded a simple tap in.

Ian Rush and David Hodgson both scored late on to give Liverpool a narrow victory on the night, but Widzew's resolute defence held strong to ensure progression to the semi-finals, matching Legia's achievement 13 years earlier. In the space of just seventeen years, the club had risen from the very bottom of the Polish football ladder to become immortalised in the country's sporting history. For a chance to surpass the Polish trailblazers of the seventies, the rebuilt team would be paired against a name with which they were all too familiar...

***

Following his move to Juventus, Zbigniew Boniek quickly established himself as a fans' favourite at the Stadio Comunale. The midfielder's performances during evening games in particular, led the club's president Gianni Agnelli to bestow upon him the nickname *Bello di Notte*—'beauty at night'—and under the floodlights he netted goals against both Danish club Hvidovre and reigning European champions Aston Villa to help *La Vecchia Signora* progress through the early rounds of the competition. Though Giovanni Trapattoni may have often struggled to find Boniek's most-effective position, his partnership with Michel Platini—a fellow new signing, bought from French club Saint-Étienne—quickly became a formidable one.

A swift return to Łódź may have been a tantalising draw for Polish fans, but Boniek himself saw it as a disappointment. He had watched his former teammates perform so strongly against Liverpool, and hoped he would meet them in the final. Instead, he and his new colleagues helped to ruin Widzew's chances of reaching the showpiece event in Athens; and while failing to make a mark on the score sheet himself, Boniek was heavily involved in the goals which eventually decided each of the two legs.

Marco Tardelli gave Juve the lead inside the Stadio Comunale, with a shot that took a significant deflection off of Andrzej Grębosz in order to deceive Młynarczyk. Boniek then helped to manufacture his team's second, finding space inside the Widzew box to test Młynarczyk, before Roberto Bettega followed up into the empty goal. In Łódź, Paolo Rossi turned the two-goal lead into three after the half-an-hour mark, playing the ball through the goalkeeper's legs after a delightfully placed chip from Platini. The gulf in class between the two teams was easily apparent.

Widzew, though, didn't give up, and found a lifeline thanks to Krzysztof Surlit's cool finish nine minutes after the restart. The Poles were then able to maintain momentum, despite a short delay caused by a fan striking the Dutch linesman with an empty beer bottle; with nine minutes remaining, Surlit wrong footing the already-committed Dino Zoff from a free kick, giving the hosts the lead on the night and setting up a grandstand finish to the tie.

Yet it was a lead that lasted barely 180 seconds. Before Widzew had a chance to mount another attack, Boniek was tumbled to the floor by his former banda czworga ally Młynarczyk. Zibi walked away quietly, refusing to celebrate the referee's decision against his countrymen; Platini, meanwhile, sent Młynarczyk in the wrong direction, salvaging *I Bianconeri*'s unbeaten run in the competition at the death.

For Wielki Widzew, the full-time whistle signalled, not only their elimination, but ultimately also the beginning of the end of their dominance in Polish football. Over the next seven weeks, three league trips to Upper Silesia proved to be their downfall; one-goal defeats to Ruch Chorzów and GKS Katowice, and a 1-1 draw at Górnik Zabrze, meaning that their title was surrendered to Lech Poznań by the narrowest of margins. Though the Czerwono-Biało-Czerwoni were still able to maintain a position on the podium for the next three years, the third title—and a return amongst the elite of European competition—would remain elusive for the time being.

Juventus also wouldn't return to the European Cup for the following season. Defeat to Hamburg in the final, and a second-place finish behind AS Roma in Serie A, meant that Boniek and his teammates' European adventures would come only in the form of a Cup Winner's Cup campaign. There, five months after the trip to Łódź, Boniek would again return to face a team from his homeland.

FROM PARTITION TO SOLIDARITY

***

As Juventus were lifting their seventh Coppa Italia trophy by virtue of a two-legged victory over Hellas Verona, a new name was being etched upon the Puchar Polski: that of Lechia Gdańsk. Lechia's success had come as a shock across the country—the first team from the III Liga to lift the trophy; a 2-1 victory over second-tier Piast Gliwice following on from victories over the top-flight trio of Widzew in the fourth round, Śląsk in the fifth, and Ruch in the semi-final. It also meant they would become the first club from outside of the top division to represent Poland in Europe; and while a handful of doubters may have raised the prospect of their place instead being handed to one of the country's elite clubs, the PZPN were quick to stress that the *Biało-Zieloni*'s place in the first-round draw was secure.

In Juventus, Lechia were handed probably the toughest draw possible. Though Dino Zoff had now retired, five World Champions still graced their squad—that even before mentioning the two further World Cup medallists in Boniek and Platini. In contrast, the Italian press reported that their team would face a squad of bricklayers and builders; a part truth, with the majority of the Lechia squad employed by one of several construction companies helped run by club president Andrzej Januszewski. Their full name, 'Budowlani Klub Sportowy Lechia' also alluded to the fact.

Nevertheless, the Italian journalists always reported on the *Lechiści* with respect—even more so after their 1-0 defeat of league champions Lech Poznań at the end of July, to become the inaugural winners of the Superpuchar Polski. Trapattoni also showed respect to his opposition, and well aware of the threat that Lechia could pose, he chose to field a full-strength XI for the opening fixture at the Comunale.

The first-round tie was practically over within the first thirty minutes. Braces for both Platini and Domenico Penzo put Juventus well on their way to a 7-0 victory in Turin—a scoreline which could have been even higher, had it not been for goalkeeper Tadeusz Fajfer palming away a second half Rossi penalty. Back at Gdańsk's Ulica Traugutta, there would be little for Lechia to play for other than pride.

> "The Lechiści did not disgrace themselves. They may have been second best, but they were second best to Juventus".
> - "Głos Wybrzeża", Albert Gochniewski and Jerzy Konopka

The crumbling terraces at Ulica Traugutta had required mass renovations, to the tune of around 60,000,000 złotys, in order to meet UEFA's requirements to host the second leg. Completed only the day before the game, each of the stands were filled by 1pm—two-and-a-half hours before kick off. Officially 30,000 fans crammed into the stadium, yet in reality there were well over 40,000; many climbing on to ledges, roofs, trees and poles in order to gain the best possible vantage point.

At precisely half-past-three, English referee Keith Hackett blew to signal the start of the game; but though the home crowd began raucously, Beniamino Vignola quietened them within 20 minutes with a low, drilled shot underneath Fajfer. Worries spread that Lechia were about to suffer another mauling.

***

Supporters of Lechia have always had a long history of anti-communist and anti-militia protest. Many of the city's striking shipyard workers were fans of the club, and besides the docks, Ulica Traugutta was one of just a handful of other places where there was a relative freedom for them to protest. On away trips, Lechia's travelling contingent would also help to spread the word of the anti-communist opposition across the country, with chants in support of Solidarność frequently audible inside each stadium that they visited.

Nevertheless, Solidarność was still a banned entity, and there was a continued attempt by the government to delegitimise the former organisation. Following his release from incarceration in late 1982, the communists agreed that Lech Wałęsa was to be treated as a regular member of the public rather than some kind of anti-establishment hero. Despite rumours of his planned attendance at the second leg against Juventus, this status meant that should he enter the stadium, there was no lawful reason for him to be stopped by the militia.

The evening prior to the game, state-run television broadcasted a heavily edited discussion between Wałęsa and his brother Stanisław, in which they were portrayed as greedy and only motivated by their own financial gain. Timed in the hope of derailing his nomination for the upcoming Nobel Peace Prize, and titled simply '*Pieniądze*' ('Money'), the pair reportedly discussed cash that they allegedly held in foreign bank accounts and also criticised leaders of the Polish church. Now, rather than prevent him from entering the stadium, the government actually hoped that Wałęsa would be seen by the principled Lechia supporters and then widely booed.

Obviously Wałęsa, with his distinctive moustache, was immediately recognised by the die-hard Lechia fans amongst whom he immediately positioned himself on the terraces. His location away from the main grandstand did mean that the majority inside the stadium were not aware of his presence, and the few minor chants which did break out in support of Solidarność struggled to gain any traction. However, during the half-time break, things changed. Piotr Adamowicz, an activist friend of Wałęsa, had days before alerted correspondents from several US television networks to both Wałęsa's possible attendance and where inside the stadium he would be located. As the cameramen noticed and began to swarm towards Wałęsa, the commotion attracted the attention of fans across the ground, and within minutes the chants of "Solidarność, Solidarność" and "Lech, Lech" were deafening.

Though official reports of the match would later state that the chanting had emanated from merely a few thousand troublemakers protesting against the state, in reality it was the entire stadium. Lechia coach Jerzy Jastrzębowski later admitted that he and his players too could hear the fans from inside the locker room, and their raucousness was enough to send "shivers all over [his] body". Meanwhile, in the opposite dressing room, Boniek attempted to explain the context of the situation to his perplexed Italian colleagues. The authorities, no longer smug and contrite, were by now concerned enough to order the delay of the television broadcast by several minutes, and eventually ordered the second half to be shown without any sound at all. Those acts were enough to suggest to viewers at home that something big was being concealed.

Upon returning to the field, Lechia were boosted by the atmosphere being generated, and within as many second-half minutes as it had taken the Italians to score in the first, the Biało-Zieloni managed to turn the game on its head. Marek Kowalczyk levelled soon after the break, with a low drive settling in Stefano Tacconi's net via a deflection. Then, twelve minutes later, Jerzy Kruszczyński sent the crowd into a frenzy with a well-executed penalty.

Alas, there would be no fairytale ending for Jastrzębowski and his charges; with 77 minutes on the clock, substitute Roberto Tavolo equalised with a tremendous left-footed volley. It was then left to Boniek to have the final say: cutting in from the left-hand side, his low shot crept in at Fajfer's near post with only seven minutes remaining.

While Lechia's dreams of a historic victory were fading, for Wałęsa and his associates, their own job was completed. With Solidarność very much thrust back into the public consciousness, a few minutes before Hackett's final whistle he was ushered out of the stadium so as to not be caught up in any trouble.

But trouble was the last thing on the minds of the Gdańszczanin audience: their players had put on a proud performance against one of the best teams in Europe, and they themselves had assisted to deal a hammer blow to the country's communist authorities. It was a blow which, before long, would begin to resonate across not only Poland, but the entire continent.

CHAPTER TWENTY-TWO
FREEDOM (THE LAST KINGS OF SILESIA)

"The teeth of bars pull from the walls! Tear off the shackles, break the whip! The walls shall fall down, fall down, fall down; and they'll bury the old world."
- *"Mury"; Jacek Kaczmarski*

THE POLAND ELEVEN that began their Euro '84 qualifying campaign against Finland in Helsinki bore only six names in common with that which had walked on to the field in Alicante. That number dropped to four for a 2-1 defeat to Portugal in Lisbon just a month later. By the time that back-to-back home draws against the Finns and the Soviet Union left a maiden appearance at the European Championships unattainable, Piechniczek's squad were unrecognisable to that which had finished third in the world.

The holes left by Szarmach and Lato had been difficult to fill, Żmuda's unsuccessful stint in Verona left him cast from the coach's favour, while both Kupcewicz and Janas had played their final games for the Białe-Orły during the unsuccessful campaign. In their places, those who had previously been considered as back ups were now thrust into starting positions.

There were, however, many positives: Boniek's blistering form continued for Juventus, as did Młynarczyk's and Smolarek's for Widzew. Several of those in peripheral roles during their time in Spain—Roman Wójcicki, Andrzej Buncol, Stefan Majewski—also stepped comfortably into more-senior roles, while the return of midfielder Waldemar Matysik, from a life-threatening bout of dehydration and exhaustion following the '82 World Cup, was extremely welcome. The qualifiers and friendlies had also been used by the Selekcjoner to bring the next generation into the fold: Dariuszes Wdowczyk and Kubicki of Legia, and Dziekanowski of Widzew, and Śląsk Wrocław's Ryszard Tarasiewicz in particular. As the qualifying round for the upcoming World Cup in Mexico appeared on the horizon, Piechniczek was confident that his newly rebuilt squad had the attributes to reach a fourth successive World Cup tournament.

A combination of both the old and new gave Poland their opening victory; from one-nil down at half-time, Smolarek's equaliser and a Dziekanowski brace established an eventual 3-1 scoreline over Greece in Zabrze. But though the margin of victory was extended when the two sides met in Athens seven months later, by that point Piechniczek's charges found themselves in a precarious position within Group One, having since suffered defeat away in Belgium and only just salvaged a point in Mielec with Albania. Fortunately, both the Belgians and Albanians had also dropped points against each other, and with a narrowly superior goal-scoring record, Poland headed into their return matches still holding destiny in their own hands.

The Poles' penultimate game, in Tirana against Albania, had been poorly scheduled for Piechniczek. The 30 May fixture kicked off fewer than 24 hours after the 1985 European Cup Final between Juventus and Liverpool, in which his star man Zbigniew Boniek played a key role. Zibi drew the penalty which earned Juve a 1-0 victory, making him the first Pole to lift the iconic trophy; however, it was success marred by tragedy, with the death of 39 Juventus supporters inside Brussels' Heysel Stadium. Boniek himself didn't find out the extent of the devastation until the following morning when, 900 miles away in Bari, he read about it in the early editions of the local newspapers. He would later donate his prize money to the victims of the disaster and their families.

Boniek's appearance in the crucial qualifier was only possible with the help of Juventus' president Agnelli who, in thanks for his service to the club and before his impending transfer to AS Roma, organised a private jet to fly his 'Bello di Notte' to the Albanian capital. Though understandably exhausted, Zibi showed little sign of being so as he fired Poland into a 24th minute lead from outside the penalty area—an advantage they held on to, to move above Belgium on goals scored, ahead of their showdown at the Stadion Śląski three months later. Needing just a single point to ensure a place at the World Cup, that fixture would be decided, not by goals, but rather an exemplary goalkeeping performance; Młynarczyk keeping his clean sheet unsullied despite the visitors' desperation in throwing everything towards the Polish goal.

The manner of qualification had not been one befitting of a team now considered as being amongst the world's best and, once again, neither were their pre-tournament preparations. Firstly, the squad were assembled only days after the end of the domestic season, giving the players little chance of a rest. The team's Mexican base of Monterrey was then crippled by public disorder, when the city's state-owned steelworks was declared bankrupt and around 10,000 workers lost their jobs. Confined to their resort for two weeks prior to their opening game, tensions between the players—particularly those from rivals Legia and Górnik—quickly grew.

In hindsight then, a goalless draw against the eventual group winners was perhaps not a bad result; but Morocco, playing in their first World Cup for 16 years, were a team that Piechniczek's charges had been expected to defeat with ease. No stranger to pointing out the Poles' flaws, Brian Clough commented on television after the match that they "looked sluggish and out of sorts"—a remark this time echoed across the following day's newspapers back home. Some improvements were seen for the second match, against a Portuguese team which had not appeared on the training field for several days beforehand. A dispute with the country's football association had left the Iberians thoroughly underprepared; and Smolarek took advantage twenty minutes from time, sending Poland to the top of Group F, one point ahead of the Moroccans and two ahead of their final opponents, England.

While Piechniczek remained unwavering in his commitment to not change a winning team, Bobby Robson's Three Lions went into the game weakened after their own goalless draw against Morocco—during their match, they had lost both their captain Bryan Robson and vice-captain Ray Wilkins, to injury and suspension respectively. The armband was instead handed to ageing goalkeeper Peter Shilton, who had a demon still to exorcise 13 years on from the two sides' meeting at Wembley. It was exorcised, but largely thanks to his fellow Leicesterian Gary Lineker; twice the striker edged past Majewski to poke home, and then completed his 28-minute hat-trick by capitalising on an uncharacteristic Młynarczyk mishap. The 3-0 result was plenty enough to nudge England above the Poles on goal difference, and left the White Eagles clinging on to a place in the knock-out rounds only as one of the best third-placed teams.

Though provided with a back door into the second round, it would only be a temporary stay of execution. At the second stage they were met by a Brazilian team which had won its opening games without concession, all whilst contending with the tropical heat and high altitude of Guadalajara's Estadio Jalisco that would host the two sides' impending meeting. Arriving with only a few days to acclimatise from the desert-like heat of their own base in Monterrey—some 1,000m closer to sea level—adaptation proved to be a problem for the Poles.

Despite Tarasiewicz hitting the post after 70 seconds and then Jan Karaś rattling the crossbar ten minutes later, the Brazilians put an end to the Poles' energetic start within the opening half-an-hour. Legendary midfielder Socrates calmly placed his penalty, theatrically won by Careca, into the top corner to put Brazil in front; and as the midday sun rapidly drained the Poles' energies, the South Americans went on to plunder a further three goals in the second half. An ambitious right-footed bicycle kick from Boniek—which could have even rivalled Diego Maradona's solo effort for goal-of-the-tournament, had it edged just the other side of Carlos' post—did come close to reducing the deficit late on, but it would have been nothing more than a consolation.

The journey back to Warsaw proved to be the final one for some: Majewski, Młynarczyk, Żmuda; all would never again wear the *Orzeł Biały* on their chest. Boniek, meanwhile, would only do so on two more occasions, finally closing the curtain on his international career in 1988.

After five-and-a-half years and 59 games, elimination also brought Antoni Piechniczek's time in charge of the national team to an end. Saying goodbye to his players in the Estadio Jalisco dressing room, he then announced his resignation to the public in a post-match interview with the Polish press. "Decades will pass before another coach repeats my result", the frustrated Piechniczek uttered to journalists as the team returned to Okęcie. *Klątwa Piechniczka*—'Piechniczek's curse'—has yet to be lifted.

***

Piechniczek's absence from football lasted for little over three months. In the middle of October 1986, he made a return to the dugout in his native Upper Silesia, taking over from former international midfielder Lesław Ćmikiewicz at Górnik Zabrze. In doing so, he inherited a dressing room filled with strong personalities which had, after only ten games of both the league season and Ćmikiewicz's reign, grown weary of the ex-Legia midfielder's training methods and lack of authority.

It was understandable that the Górnik board had reacted so quickly; Ćmikiewicz had large expectations to live up to. His predecessor, former Górnik keeper Hubert Kostka, in his first full season had brought the Polish championship back to Zabrze after a thirteen-year absence. He then retained the trophy a year later. From almost nowhere, Górnik had managed to reclaim their place at the summit of the Polish game, and they were not keen to relinquish it.

Górnik's initial success was in that, unlike many of the league's other teams, they were not heavily reliant on one player. While elsewhere a total of five players finished the 1984/85 season with a goal tally in double digits, no Górnik player hit the back of the net more than seven times; that despite the team's goal-scoring record being bettered only by the dethroned Lech Poznań. Defensively they were sound too; just sixteen conceded left only Widzew on a par. It was the Łodzianins whom the Trójkolorowi netted twice against on the final day, to pip Legia at the top by a single point.

Stability was essential for Kostka: of the 19 players utilised during the successful campaign, eleven appeared on more than 27 occasions. Three Górniczy—midfielders Marek Majka and Waldek Matysik, and attacker Andrzej Pałasz—even started every single one of the club's 30 league games. Though the post-season signings of Zagłębie Sosnowiec midfielder Jan Urban and Wisła Kraków striker Andrzej Iwan added depth to the squad, consistency remained a feature throughout their sophomore season, too. Nine of the squad participated in at least 90 per cent of league games during the 1985/86 season; only this time striker Andrzej Zgutczyński's 20 goals were enough to earn him the golden boot. But, while the lead over second-placed Legia was this time extended to four points, and their attacking record strengthened even further, Kostka was ousted at the end of the season—a breakdown in relations, not only with the players, but also the club's leadership, to blame.

A return amongst the elite of Polish football was little due to the influence of the club's president Marian Polus, but rather his predecessor —and by now the director of the Zabrze Mining Corporation—Jan Szlachta. Though Szlachta had resigned from his role at the club in February 1984 to concentrate on his political ambitions (in 1986 he was appointed as the Minister of Mining and Energy), he continued to be heavily involved in its running from within the shadows. With money and supplies diverted from the mines, the club were quickly and easily able to assemble the strongest squad in the country by some distance. The sums now on offer at Ulica Roosevelta were huge; upon signing from relegated Wisła, Andrzej Iwan was able to, not double or triple, but almost quadruple his wages. On top of that, bonuses—especially for defeating local rivals such as Ruch Chorzów and GKS Katowice—were mind boggling, while, providing the successes continued, Szlachta was more than happy to cater to the players' every whim.

Piechniczek was greeted by an air of familiarity within the dressing room upon his arrival in Zabrze: goalkeeper Józef Wandzik; and a midfielder four of Urban, Matysik, Pałasz and Ryszard Komornicki, were all players he had taken to Mexico for that summer's World Cup. The coach's 1982 selection Iwan also remained at the club; however, a sixth member of the '86 squad—Zgutczyński—had since moved to France.

The 1986/87 season also coincided with a rule change put in place by the PZPN, in order to encourage attacking football: any victory by three-goals-or-more was rewarded with a bonus point, whilst a defeat by the same margin was punished by the deduction of a point. Free-scoring Górnik managed seven bonus-point wins—four of them within Piechniczek's first five games. The changes served only to increase Gornik's lead over second placed Pogoń Szczecin, from four points to five.

However, a final-day defeat to relegated Motor Lublin was the last of Piechniczek's short stint in charge, as he left Poland for the head coaching position at Tunisian club Esperance Sportive de Tunis. His replacement Marcin Bochynek, promoted from fellow mining club Górnik Knurów, was given a simple brief: guide the club to its fourth-successive championship, and fourteenth overall—and surpass great rivals Ruch Chorzów in the process.

***

Though martial law had been abolished two months prior to Wałęsa's appearance at Ulica Traugutta, and amnesty granted to thousands of the political prisoners holed up in detainment camps across the country, this had by no means constituted a political thaw. If anything, the brutality shown by both the militia and the *Służba Bezpieczeństwa* (Security Service) had since only grown to an unprecedented level.

A second Papal visit in 1983, in which John Paul II openly criticised the communist elites in front of a million-strong Silesian audience, only served to antagonise the government. The following crackdown on both trade union activists and the Catholic Church saw thousands more persecuted, beaten and imprisoned, while the torture and murder of pro-democracy priest Father Jerzy Popieluszko in 1984 proved so shocking that the government were left with no choice but to take action against the SB officers responsible. Further harassments followed with a purge of the educational system in late 1985, which saw thousands of academics dismissed from their positions. The general public were also suffering worse than ever before, with the number fleeing westwards to escape both the rationing and shortages of basic commodities increasing at an alarming rate.

Wałęsa's Nobel Peace Prize victory in 1983 put paid to any thoughts he may have had of returning to work in the shipyards, and by 1984 he was once again fully re-immersed in Solidarność's underground activities. Though the organisation's influence had reduced whilst in the shadows, it had not completely diminished; almost every major Western diplomat which visited the country—even as senior as American Vice President George Bush—visited Wałęsa and his colleagues to discuss the effects of the sanctions being placed upon Poland at the time.

The implementation of martial law, and every other of Jaruzelski's attempts to bring Poland back under Muscovite command, had all been on behalf of former Soviet Premier Leonid Brezhnev; however, his death in 1982 brought significant change behind the Iron Curtain. Though hardliners Yurii Andropov and Konstantin Chernenko had followed, the 1985 election of Mikhail Gorbachev as First Secretary of the USSR was a turning point; faced with both a collapsing economy and a losing position in the Cold War, Gorbachev's policies of *glasnost* and *perestroika* ('openness' and 'reorganisation') were the very opposite of what his predecessors had strived for. The country's new vision involved a significant change of direction, notably the ridding of its satellite states to the west which had become both social and economic burdens.

Gorbachev's position was a hammer blow to Jaruzelski, and threatened to undermine the General's entire leadership—even more so when the Soviet hegemony publicly declared the abandonment of Brezhnev's doctrine, which had authorised military intervention in support of Eastern Europe's communist regimes. Every action that Jaruzelski had until then taken against the Polish people had been argued as being in order to prevent Soviet intervention. No longer able to use that excuse, any legitimacy of his leadership that still remained was swiftly lost.

Though technically still outlawed, Solidarność had continued to push for dialogue between themselves and the government, even if Jaruzelski's refusal to acknowledge their presence made this difficult. Eventually though, in response to the threat of nationwide strikes in 1988, the First Secretary finally caved in. Growing weaker by the day, the government were eventually given no option but to negotiate with their opposition, and in September preparatory talks between the parties began.

After much disagreement over who would be involved and what would be discussed, on 6 February 1989 the 'Round Table talks' began; 57 people from all sides coming together to discuss the future path of the country, with the eventual goal of non-confrontational elections. By the time that the talks finished eight weeks later, Solidarność had not only regained its legal status as a trade union, but had also become an official political party in opposition to the government. Constitutional changes had also been made: the role of President was reinstated, and elections scheduled for June. In doing so, the Communist Workers' Party were effectively signing their own execution order.

The elections would be only partly free: 65 per cent of seats in the Sejm (lower house of parliament) were reserved for PZPR members in order to maintain their position of power, while opposition parties were allowed only to contest the remaining 35 per cent. In the Senate, however, all elections were unrestricted. With most Poles never having been given such a role in deciding the future of their country, no one was entirely sure how the voting would play out. Jaruzelski had begun to prepare for a narrow communist majority, yet in private he and PZPR officials partook in discussions about how it may be perceived in the west should Solidarność fail to collect even a single seat.

However, on 4 June, the communists were crushed. Despite a low turnout and voter apathy from an electorate which truly believed that nothing would change, Solidarność claimed every single one of the seats they had been able to contest in the Sejm and all-but-one of the 100 seats in the Senate. To rub salt into the wound, 33 of the Workers' Party members that had seats reserved for them failed to get even the minimum number of votes required to take them. The establishment hadn't just been embarrassed, they had been humiliated.

Prior to the election it had been presumed that Jaruzelski would emerge as Poland's president; but needing to be elected by both houses of parliament, in which Solidarność were now the majority, that was no longer a certainty. Having convinced two communist-aligned parties to switch allegiance, the Workers' Party were unable to form a government —scrapping their plan of appointing only a few Solidarność activists in token cabinet posts. Eventually, a compromise was drawn up: Jaruzelski as president and Wałęsa-nominated Tadeusz Mazowiecki as Prime Minister.

While the world watched in awe at the symbolic felling of the Berlin Wall, in Poland, where the dominoes had first begun to topple, the government were already dealing with the repercussions of transforming into a market economy under an accelerated schedule. State-owned industries were quickly privatised, and immediately proved to be inadequately prepared for capitalist competition. The economic reforms put in place by new Finance Minister Leszek Balcerowicz also crippled foreign trade and sent the country spiralling into recession, while thousands lost their jobs—even if the goals of controlled inflation, a stabilised currency and foreign investment were ultimately achieved.

Having pushed for early presidential elections to take place in 1990, Wałęsa replaced Jaruzelski as Poland's head of state—the first to be democratically elected in over sixty years. Within less than twelve months, the landscape of both Poland and Europe had changed completely: domestically, the Workers' Party had dissolved itself, while Poland's western border with the reunited Germany was resolved; internationally, the Warsaw Pact was torn up in July 1991, while the Soviet Union was torn apart just a matter of months later.

Most importantly, the parliamentary elections in October 1991 officially brought an end to the era of communist party rule in Poland after well over 40 years. The transition to a western-style democracy was complete; but however welcome, it would take the country some time to adjust to its new status.

***

Marcin Bochynek's maiden league campaign in charge of Górnik could not have gone better. Urban, Ryszard Cyroń and Krzysztof Baran all notched up double-figure goal scoring records as the Trójkolorowi collected a fourth successive championship—a record eleven points clear of their nearest challengers.

In the shadow of Górnik's successes, fellow mining club GKS Katowice had risen to become the newest pretenders to the throne. With senior PZPN official Marian Dziurowicz as their president, *GieKSa* were unlike other mining clubs in that Jan Szlachta was unable to exert any of his vast influence upon them. Having bettered their third-place finish in

1987 to claim the title of *Vicemistrz* in '88, there had developed a feeling in Katowice that the 1988/89 season could see a new Silesian champion crowned.

That was a feeling shared just a few miles away in Chorzów where, fresh from a stint in the second tier, Ruch had developed a determination to bring the championship back to Ulica Cicha for the first time in a decade. With a majority of their team forcibly tied to the club following a first relegation in its 67-year history, Ruch powered back to the top flight with only eight points dropped. Both the settled squad and continued success bred confidence within the team, and they returned to their rightful place amongst the country's elite with aspirations much higher than just battling for survival.

Of course, the Huta Batory Steelworks were not able to provide the same financial backing for Ruch as the mining industry had for Górnik and GieKSa; however, at a time when rationing and empty shelves in grocery stores had become the norm, money wasn't necessarily the be-all and end-all. Through the contacts of one of the club's activists, entrepreneur Krzysztof Kubowicz, the Niebiescy's players had need not worry about such matters; and with both food cupboards and petrol tanks full, they were able to focus solely on football.

From the embryonic stages of the 1988/89 season, the league's leadership was solely reserved for one of the Silesian giants; GKS escaping from the blocks quickest, before Górnik soon took their familiar position at the summit—all whilst Ruch remained within touching distance. By the third week in May all three sat together on 40 points, waiting for the others to stumble.

That stumble came in early June, during a tempestuous *Wielkie Derby Śląska* ultimately decided by a pair of penalties: Ruch's converted by Krzysztof Warzycha and Górnik's palmed away by goalkeeper Ryszard Kołodziejczyk. Having maintained their position at the summit for much of eight months, two further defeats left Górnik dethroned and slumping into a third-place finish. Meanwhile, in leaving Zabrze with a 2-1 victory, the Niebiescy also left with a one-point lead over GKS Katowice; an advantage that would be extended to five by the end of the campaign. A fourteenth title for Ruch, to put them back on level terms with their great rivals once again.

Since before even the 'Pacification of Wujek', coal mining had been at the heart of the Solidarność revolution. It had been miners in Jastrzębie-Zdrój who led strikes during the summer of 1980, and later they who had also kick-started the August 1988 protests that eventually forced the communists into negotiation. For a heavily industrialised country such as Poland, coal was almost as valuable as gold—the black blood running through its veins, keeping it alive. If coal mining stopped, the country would stop; and when the country stopped, the government was forced to listen.

Unfortunately, coal mining was also one of the first industries to suffer from Poland's transformation to a capitalist economy. As with most areas of heavy industry, mining was quickly found to be over-employed and inefficient; and costs that had previously been financed by the public coffers were immediately shed just to try to keep the pits open. Jobs were lost; the companies' luxury facilities, reserved for employees, were sold. The sports clubs to which the industries had been inextricably linked for over three decades were also quickly deemed as expendable.

By the summer of 1988, Górnik's downfall had already begun: like the mines themselves, from a position of wealth it was now pinching for pennies. Not only the playing staff, but any asset that the club possessed was auctioned to the highest bidder, just to allow it to stay afloat. The mining company had even begun to take back from the club everything that had belonged to it, leaving the offices and corridors in the stadium completely bare. Several of Gornik's championship-winning squad had sensed the impending changes within both the country and the club, and were able to engineer moves abroad to escape the situation. Marek Kostrzewa, Waldek Matysik and Andrzej Pałasz moved west following the 1987 championship, while Andrzej Iwan and Marek Majka left a year later. By the time that Joachim Klemenz, Jan Urban and Ryszard Komornicki were readying to depart for Freiburg, Osasuna and Aarau during the 1988/89 season, the tide could not be stopped from turning.

Ruch were also dragged into the financial quagmire, as the steel industry joined the many others struggling with the transition to capitalism. The sale of Warzycha to Panathinaikos midway through the defence of their title temporarily eased the strain on the purse strings, but the impact on league form was severe; with just six goals scored and one victory claimed in the fifteen games following the striker's departure, the Niebiescy plummeted from third to twelfth place. The league trophy was effectively surrendered in the penultimate game of the season, as champions-elect Lech Poznań gained a 2-0 victory over the incumbents. More than a quarter-of-a-century later, fans in both Chorzów and Zabrze are still yet to see its return.

Act VI
A Free Poland

CHAPTER TWENTY-THREE
THE THIRD REPUBLIC

"We hold our heads high despite the price we have paid, because freedom is priceless."
- Lech Wałęsa

HAVING ALREADY BEGUN TO SLOW through the 80s, following the collapse of communism, the Polish Army's sponsorship of Legia began to dry up completely. On the pitch, league form had diminished too, with back-to-back bottom-half finishes to begin the decade, and even a relegation battle until the penultimate day of the 1991/92 campaign. Legia's sole reason for celebration was their performance in the cup: Puchar Polski victories in both 1989 and 1990, twice giving them entrance to European competition. The first of the Wojskowi's two Cup Winner's Cup appearances ended abruptly, at the hands of Catalan giants Barcelona. The second, however, was a marked improvement: Luxembourgish side Swift Hesperange, Scotland's Aberdeen and Coppa Italia winners Sampdoria—all beaten on their way to a last-four berth. Defeat to eventual winners Manchester United was far from a disgrace.

On the international stage, Poland had entered a period of free-fall. Former Lechia Gdańsk and Lech Poznań coach Wojciech Łazarek proved to be an unsuccessful appointment, having taken over the national team in the wake of Antoni Piechniczek's departure. Fourth of five in qualifying for Euro '88 was followed in 1989 by back-to-back defeats in Sweden and England; by the time that Łazarek left the job after the 3-0 loss at Wembley, his successor Andrzej Strejlau would have needed to perform miracles in order to reach Italia '90.

While Poland's second golden generation may have largely disappeared, a new group of talented prospects were steadily beginning to emerge. Steered to the quarter-final of the 1992 European Championships by former Jagiellonia Białystok coach Janusz Wójcik, Poland's under-21 squad, as a result, also qualified for that summer's Olympics in Barcelona. It may only have been on a technicality due to semi-finalists Scotland's inability to represent the united Great Britain team, but it was still both their first appearance since professionalism had been allowed in the Olympics, and also the first since Górski's silver medallists 16 years earlier. Spearheaded by seven-goal striker Andrzej Juskowiak, Poland's tournament was a success. Wójcik's Olympians repeated the feat of their predecessors by progressing past Italy, USA and Kuwait in the group stage, and Qatar and Australia in the knockout rounds. Although they eventually succumbed to their strong Spanish hosts in the Gold Medal Match, the young Eagles had built a platform from which it was hoped the Polish game could expand upon.

**

Still shy of his 22nd birthday, Juskowiak had emerged almost three years prior to the Olympics: the league's top scorer as Lech Poznań claimed the first championship of post-communist Poland. The *Kolejorz* had been buoyed by the return of coach Jerzy Kopa—the man whose spell in charge in the late 70s had paved the way for the club's first two titles soon after. They were also aided by the fact that, unlike the heavy industries and their associated clubs in Upper Silesia, the railways hadn't *immediately* withdrawn their sponsorship of the Poznaniaks.

However, it was the second champions of the Third Republic—a new name on the trophy, Zagłębie Lubin—who set the template for others to follow, away from the now-defunct socialist, centralised system. While the Upper Silesian coal mining industry had withered, Lower Silesia's now-privatised copper mining industry was burgeoning, and able to plough funds into the small-town club located next to its biggest mine, the state enterprise KGHM were able to quickly build on the club's previous minor successes.

Zagłębie had been little more than a mid-table side during the 1980s—in fact, until 1982 the *Miedzowi*'s best years had been spent yo-yoing between the second and third tiers. Still, much of KGHM's investment was spent, not on personnel, but rather infrastructure; a new stadium and training facilities in 1985—amongst the largest and most modern in Poland—highlighting the club's ambitions. Only a handful of additions were made to the 1989 promotion-winning team, which went on to surprise Poland with a runners-up spot behind Lech in 1990. Just 12 months later, largely the same set of players captured the unlikely championship, two wins clear of both the fading Górnik Zabrze and a resurgent Wisła Kraków.

Still under the auspices of the railways, Lech were able to reclaim their title in 1992. But with the purchase of Legia by businessman Janusz Romanowski in the autumn, and the club's multi-billion-złoty sponsorship deal with Warsaw-based automotive company FSO (equating to approximately 2.4 million PLN after the currency's 1995 re-denomination), a new era in Polish football was beginning. Success was no longer solely about pride in a city or an industry, but rather a return on investments. Money had become king. Winning was now of even greater importance.

***

With so much now riding on success, the fall of communism only served to expose the seedy underworld of Polish football. Corruption, in particular match fixing, reared its ugly head in the early 90s; this was made more apparent as, without a government to protect its leading officials in charge of the clubs, it was not so easy to cover up.

Accusations had already been levelled at the Silesian champions during the 80s: Ruch's 1989 title win was deemed suspicious due to Krzysztof Kubowicz's position as head of the committee responsible for organising referees, while Jan Szlachta's interference with other mining clubs during Górnik's earlier domination of the league was also called into question. Also in 1989, director Janusz Zaorski premiered his now-cult movie *Piłkarski Poker* ('Football Poker'); the story of Jan Laguna, an ex-player-turned-referee looking for a final payday, and a group of club presidents hoping to rig the final round of league matches. Could Zaorski have known how close his film—so extreme that at the time it surely could only have been considered as a surreal comedy—actually mirrored the supposed reality? He later confirmed that the tale was based upon real events that had been relayed to him by journalist friends. Still, in the case of both Górnik and Ruch, their guilt was never proven.

Yet no incident garnered more attention than the culmination of the 1992/93 season, in which three sides remained in the hunt for the title on the final day. Legia led the way on goal difference from second-placed ŁKS Łódź—a win at mid-table Wisła Kraków likely enough to see the title return to Warsaw for the first time in 23 years. However, if the Łodzianin side could engineer a four-goal swing in their home game with relegated Olimpia Poznań, the title would become their property for the first time since 1958. A point further back in third, reigning champions Lech were hoping to take advantage on the slim chance that both of their rivals should slip up.

While ŁKS ran out 7-1 victors, Legia won by a six-goal margin themselves—results which were both declared null-and-void several weeks after Legia lifted the trophy. No hard evidence pointed to either clubs' wrongdoing, yet the title was snatched from Janusz Wójcik's Wojskowi by the PZPN. It was instead handed to Lech, whose 3-3 draw with Widzew was enough to place them top of the pile due to a significantly superior goal-scoring record. The events eventually became known, particularly in

Poznań, as the 'Sunday of Miracles'—a name bandied by corrupt referee Laguna in Zaorski's film.

> *"All of Poland saw, and you are blind?!"*
> *- PZPN vice-president, Ryszard Kulesza*

> *"Kulesza furrowed, and [PZPN President, Kazimierz] Górski hid his head in the sand."*
> *- Janusz Wójcik, "Wojt: Jedziemy z frajerami! Całe moje życie"*

Legia's long-awaited fifth league championship was finally claimed twelve months later—although once again it was mired in controversy. Last-day opponents Górnik had one hand placed on the trophy by virtue of the new 'head-to-head' rule brought in after the previous season's cause célèbre. However, reduced to eight men by a card-happy referee, their one-goal lead at Ulica Łazienkowska—and a record 15th title—was surrendered in the final half-an-hour of the season.

Like had been the case with corruption, the rise of hooliganism within Polish football during the 1970s and 80s had too been largely brushed under the carpet by the communist authorities. In this period no official statistics were recorded, while incidents were largely sporadic—many taking place in streets and train stations around the stadiums, rather than actually inside of them. It took until 1981 for the first organised incident to be reported on by the media, during a league match between Legia and Widzew. Both the fighting within the stands and subsequent pitch invasion were captured by television cameras and broadcast across the entire country, thus making it impossible for the communist government to conceal.

The hooliganism problem steadily increased throughout the 80s, and in a post-communist society began to spiral rapidly out of control. Now no longer bankrolled by their state-sponsored benefactors, clubs were forced to yield power to hooligan groups, in fear that they could withhold much needed matchday income. At the same time, the groups saw their membership numbers skyrocket—perhaps encouraged by a fall in employment levels and a lack of opportunities for young men whose communities had been decimated by the collapse of industry.

Though the number of recorded violent incidents continued to increase for several years more, none were more damning than those which took place on 29 May 1993, as the Stadion Śląski hosted Poland and England for a World Cup qualifier. After fighting the visiting fans through the streets of Katowice, the Polish hooligans started to battle amongst themselves over club allegiances, and then also with the police as they tried to intervene. The pre-match death of a Pogoń Szczecin supporter at the hands of a rival team's hooligans had already set a tense atmosphere in the stadium, and not only led to a further increase in hostilities between groups for many years to come, but continues to shape the landscape of Polish fan culture to this day.

***

As the 100th anniversary of Włodzimierz Chomicki's maiden goal passed on 14 July 1994, the Polish game stood on the edge of a precipice; whilst the plagues of corruption and hooliganism tarnished it off-the-field, there were also problems on it. A series of poor results under Strejlau and then his successor Lesław Ćmikiewicz had meant the national team were unable to translate their 1992 Olympic success into qualification for the World Cup in America two years later. The domestic game was arguably weakening too, as the free market now allowed the country's best players to move westwards for better money at a much younger age. Given the vast changes and hardships across Poland since Sokół's exhibition match in 1894, it is perfectly plausible that the lack of commemoration of Chomicki's exploits that day was purely due to forgetfulness. However, given the state of the game at the time, it was just as likely because there was very little about which to celebrate.

Yet a handful of signs did suggest that better times may be on the horizon. In the summer of 1995, French TV network Canal+ acquired the broadcasting rights to show top-flight football, and as Polish fans lined up to buy the new satellite decoders in their droves, clubs watched their bank balances begin to swell. While the deal was being signed, a two-legged victory over IFK Göteborg earned Legia the right to represent Poland in UEFA's Champions League group stage—the first club to do so since the competition's rebranding three years earlier. Adding the influx of TV cash to Romanowski's own investments meant they were able to compete amongst Europe's elite; a pair of wins against Norwegians Rosenborg and victory at home to Premier League champions Blackburn Rovers yielding a spot in the last eight. When they were eventually downed, there was at least still some national pride in that it was a Polish duo which were instrumental in doing so: Józef Wandzik keeping a clean sheet and Krzysztof Warzycha bagging a second-leg brace as Greek champions Panathinaikos progressed to the semi-final at the Varsovians' expense.

While Polish football had begun its first century with a fight for recognition and autonomy, its second had started with a battle to rid itself of the remaining vestiges of its past. To cleanse and modernise itself after decades of partition, occupation and oppression. To try to keep pace with a game rapidly developing across the rest of the continent. To change the attitudes of those in charge of the clubs, the PZPN, the fans, the players...

It wouldn't be easy. But if any lesson could be taken from a century of Polish football history, it is that nothing—ever—has been easy.

EPILOGUE
THE SECOND ONE-HUNDRED YEARS

"Who wants to live with one foot in hell just for the sake of nostalgia? Our time is forever now."
- Alice Childress

ON 18 APRIL 2007, at UEFA's Executive Committee meeting in Cardiff, the joint bid presented by Poland and Ukraine to host the 2012 European Championships was confirmed as successful by President Michel Platini. The weakest package, from Hungary and Croatia, received not a single vote, while the rival Italian bid had been rocked by both the high-profile *'Calciopoli'* corruption scandal and the recent death of a policeman during football-related riots in Catania. Platini's election just three months earlier had come with the overwhelming backing of the 24 Eastern European nations that had emerged from behind the Iron Curtain. The selection of the Slavic neighbours as hosts was widely perceived to be his 'thank you'—a long-overdue welcoming for the former Eastern Bloc nations into the European football family.

Prior to the vote, Poland had suffered a scandal of its own which threatened to scupper their bid. While not as high profile as Calciopoli, a 2006 audit of the PZPN found evidence of widespread match fixing within the Polish game, of which the government accused the football association of failing to act upon. Starting with a suspicious-looking game in Lower Silesia, investigators soon uncovered a web of corruption which spread right across the country; eventually hundreds of referees, coaches, players and even high-ranking PZPN officials were found to be entangled. Arrests numbered into the hundreds. Just three months prior to the Euro 2012 vote, the Ministry of Sport made the drastic decision to suspend the entire board of the PZPN, incurring the wrath of both bodies of World and European Football. Threatened with suspension from international competition by FIFA and having their bid for Euro 2012 torn up by UEFA, the Polish government quickly backed down. It did not stop them from trying to repeat the process eighteen months later, with a similar outcome.

For their roles in the scandal, a number of clubs received punishments of varying degrees: Arka Gdynia, KSZO Ostrowiec Świętokrzyski, Zagłębie Sosnowiec, Korona Kielce, Widzew Łódź and Zagłębie Lubin were all relegated one level; Górnik Łęczna and Górnik Polkowice were both demoted two. Many others, including Jagiellonia Białystok, received severe financial penalties. Whilst it has taken some clubs a number of years to return to their previous level, financial problems have sunk others even further. Today still, the scar upon Polish football remains deep.

The bleakness off-the-field had been preceded by bleakness on it, too. Though Widzew had followed Legia into the Champions League for the 1996/97 season, no one could have known at the time that it would be another two decades before Poland would again be represented amongst Europe's elite. The national team's absence from the world stage was only slightly shorter, with a sixteen-year gap between Mexico '86 and their next appearance in 2002. A sole victory against the already-qualified United States side saw Jerzy Engel's side leave South Korea much earlier than they had hoped. It was a similar story four years later, with a 2-1 victory over Costa Rica in the Group A dead rubber the only remotely positive experience during the team's time in Germany. One result in particular from that tournament earned sharp criticism from the frustrated Polish press: after the 2-0 opening defeat to Ecuador, the particularly aggrieved daily tabloid *Fakt* provided the most infamous headline, splashing the words "Shame, embarrassment, disgrace, dishonour, pushovers" across its front page, before following it up with a simple message to Paweł Janas' defeated charges: "do not return home".

***

As Poland fought to pull away from the grasp of its communist past, it fell into the welcoming arms of a much more tolerant and progressive West. The European Union could trace its roots to the 1950s, where several neighbouring countries sought to tie their individual coal and steel industries together in order to "make war unthinkable and materially impossible". With such a rich history in both industries, and as the battleground for a large portion of the deadliest conflict in human history, Poland's accession to the organisation in 2004 seemed to make perfect sense.

EU membership brought with it a wealth of redevelopment across the country: new hospitals commissioned, new schools built, new skyscrapers raised. Within the first ten years almost €70 billion was spent on rebuilding Poland's crumbling infrastructure, while the country's GDP more than doubled. Helped by the major boom in the construction industry, Poland was the only EU country to avoid slipping into recession during the global financial crisis of 2009.

It could be reasonably claimed that the fast-approaching European Championships contributed heavily to the construction boom, with large amounts of the EU development cash earmarked for projects both directly and indirectly related to the tournament. Hotels were built across the four host cities, whilst airports, roads and railways were constructed to shift the fans around. It wasn't long before cranes, excavators and high-visibility jackets had become a common feature on the Polish landscape.

And, of course, no major tournament would be complete without its new stadia. Poznań's reconstructed Stadion Miejski was the first of the Polish venues to be completed, opening its doors to more than 43,000 fans in late September 2010. The brand new, amber-cladded PGE Arena in Gdańsk and the paper-lantern-like Stadion Miejski in Wrocław followed in August and September of the following year; each one slightly larger than, and just as aesthetically pleasing as the one before it.

However, Poland's fourth-and-final stadium for the tournament was not solely another stunning piece of architecture—it also represented the beginning of yet another new era for Polish football. Having led a nomadic existence since the 2009 closure of the ailing Stadion Śląski, the national team finally found its new home in the Stadion Narodowy—on Warsaw's right bank—almost thirty years after its predecessor, the Stadion Dziesięciolecia, had hosted its final game.

The move from Chorzów to Warsaw was one that mirrored the earlier transfer of power in the Polish game, from the industry-backed clubs in Silesia to the privately owned teams of capitalist Poland. It also followed the shift in the economic centre of the country, from the post-industrial Silesian wasteland to the up-and-coming commercial hub in the capital. But most of all, the Narodowy's majestic red-and-white aluminium façade and retractable fibreglass roof were symbolic of a rapidly evolving Poland; one starting to look forward to its ever-brightening future rather than back to its heavily chequered past.

***

Now, many of those crumbling, weed-strewn terraces have been replaced by pristine, pre-fabricated stands. Those faded plastic chairs have been removed in favour of ergonomic seating, providing comfort in both the most-blistering heat and the heaviest, coldest snowfall. The rusting metal fences are now freshly painted and fit for purpose. The walkways trodden by men, women and children are no longer the same ones as their fathers and grandfathers decades before.

Still, though, there is the familiar scattering of seed shells. Still, the setting sun shines through the smog to create a beautifully haunting, orange haze. Still, there is the scent of freshly grilled kiełbasa and cheap, strong lager, soon giving way to the overpowering, yet somewhat tantalising whiff of firecrackers and flares.

But most importantly: still, everything feels... right.

ACKNOWLEDGEMENTS

IF YOU'D HAVE SAID ten years ago that I would eventually write a book—on Polish football, nonetheless—I'd have likely laughed in your face. But here we are. A proper book. And there are a lot of people who I need to thank for getting me here—some of whom won't have even realised how much they've contributed:

The first 'thanks' is offered to Jeff Livingstone, David Hartrick and Ben Shave—the co-conspirators behind *In Bed With Maradona*, who back in 2010 published my first ever article. It was terrible. But it sparked a joy inside of me, which has ultimately paved the way to this very book. I can't thank you guys enough for the help and support you offered in those early years. Huge thanks can also extend to ESPN FC, Goal.com, Mirror Football, Daily Record, FourFourTwo, and all of the other places where my writing has ended up over the years.

Next, a huge thanks to Łukasz Lesiński, Andrzej Kozłowski, Adrian Płaczek, and all the other Polish guys who got me into the Ekstraklasa all those years ago, when Leicester City were far from good enough to bear watching every week.

Michał Zachodny, my one-time collaborator with *#Ekstraklasa Magazine* and *EkstraklasaReview.co.uk*, for your help and guidance over the years, and for letting me sleep on your sofa while I finished chapter twelve.

ACKNOWLEDGEMENTS

Robert Błaszczak, for (metaphorically) holding my hand on those first SportsTonight Ekstraklasa broadcasts, and for all your help and masses of encouragement along the way.

Gareth Lloyd—the best mate I could ask for, really. For being my best man, for all of the *Alan Partridge* and *Father Ted* quotes, for constantly letting me use your season ticket down at the KP, and so much more. I have a marker pen on standby.

I cannot even begin to list everything that both of my parents have done for both myself personally and my family. No amount of 'thanks' can ever be enough. The same goes for my sister Charlotte, and my wonderful in-laws too.

My penultimate thanks go to the two most important people in my life. My world. To my beautiful wife Melissa: the support, the happiness, the fun, the relief, and the endless cups of tea you continue to provide, make me confident that I am the luckiest person in the world. To my amazing son Rivers: every day you continue to astound me with how intelligent, kind and caring you are, and I cannot even begin to express how proud you make both mummy and daddy. You have the ability to achieve anything if you put your mind to it.

Finally the last, and the biggest 'thank you' is to you—the person reading these very words. It has always seemed to me somewhat bizarre that people have been prepared to spend their time (and sometimes even their money) to read something which I have written. The fact that you have, whether it be this book or anything I have put together previously, is forever humbling.

BIBLIOGRAPHY

BOOKS

Apiecionek K., **Mundial '74: Dogrywka** *Published by Wydawnictwo Olesiejuk, Ożarów Mazowiecki, 2012*

Bogusz A., **Dawna Łódź Sportowa: 1824-1945** *Published by Muzeum Historii Miasta Łodzi, Łódź, 2007*

Bołba W., Brychczy L., et al. **Kici: Lucjan Brychczy** *Published by Grupa Wydawnicza Foksal, Warszawa, 2014*

Braciszewski J., Gawkowski R. and Laskowski K., **Historia Polskiej Piłki Nożnej** *Published by Wydawnictwo SBM, Warszawa, 2016*

Bryl J., **Wacław Kuchar** *Published by KAW, Warszawa, 1982*

Chełmecki J., Dudek D., et al. **The Origins of Football in Poland** *Published by Museum of Sports and Tourism, Warszawa, 2012*

Czado P. and Żurek B., **Piechniczek: Tego nie wie nikt** *Published by Agora SA, Warszawa, 2015*

Dziekanowski D. and Nakoniecznik A., **Dariusz Dziekanowski. Dziekan** *Published by Akurat, Warszawa, 2015*

Gowarszewski A., **Encyklopedia Piłkarska Kolekcja Klubów Tom.1: Ruch Chorzów** *Published by Wydawnictwo GiA, Katowice, 1995*

Gowarszewski A., **Encyklopedia Piłkarska Kolekcja Klubów Tom.3: Wisła Kraków** *Published by Wydawnictwo GiA, Katowice, 1996*

Gowarszewski A., **Encyklopedia Piłkarska Kolekcja Klubów Tom.4: Lwów i Wilno** *Published by Wydawnictwo GiA, Katowice, 1997*

Gowarszewski A., **Encyklopedia Piłkarska Kolekcja Klubów Tom.5: Widzew Łódź** *Published by Wydawnictwo GiA, Katowice, 1998*

Gowarszewski A., **Encyklopedia Piłkarska Kolekcja Klubów Tom.7: Polonia, Warszawianka, Gwardia** *Published by Wydawnictwo GiA, Katowice, 2003*

Gowarszewski A., **Encyklopedia Piłkarska Kolekcja Klubów Tom.8: Lech Poznań** *Published by Wydawnictwo GiA, Katowice, 2003*

Gowarszewski A., **Encyklopedia Piłkarska Kolekcja Klubów Tom.10: Cracovia** *Published by Wydawnictwo GiA, Katowice, 2006*

Gowarszewski A., **Encyklopedia Piłkarska Kolekcja Klubów Tom.11: Górnik Zabrze** *Published by Wydawnictwo GiA, Katowice, 2009*

Gowarszewski A., **Encyklopedia Piłkarska Kolekcja Klubów Tom.13: Legia najlepsza jest...** *Published by Wydawnictwo GiA, Katowice, 2013*

Gowarszewski A., **Encyklopedia Piłkarska Tom.2: Biało-Czerwoni** *Published by Wydawnictwo GiA, Katowice, 1991*

Gowarszewski A., **Encyklopedia Piłkarska Tom.12: 75 lat PZPN** *Published by Wydawnictwo GiA, Katowice, 1994*

Gowarszewski A., **Encyklopedia Piłkarska Tom.14: Biało-Czerwoni** *Published by Wydawnictwo GiA, Katowice, 1995*

Gowarszewski A., **Encyklopedia Piłkarska Tom.16: Biało-Czerwoni** *Published by Wydawnictwo GiA, Katowice, 1996*

Gowarszewski A., **Encyklopedia Piłkarska Tom.20: Biało-Czerwoni** *Published by Wydawnictwo GiA, Katowice, 1997*

Gowarszewski A., **Encyklopedia Piłkarska Tom.25: Liga Polska** *Published by Wydawnictwo GiA, Katowice, 2000*

Haarke K. and Kachel G., **Die Lebensgeschichte des Fußball-Altnationalspielers Ernst Wilimowski** *Published by Laumann-Verlag, Dülmen, 1996*

Iwan A. and Stanowski K., **Spalony** *Published by Buchmann, Warszawa, 2012*

Kołodziejczyk L., **One hundred years of Cracovia Stadium** *Published by Dystrybucja Kziążek, Kraków, 2012*

Kołtoń R., **Deyna, czyli obcy** *Published by Zysk i S-ka Wydawnictwo, Poznań, 2014*

Kordek M. and Nawrocki K., **Lechia – Juventus. Więcej niż mecz** *Published by Wydawnictwo Bernardinum, Pelplin, 2013*

Kurowski J. and Szarmach A., **Andrzej Szarmach: Diabeł nie Anioł** *Published by Wydawnictwo Dolnośląskie, Wrocław, 2016*

Lubański W. and Olszański M., **Życie jest Dobry Mecz: Włodzimierz Lubański w rozmowie z Michałem Olszańskim** *Published by Wydawnictwo Literackie, Kraków, 2016*

Lubański W. and Słowiński P., **Włodek Lubański: Legenda Polskiego futbolu** *Published by Wydawnictwo Videograf, Chorzów, 2008*

Mielech S., **Gole, Fauly i Ofsaidy** *Published by Sport i Turystyka, Warszawa, 1957*

Nahorny R. and Terlecki S., **Pele, Boniek i Ja** *Published by Zysk i S-ka Wydawnictwo, Poznań, 2006*

Wawrzynowski M., **Wielki Widzew** *Published by Wydawnictwo QSB, Warszawa, 2013*

Wójcik J. and Ofiara P., **Wójt. Jedziemy z frajerami! Całe moje życie** *Published by Wydawnictwo Sine Qua Non, Kraków, 2014*

Zamoyski A., **Poland: A History** *Published by William Collins, London, 2009*

PAPERS & EXHIBITIONS

Kobiela F., **From State Socialism to Free Society. Sport in Poland from 1945 until Present Day** *Published in: 'The Interaction of Sport and Society in the V4 Countries', Budapest, 2011*

Łoniewski K., **Mundial—Meksyk '86. Polscy piłkarze w otoczeniu esbeków** *Published in: 'Biuletyn—Instytutu Pamięci Narodowej' Nr.6, Warszawa, 2006*

Muzeum Historii Polski, **Futbol Niezwyczajnych Dni—Sport w Okupowanej Warszawie** *Exhibited in Warszawa, 2014*

Piotrowski P., **Soccer Hooliganism in Poland. Extent, Dynamism and Psychological Conditions** *Published in: '(Re)constructing cultures of violence and peace', Amsterdam and New York, 2004*

INTERNET

http://90minut.pl, http://boisko.info, http://dzieje.pl, http://ekstraklasareview.co.uk, http://fifa.com, http://footballia.net, http://historiaruchu.pl, http://historiawisly.pl, http://hppn.pl, http://lechiahistoria.pl, http://przegladsportowy.pl, http://pzpn.pl, http://rfbl.pl, http://rightbankwarsaw.com, http://rsssf.com, http://sport.pl, http://uefa.com, http://wikigornik.pl, http://wikiliga.pl, http://wikipasy.pl, http://youtube.com

CLUB WEBSITES

http://cracovia.pl, http://gornikzabrze.pl, http://legia.com, http://lechia.pl, http://lechpoznan.pl, http://lkslodz.pl, http://pogon.lwow.net, http://ruchchorzow.com.pl, http://widzew.com, http://zaglebie.com

DOCUMENTARIES AND FILMS

Mundial: Gra o Wszystko Directed by Michał Bielawski, *Against Gravity*

Piłkarski Poker Directed by Janusz Zaorski, *Zespół Filmowy Dom*

NEWSPAPER ARCHIVES

British Library, London; Biblioteka Narodowa, Warszawa.

Printed in Great Britain
by Amazon